D0596097

# The
# SPIRITUALITY
## of
# WELCOMING

## HOW TO TRANSFORM
## YOUR CONGREGATION
## INTO A
## SACRED COMMUNITY

## Dr. Ron Wolfson

*For People of All Faiths, All Backgrounds*

**JEWISH LIGHTS Publishing**

Woodstock, Vermont

*The Spirituality of Welcoming:*
*How to Transform Your Congregation into a Sacred Community*

2011 Quality Paperback Edition, Fifth Printing

All rights reserved. No part of this book may be reproduced or reprinted in any form or by any means, electronic or mechanical, including photocopying, recording, or by any information storage and retrieval system, without permission in writing from the publisher.

For information regarding permission to reprint material from this book, please write or fax your request to Jewish Lights Publishing, Permissions Department, at the address / fax number listed below, or e-mail your request to permissions@jewishlights.com.

© 2006 by Ron Wolfson

**Library of Congress Cataloging-in-Publication Data**
Wolfson, Ron.
The spirituality of welcoming : how to transform your congregation into a sacred community / by Ron Wolfson.
p. cm.
Includes bibliographical references.
ISBN-13: 978-1-58023-244-9 (pbk.)
ISBN-10: 1-58023-244-2 (pbk.)
1. Synagogues. 2. Hospitality—Religious aspects—Judaism. 3. Fellowship—Religious aspects—Judaism. 4. Community—Religious aspects—Judaism. 5. Spiritual life—Judaism.
I. Title.
BM653.W65 2006
296.6'5—dc22

2006008081

10   9   8   7   6   5

Manufactured in the United States of America

Cover Design: Sara Dismukes

Published by Jewish Lights Publishing
A Division of LongHill Partners, Inc.
Sunset Farm Offices, Route 4, P.O. Box 237
Woodstock, VT 05091
Tel: (802) 457-4000      Fax: (802) 457-4004
www.jewishlights.com

## Also Available by Dr. Ron Wolfson

*God's To-Do List*
*103 Ways to Be an Angel and Do God's Work on Earth*

*The Seven Questions You're Asked in Heaven*
*Reviewing and Renewing Your Life on Earth*

*A Time to Mourn, a Time to Comfort*
*A Guide to Jewish Bereavement*

*What You Will See Inside a Synagogue*
(co-authored with Rabbi Lawrence A. Hoffman, PhD)

## The Art of Jewish Living Series

*Hanukkah,* 2nd Ed.
*The Family Guide to Spiritual Celebration*

*Passover,* 2nd Ed.
*The Family Guide to Spiritual Celebration*
(with Joel Lurie Grishaver)

*Shabbat,* 2nd Ed.
*The Family Guide to Preparing for and Celebrating the Sabbath*

For Abram Kukawka
In Memory of Hildegarde Lieball Kukawka,
Uncle George Kukawka, and the Kukawka Family

# CONTENTS

# INTRODUCTION

**I love synagogues.**

I have loved synagogues ever since I was a little boy in Omaha, Nebraska, when my parents, Alan and Bernice, moved our family to a home within walking distance of our congregational home. I was a shul (synagogue) kid.

Many people love their synagogues. You may be one of them. You may even be a leader of your congregation—lay or professional. Your synagogue is a place where you are comfortable, where people know you, a "second home." But there are many people who don't love synagogues, people who are uncomfortable when they walk into a synagogue. Why? Because it is unfamiliar, intimidating, and often unwelcoming—especially for guests, shul-shoppers, and even for members who rarely show up.

I will never forget the time I walked into the sanctuary of a large Conservative congregation and experienced firsthand what many newcomers have encountered on their first visit to a synagogue. I had been invited as scholar-in-residence to speak on Friday evening. After I gave my talk, the rabbi emeritus, a long-time acquaintance, said, "Ron, they won't make you sit on the *bimah* [pulpit] tomorrow morning. Would you like to sit with me?" I readily agreed. The next morning, I showed up promptly at 8:55 a.m., five minutes before the start of the Shabbat morning service. As I looked around the enormous sanctuary, there were about eight people in the room: the shammes (ritual director); four or five regulars, who I assume always come on time; and three guests of that day's Bat Mitzvah who had taken the invitation time seriously! The service began, but no rabbi emeritus was in sight.

I took a seat on the aisle one row from the back of the sanctuary, hoping to see the rabbi when he came in. About ten minutes later, I felt a tap on my shoulder. I looked up and saw a sweet old man looking at me with the saddest eyes. He said, "You know, I wouldn't tell you that you are sitting in my seat." He then pointed to an empty seat directly behind me. "And I would sit there," he continued, "but, if I sat there, where would my friend who always sits there sit?" I looked around; there were 785 empty seats, but this man needed the seat I was in!

Of course, I moved immediately. Because I could identify that man. That man was a regular who had been sitting in that seat for fifty years. In a way, his need to sit in that seat is one of the great things about being a member of a sacred community. It is his *makom kavu'a,* his "established place," in the congregation. And, it is true that if his friend who sits behind him is not in his seat, then the friends who know him would be worried: Is he sick? So, I found another seat and he took his.

At the kiddush afterward, his friends who witnessed this incident really lit into him. Why? Because he kicked the scholar-in-residence out of his seat! If I had been a stranger, or someone looking for a congregation, or a guest of the Bat Mitzvah, it would have been no big deal. Anyone in my position would have felt unwelcome, but no one in the community would have batted an eyelash had it been anybody else.

This experience highlights a key problem with synagogue life: Many of our congregations are no longer welcoming places. When I meet with synagogue leaders today, I always ask: What could the man have said that would have welcomed me *and* gotten him his seat? How do we create a welcoming atmosphere that does not alienate those who already feel at home? How can we transform our congregations into sacred communities where a spirituality of welcoming permeates the physical space and all those who walk in its doors? This book is an attempt to answer these questions.

## Studying Synagogues: The Genesis of Synagogue 2000

I have spent a good part of my life studying synagogues from the inside out. I have *davenned* (prayed) in congregations of all sizes, shapes, and denominations—from small synagogues in the South to enormous cavernous sanctuaries in the Northeast, from ultra-Orthodox *shteiblach* in Jerusalem to Jewish renewal *havurot* in Berkeley, from the Sephardic synagogue in North Hollywood to the Ashkenazic shul in South Carolina, from Classical Reform services in San Francisco to the Carlebach *minyan* in Manhattan.

To this day, after visiting hundreds of synagogues throughout the world, I am amazed at how I can measure the health of a congregation within minutes of stepping into the place. Perhaps it is because of my training as a cultural anthropologist. Perhaps it is because the people who meet my flight will tell me—a perfect stranger—volumes about the congregation on the ride from the airport to the synagogue, including the scoop on current conflicts and intrigues. But in any case, I have noticed that some of the congregations are far more exciting than others; you can feel it from the minute you walk into the place. I now know it is the *culture of community* that is different.

In synagogues where the culture of community is thriving, the place is buzzing with activity. More often than not, these same synagogues offer a warm greeting to a stranger. In a synagogue where the culture of community is absent, the place looks drab, feels sleepy, and even smells bad. Newcomers are treated indifferently or completely ignored, and with whispered gossip filling the air, everyone seems to be angry at somebody. It is my goal to cultivate and restore this culture of community through a process known broadly as "synagogue transformation."

Much of my work with synagogue transformation has been in the context of Synagogue 2000, a project I cofounded with Larry Hoffman. When I first met him in 1995, Larry, a professor of liturgy at Hebrew Union College in New York, was a leading voice for the transformation of worship in the Reform Movement, influencing a generation of rabbis and cantors as one of the most beloved teachers at the college. He had also achieved great renown for his expertise in liturgy and his skill as a scintillating public speaker to audiences in the academic world as well as in Reform congregations as a popular scholar-in-residence.

Rabbi Rachel Cowan is responsible for bringing us together. I had been introduced to Rachel at a meeting of the first grantees of the

Nathan Cummings Foundation where she was the program officer for Jewish grants. After learning of our work in pioneering Jewish family education at the Whizin Institute for Jewish Family Life, Rachel asked me, "What's next on your agenda?" I replied, "Synagogues." She understood immediately: "What do you need?" I said, "Money." She said, "How about a planning grant?" I said, "Great!" Then, Rachel added, "I want you to meet my mentor and rabbi, Larry Hoffman." I called Larry the next day.

Larry and I met at the Rabbinical Assembly convention in the Catskill Mountains, where he had been invited to give a keynote address and I was offering a workshop on family education to one of my primary audiences in the Conservative Movement. That meeting over stale coffee in the dilapidated Concord Hotel changed both of our lives. Each of us thought it would be an obligatory half hour chat to satisfy Rachel's desire for us to meet. But, after what seemed like hours of animated conversation, we realized that we shared much of the same love for and critique of synagogue life and a passion to do something about it. We quickly ascertained that because of our relative standings within our movements, we could create a project that would speak to 90 percent of North American synagogues. We reveled in the fact that Larry was a rabbi and I was a Jewish educator, each bringing different skills and knowledge to the effort. He was from the East Coast, while I was from the West Coast. He was raised in a small town in Canada, while I grew up in a small town in the Midwest. He could not sit still while he talked and neither could I. We left the meeting promising each other to become partners in planning this as-yet unnamed project to deepen synagogues.

Over the next ten years, the institute we envisioned that day and later named Synagogue 2000 (S2K for short) became a leading exponent of the work of transforming the synagogue into the spiritual center of the Jewish community. When we began this project, Larry and I gathered together a group of outstanding rabbis, cantors, artists, educators, and funders to imagine the synagogue of the twenty-first century. After two days of intense deliberations, we agreed on the conception of the synagogue as a spiritual center with six entry "gates." Four of the gates represent the fundamental functions of the synagogue: *prayer, study, good deeds,* and *healing.* Two of the gates represent the processes that are essential for the synagogue to remain vibrant and enticing: *institutional deepening* and *ambience of welcome.*

Together, the first letters of each gate spell the word PISGAH, the Hebrew name for the mountaintop from which Moses looked into the future:

> Moses went up from the steppes of Moab to Mount Nebo, to the summit of Pisgah, opposite Jericho, and the Lord showed him the whole land.
>
> —*Deuteronomy 34:1*

Moses would not reach the Promised Land, but he was able to see it from the summit.

We committed to creating a process by which synagogue teams would engage in a long-term visioning of the future of their congregation. Our purpose was not to tell congregations how to create themselves as spiritual centers; we realized that every synagogue has its own individual ideology and character. We did, however, want to cast a vision of the six gates into the spiritual center:

*Prayer* that is engaging, uplifting, and spiritually moving.
*Institutional deepening* that is possible because of an
    openness to change.
*Study* for adults and families, as well as children.
*Good deeds,* the work of social justice, is a commitment
    of each and every member.
*Ambience of welcome* that creates a culture of warmth
    and outreach.
*Healing,* a sense of completeness that offers comfort and
    support at times of illness and loss.

These six gateways into a spiritual community shaped our vision of what a synagogue of the twenty-first century would look like. It would be a place where the culture of the entire community would reflect an ambience of welcome, a place not just where everyone knew your name, but a place where everyone was treated as an "image of God" living within a culture of honor. It would be a place where the building itself said "Welcome!" and where the people who served as professional and lay leaders truly served others with uncommon grace, courtesy, and compassion. It would be a place where the worship experience was dynamic and moving, where everyone was encouraged to study, where everyone was committed to repairing the world. It would be a place to turn for comfort and support in times of trouble. It would be a place that embraced the possibilities of change, a community unafraid to experiment, even to take risks. It would be a place of deep partnership between the clergy and the laity. It would be a high place, a place to stand on a summit, always looking into the future, hoping to enter the Promised Land.

Using the PISGAH vision as our template, Synagogue 2000 embarked on a ten-year period of experimentation and research to design a "synagogue transformation process" to envision the synagogue of the twenty-first century. Supported initially by the Nathan Cummings Foundation, Steven Spielberg's Righteous Persons Foundation, the Whizin Foundation, and a generous board of advisors, we chose sixteen pilot site congregations—eight Conservative and eight Reform—for our first national cohort. Two years later, we were invited to Washington, D.C., to work with five congregations in a regional cohort. The next year, we were asked to come to Denver/Boulder to work with thirteen congregations, funded by the Rose Community Foundation and the local federation. In quick succession, we began projects in Detroit/Ann Arbor with eleven congregations under a grant from the Jewish Federation of Metropolitan Detroit, a national cohort of eighteen Reform congregations supported by the Union of American Hebrew Congregations (now Union of Reform Judaism), and, finally, a group of twenty congregations in Westchester County, New York, funded by UJA-Federation of New York.

Larry and I were fortunate to assemble a talented staff of program specialists, consultants, and curriculum writers who joined our two offices—one on the West Coast at the Whizin Center for the Jewish Future at the American Jewish University and the other on the East Coast at the Hebrew Union College–Jewish Institute of Religion, New York. In addition, we identified some of the most creative synagogue leaders and resource people doing cutting-edge work on the front lines of congregations. We called them Synagogue 2000 fellows and they became our rotating staff of presenters to the cohort groups. Together, we continually developed and evaluated an innovative model of synagogue transformation that included conferences, curricula, and consulting to guide the deliberations of the synagogues as they journeyed through the Synagogue 2000 process.

In the early years of this project, we could not have envisioned just how far it would take us. But the importance of our work was apparent from our very first meeting in 1995. That year, with the community still reeling from the highly publicized intermarriage figure of 52 percent (later found to be more like 42 percent), the communal obsession with "continuity" was fueling any number of efforts to find ways to "ensure the Jewish future." It was a time to stand on the precipice of the twentieth century and look forward into the next millennium. Larry and I were convinced that synagogues represented the best hope for reaching the largest number of Jews, if only the leadership of the synagogues and the community invested serious energy, effort, and resources into renewing and deepening the institution.

## The Transformation of American Judaism

I am willing to stake my career on this proposition:

The future of the Jewish community in America is directly connected to the effectiveness of synagogues in transforming the Jewish people. By "transforming," I refer to two things: (1) the *spiritual transformation* of Jewish individuals and families and (2) the *physical transformation* of the Jewish community through incentives to increase our numbers through population growth, outreach to unaffiliated Jews, and welcoming and encouraging of non-Jews in Jewish relationships and families to become Jewish and/or to raise their children as Jews.

Transformation is about changing people's lives. It is not about membership or affiliation. It is not about numbers. It is about transforming the spiritual lives of individuals, one at a time. It is about "forming" a Jewish identity through the experience of living in a sacred community. Spiritual formation requires the planting of seeds in the soil of the soul, seeds that must be tended and nurtured. Synagogues can be the garden in which growth occurs, but ultimately, it is God who transforms lives. Synagogues are the sacred communities that can create the conditions for spiritual formation by engaging the individual in uplifting prayer, serious study, works of social justice, acts of healing and comfort, and connectedness to others. But, ultimately, it is God who transforms lives.

Synagogues are the best hope for the physical transformation of the Jewish people. The twentieth century saw the development of synagogues as bedrock institutions of the Jewish community. More Jews affiliate with synagogues than with any other institution or group in the Jewish community, by far. The potential of synagogues to reach more people—Jews and non-Jews—and to empower them to become active citizens of the Jewish community is enormous. Most synagogues are good at what they do, especially with their typically limited staff and resources. To move from good to great, synagogues will need to accept this challenge of growth and deepen their most important work of creating inspiring and empowering spiritual communities.

This new vision of the twenty-first-century synagogue can be stated in a simple sentence: The synagogue is the spiritual center of people's lives. It is a *kehillah kedoshah*, a "sacred community," where relationships are paramount, where worship is engaging, where everyone is learning, where repair of the world is a moral imperative, where healing is offered, and where personal and institutional transformation are embraced.

The twenty-first-century synagogue must become a gateway of welcome for those who seek a spiritual community. When people interact with the institution, they should encounter a culture characterized by an understanding that *every* human being, not just the *machers* (leaders), is a *b'tzelem Elohim*, a person "made in the image of God." When congregations take this charge seriously, every interaction with members and potential members is looked upon as an opportunity to create a unique, special, holy, *sacred* community. This is the first step in establishing a synagogue of relationships.

To accomplish this goal, the leadership of individual synagogues, denominational movements, and federations as well as philanthropists will need to invest the resources required to substantially increase the infrastructure and capabilities of synagogues to establish meaningful relationships with each and every person who comes into their orbit. The synagogue of the twenty-first century envisioned here will need the resources to add staff (rabbis, cantors, musicians, artists, membership directors, spiritual directors, and teachers), to renovate aging buildings, to build new campuses, and to empower lay leadership to join the professionals in creating synagogues where relationships are sacred and lasting.

When individual Jews have these kind of relationships, their lives are transformed and their commitment to Judaism, to the local Jewish community, to Israel, and to the future of the Jewish people is strengthened. This is the great goal for the synagogue of the twenty-first century.

I believe the critical challenge to Judaism in the twenty-first century will be whether we can achieve this goal of growing the Jewish people. I recall vividly conversations in the late 1960s and early 1970s about the future of the Jewish community in North America. Dire predictions were everywhere that the declining birthrate and increasing percentages of young adults intermarrying would decimate our numbers. Clearly, this has not happened.

Yet, observers of North American Jewry continue their attempts to divine the Jewish future. Sociologist Steven M. Cohen predicts that assimilation is such a powerful force that nothing can prevent the loss of as many as one million Jews, while Gary Tobin believes that, using his definition of "who is a Jew," there are tens of thousands of Jews uncounted in the National Jewish Population Survey. Most scholars agree with historian Jonathan Sarna who summarizes the current situation succinctly in his outstanding history *American Judaism* by pointing out two competing forces at work: the slow diminution of the Jewish population and the intensification of Jewish commitment and expression among those who remain Jews.

In an age-old debate, some leaders have argued that the Jewish community has always survived because of a "saving remnant," a small group of dedicated Jews who keep the religion and culture alive. Others have dismissed this view as pessimistic and fatalistic, preferring to believe that Judaism as a religion, culture, and people is so deep, so inspiring, so meaningful that the only reason we have not grown is a centuries-long resistance to proselytizing. In other words, we have a great product; our marketing stinks.

This is not an insignificant issue for synagogues. There are those in congregations who believe that the purpose of the synagogue is to serve those who are already committed to Judaism and not worry about those who have yet to demonstrate such commitment. The problem today, however, is that many of our congregations, particularly in the so-called liberal movements, are populated with increasing numbers of Jews who have married non-Jews. One need not reach out too far to find people who could become Jews; they are often sitting in our pews.

This hesitancy to proselytize is deep-seated in our culture, shaped by centuries of anti-Semitism, creating fear and distrust of the "other." There was good reason for the practice of requesting that those who sought entry into the Jewish people ask three times before being taken seriously. Then, once accepted as a potential member of the community, the bar for entry was set very high: knowledge of Jewish practice, language, values, Torah, and, in the case of males wanting in, a certain surgical procedure that would give any adult man pause.

While this cautionary approach worked well in the past, it is a disastrous prescription for growing the Jewish people. This is not to say that standards and boundaries are unimportant; there is a legitimate concern of maintaining the integrity of the community. However, with our children waiting longer and longer to get married, and with a birth rate of well under two children per family, we will not come close to maintaining our current population. How else are we to sustain our numbers except by retaining the people we have and recruiting new Jews?

I believe that synagogues can become the most powerful vehicle for growing the Jewish people. It is commonly thought that the Jewish Community Centers are the most logical gateways into the Jewish community for intermarrieds and others who stand on the periphery of the community since the religious boundary issues are not applicable. I completely support the community center movement as a vital arm of the Jewish institutional world—some of my best friends are JCC leaders. As noted above, however, at any one time, more than twice the number of Jews affiliate with synagogues than with JCCs (in 2000, 46 percent belonged to a synagogue; 21 percent belonged to a JCC). The question is: Will congregations take on the task of bringing the "un-synagogued" into their midst?

The concept of outreach is often referred to (in the more traditional religious communities) by the Hebrew term *keiruv*, literally, "to bring closer." The idea is that the community is obligated to bring the stranger closer to Judaism. Thus, a variety of synagogues and continental organizations have *keiruv* committees and *keiruv* projects.

This is a far too limiting view of outreach. It has often been noted that, today, all Jews are Jews by choice. The import of this statement is that all Jews, even those who are born Jewish, must make a conscious effort to "be Jewish" in the face of assimilation and competing cultural norms. Arnold Eisen and Steven M. Cohen make a persuasive argument in their excellent volume *The Jew Within* that many Jews make nearly daily choices about how "Jewish" they will be at any one moment. American Jews do not, with few exceptions, feel commanded or obligated to conform to even the most basic of Jewish standards of behavior. Synagogues are competing for the hearts and minds of all Jews, those born Jewish and those not yet Jewish. The concept of *keiruv* itself may be insufficient to confront this challenge. We need new language—spiritual language—to describe how we can best issue the invitation to our community.

## A New Kind of *Aliyah*

Consider this question: When in modern history has there been a need to grow a Jewish community? Answer: in 1948 in the state of Israel. The Jewish population, mostly refugees from Europe, found themselves surrounded by hostile neighbors, fighting for their very survival, and succeeding beyond even their wildest dreams. The leaders of the new country knew that measures had to be taken to stimulate the growth of the community, to gain numbers of people—rapidly. And, so, a plan to increase the population began to take shape.

Two major efforts grounded this daunting task. The first was the remarkable call for Jews from all over the world to immigrate to Israel. *Aliyah,* the Hebrew term meaning "ascend," was a plea for Jews to return to their ancient homeland, to rebuild it as a modern state. Hundreds of thousands of Jews did so voluntarily, while thousands more were rescued from inhospitable countries in the Middle East, Africa, and the former Soviet Union.

The second strategy to grow the community involved an incredible social experiment. The government put in place incentives for parents to have more children. Taxes were reduced, stipends were provided, housing was built, and communities were founded—all with the intention of making it easier for families to grow in numbers. The theory was simple: Reduce the costs and burdens of having children and we'll have more children.

Amazingly, it worked. The Jewish population of Israel in 1948 was 650,000. In 2004, the Jewish population was estimated to be 5,180,000.

The point is that when a Jewish community is intentional about growing itself, it can be done. Can we grow the Jewish population in America? I believe we must, and synagogues will have a major role in the effort.

We need a new *aliyah*, an *aliyah* to Judaism—a call to born Jews, to Jews by choice, to non-Jews, to members, and to not-yet members of our synagogues to affirm their desire to be within the Jewish community.

*Aliyah* literally means going up, ascending to a higher place, a place of meaning and purpose. It is a term, of course, borrowed from Jewish ritual. The act of pronouncing the blessings before and after the public reading of the Torah in the synagogue is called an *aliyah*. It is considered one of the highest honors in Jewish religious life. The actual moment a child demonstrates the ability to take on the religious obligations of Judaism as an adult is her or his *aliyah* during the Bat Mitzvah or Bar Mitzvah ceremony. In many synagogues, the honor of an *aliyah* is highly coveted.

To me, the most thrilling moment of having an *aliyah* is when I am literally *called by name* to bless God before and after the Torah reading. *"Ya-amod, Gershon ben Avraham u'Vracha!"*—"Arise, Gershon, son of Avraham and B'racha [the Hebrew names of my father and mother]." I am *called* to rise, to stand up, to come forward, to ascend the pulpit, to encounter the Torah.

*Aliyah* is a warmer invitation to Judaism than *keiruv*. *Keiruv* can be construed as a "yanking in"; *aliyah* is a "calling up." *Keiruv* is what Jews do to bring in the "other"; *aliyah* is a spiritual act experienced by the potential Jew.

*Aliyah* is for everyone. For born Jews, the *aliyah* of their young adolescence must be renewed. To borrow a term, they must be reborn as real adult Jews who respond to the call to a life of Torah, who actualize the covenant with God through a life filled with prayer, study, social justice, healing, and connection to sacred community. For converts to Judaism, they have accepted the call and are considered as Jewish as any born Jew. For non-Jews who have not yet converted or will never convert, we need a new category of inclusion in our sacred communities, a subject I will discuss at greater length in chapter 5, "Welcoming Membership."

We will need incentives for this new *aliyah*. Just as Israel realized it had to remove the financial obstacles that blocked the expansion of the Jewish community, the cost of living a Jewish life has become burdensome for many. I often quip that day school tuition and synagogue dues are the most effective form of Jewish birth control yet invented. It isn't funny. Those who resonate with this call for *aliyah* to Judaism will need to devise strategies for overcoming the barriers to entry and making it financially feasible for more people to affiliate.

## What Are the Major Challenges Facing Synagogues Today?

In order to make this call to *aliyah*, we need to take stock of where we stand today. To that end, Larry Hoffman and I began Synagogue 2000 with an honest critique of the challenges facing the synagogue as it evolved in the twentieth century. As one of the foremost analysts of the sociology of religion, Larry has written most eloquently on this topic. In sum, we agreed that leaders of synagogues rarely asked the deep questions of purpose: Why synagogue? What does synagogue do for people? What constitutes success in synagogue life?

During our extensive visits to synagogues throughout North America, we found many who seemed to be doing well; in fact, some were becoming quite large. Yet, sheer numbers of members is not a reliable indication of success. As one rabbi of a major metropolitan synagogue that serves more than a thousand family units told us in a brutally honest moment: "My synagogue is full, but empty."

What the rabbi meant to imply was that though the four thousand individuals who belonged to his synagogue came in droves to the many programs that the institution offered; though the large campus was crowded with people, mostly children who were dropped off in carpool lines that snaked across the expansive parking lot; though the weekly Bar or Bat Mitzvah service attracted hundreds, most of whom were guests of the family celebrating the *simcha* (happy occasion); though there was a very small core of regulars who attended everything and who could be counted on to help out the large professional staff; though it was a place full of activity for virtually every age group, it nevertheless was "empty" of spiritual significance in the lives of most of its members.

Larry describes this kind of synagogue as a "limited-liability" community. There is a tacit understanding between the institution and the members. For the members, it goes something like this: "We pay you a fee [dues] for services rendered. We expect a religious school for our children, a rabbi on call when we need her or him, and seats for the High Holy Days. Other than that, we expect you to offer programs that may or may not attract our attendance, because, after all, we are very, very busy people and synagogue is not exactly our top priority. We like the fact that you are there when we need you, but don't expect or exact too much more of a commitment from us." For the professional staff and leadership, it goes something like this: "We depend on attracting enough members to pay dues to cover our expenses—professional salaries, building maintenance, and program costs. We will provide the basic functions of a synagogue; religious school; access to rabbis; Bar or Bat Mitzvah training; High Holy Day, weekly, and, where applicable, daily religious services; and lots and lots of programs. Heaven help us if more than a small percentage of people actually want to engage the professional staff on a more intensive basis, because frankly, we don't have the time." The synagogue that developed in the twentieth century is good at serving its small core of regulars and an ever-changing group of families who join primarily to have their children receive some form of Jewish education and become Bar or Bat Mitzvah. The regulars somehow (often due to consistent attendance at worship services or by volunteering in leadership roles) find their way into a committed relationship with the congregation; the majority of members do not. Thus, the first obstacle to overcome is this: The synagogue itself—especially its spiritual and lay leadership—will need to accept the challenge of welcoming all who come within its orbit and become a *synagogue of relationships.*

This will require far more than an increased number of programs. Synagogues can have the appearance of success by sending flier after flier (nowadays, e-mail after e-mail) in an attempt to attract attendance; I call these congregations "frequent-flier synagogues." It is not rocket science to offer interesting and varied programs, and often the programs do bring more people into the building. That is a good thing, but it is nowhere near sufficient in creating the kind of sacred community that is envisioned here.

Ask yourself this question: Why is it that so many individuals and families affiliate with synagogues at one time or another in their lives but then move to the periphery of the congregation or leave altogether? Certainly, there are a variety of reasons, but if you unpack the usual reasons given, the bottom line is that most synagogues fail to establish a connection between the individual and the congregation that is so valuable, so meaningful that it would be unthinkable to sever it. This is the most serious indictment of the twentieth-century-synagogue model.

The relationship between synagogue and individual is limited. And the result is that many congregations have a revolving door in the main entrance, with members both coming and leaving.

According to the 2000 National Jewish Population Survey, 46 percent of American Jews belonged to a synagogue in 1999 when the survey was conducted. Most North American Jews (estimates range from 75 to 80 percent) join a synagogue at one time during their adult life, but a much smaller percentage remain members throughout their lives. (This is less true in most Orthodox and some Conservative congregations, particularly in the East and Midwest where synagogue membership tends to be a lifelong commitment.) This is both the challenge and the promise of congregations. Synagogues are the "retail outlets" of Judaism in North America. We get them in the door. The question is: Why don't we keep them?

In fact, we know when many people drop out of synagogue membership. As soon as the youngest child in the family becomes a Bar or Bat Mitzvah, not only does the teenager go missing in action, the parents stop coming around as well. If one of the major motivations for synagogue membership is to get the kids to the *bimah* for the big BM, then what would keep them involved after it's over? This is the cost of the dependence synagogues have on children as the reason for membership and as the focus of programming. When the synagogue fails to engage the *adults* in the family during this twelve- to fifteen-year period of membership, then it should come as no surprise that they move to the periphery of the congregation or out the revolving door altogether.

Meanwhile, synagogues are woefully understaffed. The problem is exacerbated by how we count our membership. We count households or families or units. Bad mistake. We should be counting individuals. A medium-sized congregation of five hundred families may represent as many as two thousand individuals. How is one rabbi to minister to that many people? How can a staff of three or four professionals create the kind of synagogue of relationships envisioned here? It is no wonder that a regular feature at rabbinical conferences is a session on clergy burnout.

Thus, the first and—to my mind—most critical question to emerge from our critique is this: What should be the fundamental *relationship* between the member and the congregation? Can it be deeper than fee-for-service? Can it be different from the moment a prospective member walks in the door?

## Why Don't Most Jews Enjoy Synagogue?

When I visit a synagogue, everyone tells me what's *really* going on in the place. I will hear about the clergy, the lay leadership, the members, the demographics, the religious school, the youth group, trends in membership, the financial condition, and the current challenges. Sometimes, there is a specific issue that is all-consuming. For example, a synagogue might be facing the need to physically move from one neighborhood to another, or a new rabbi in the congregation down the street is enticing away members. I've been asked questions such as "What shall we do about including non-Jewish spouses in religious rituals? What is your opinion, Ron, of gay unions? We are looking for a new rabbi/cantor/educator; Ron, do you know anyone who might be interested?"

I am simultaneously amused and chagrined by these conversations. On the one hand, the challenges facing synagogues are universal and repetitive. On the other hand, these are not the questions I am coming to raise and/or answer with the congregation. I want them to reflect on questions of purpose, direction, future, meaning; they are busy putting out fires or just trying to survive. I want to talk about relationships; they want a list of programs. I want to talk about how to reach the un-synagogued; they are exhausted just dealing with the people they already have.

Then, I arrive at the synagogue for Friday night dinner and services, and I begin to meet the people. I am always warmly welcomed—I am a guest, after all—and I begin to hear the predictable and recurrent complaints and disappointments.

> When I first moved here, I went shul-shopping. At two of the congregations, I walked around after Friday night services and no one said hello. At this one, someone greeted me warmly. This is the one I chose.

> I've been a member at this synagogue for five years, and I still can't break into the cliques in the congregation.

> I tried one synagogue, but the religious school was a disaster. So I moved my kids to this one.

> I got a membership packet from one synagogue that assumed I was married with children, along with a computerized sheet with expected dues. They didn't bother to learn who I was— a single woman engaged to be married. It was like, "Pay up and then we'll get to know you."

Over the years, I have experienced a share of my own horror stories: I was once asked to talk with a board committee charged with improving the level of welcoming in a major East Coast congregation. I arrived early, as is my custom, in order to walk around the building to get a sense of the place. It was a large congregation with a four-hundred-student day school on campus, seven people in the office, and a gift shop open at 9:00 on a Monday morning. There were people everywhere. Nevertheless, it took nearly twenty minutes before someone finally said hello. His name was Winston. I knew his name because it was stitched onto a name tag on his shirt. He was the head custodian.

One advantage I have as a researcher into synagogue life is this: I am a layperson. I am not now nor have I ever been a rabbi. I view the experience of synagogue from the pew, not from the pulpit. I often recommend to clergy that one of the most valuable things to do during a process of reflection about the purpose of synagogues is to sit in the seat of the congregant.

One thing you notice when you sit in the seat of the congregant is that many synagogue spaces don't work anymore. By "work," I mean that they do not inspire or facilitate the kind of spiritual experience that many seek in a worship service. Synagogues built during the twentieth century were heavily influenced by church architecture. The traditional configuration of synagogues with the Torah reading table in the center of the space was replaced by high pulpits, imposing arks, and regal furniture. Pews were arranged in rows and fixed to the ground, focusing attention squarely on what was happening in the front and reducing the chance for interaction with others. This created distance between the congregants and the clergy, between the people and each other, between the people and their God. In fact, these "cathedral" synagogues reflected a view of God as transcendent, distant, unapproachable. For a certain generation, these spaces did work to inspire awe. For me, and for most of the generation of baby boomers and those younger, these sanctuaries are off-putting, inflexible, and unwelcoming.

The rest of the synagogue building can also be problematic. For example, few synagogues have adequate gathering space before entering the sanctuary. Lobbies are often small or nonexistent. Schools are off to one side and libraries are buried off a back hallway. Gift shops range from tiny to lovely, but most often offer the usual ritual objects and Jewish tchotchkes, not serious books of Jewish content that can help families and individuals build home libraries. Offices usually feel corporate and the rabbi's study—a very important sacred space—is often inaccessible without first negotiating the receptionist and the rabbi's administrative assistant and offers little, if any, privacy.

For many first-time visitors, the predominant feeling walking into a synagogue building is that of being lost. Most synagogues have poor signage, making it difficult to find the sanctuary, the office, the rabbi, the cantor, the school, the social hall, or the restrooms. I visited one synagogue where I could not find a way into the building. The front door was locked, and when I finally found an entrance and I mentioned my difficulty to the executive director, he said, "Well, everyone knows to come in through the kitchen!"

In sum, the model of synagogue in the twentieth century worked well in a time and place when synagogue membership was an expected social norm. It did its job of teaching children, offering services, organizing social justice projects, supporting clergy, and providing occasional programs for adults. It served the needs of ethnic Jews with an evolving corporate structure that was effective and efficient. Yet, as we approached the new millennium, it was becoming increasingly evident that a paradigm shift away from corporate synagogues as enclaves of ethnicity was under way, demanding a new vision of synagogue. Creating this new vision became the raison d'être of Synagogue 2000.

## Rethinking Spirituality

The new synagogue we envision is a spiritual center for all those who set foot inside it. It is a *kehillah kedoshah,* a sacred community, where relationships are paramount, where worship is engaging, where everyone is learning, where repair of the world is a moral imperative, where healing is offered, where personal and institutional transformation are embraced.

The times are ripe for this spiritual call. There is abundant evidence that North America is in the midst of the third Great Awakening. The first Great Awakening occurred in colonial times; the second Great Awakening happened in the late nineteenth century when a revival of religious fervor swept the continent. The current Great Awakening has been fueled by a combination of phenomena: the reaching of middle age by the baby-boom generation who are asking questions of meaning, the rise of evangelical Christianity and the emergence of the megachurch, the culture wars, the increasing blurring of state and religion, the turn of the millennium, and even the tragedy of 9/11. It is during times of great turmoil that people return to houses of worship seeking comfort, meaning, and purpose.

This should be no surprise. America has always been a very religious country. In a recent poll commissioned by *Newsweek* magazine and Beliefnet, a website devoted to religious issues, 88 percent of Americans describe themselves as either "spiritual" or "religious." Even among teenagers, more than 90 percent in a recent survey say they believe in a personal God.

Witness my friend, Rick Warren, senior pastor of the largest congregation in America, Saddleback Church in Orange County, California. On a sabbatical in 2001, Rick wrote a book called *The Purpose-Driven Life* that he intended to be used during a church-sponsored, forty-day campaign of spiritual growth. A genius at sharing his message, particularly through a network of thousands of pastors who have made the pilgrimage to Saddleback to learn its secrets of success, the book has become the best-selling nonfiction volume in history. At this writing, more than twenty-five million copies have been bought in America, and the pace of sales throughout the world is approaching one million per month. The subtitle of the book asks the key question that religion seeks to answer: What on earth am I here for?

In short, there has never been a better time for synagogues to reach those who are seeking spirituality. Rather than concede these seekers to New Age pseudo-religions and so-called centers of Jewish mysticism, the synagogue can offer an authentic community that serves the spiritual needs of human beings.

What is spirituality? For some, it connotes some sort of New Age mumbo jumbo. I can recall when we first began our work in the Whizin Institute for Jewish Family Life in the early 1990s, my philanthropic partners Bruce and Shelley Whizin suggested we focus on "spirituality" in our work. I replied, "Don't use the S word!" The vast majority of rabbis and educators, unused to hearing, much less teaching, God language and uncomfortable with touchy-feely expressions of emotion, would immediately turn off if they thought we were pushing an agenda that imitated some in the Jewish Renewal community. It was just too marginal and it was not, at the time, taken seriously.

I remember clearly my own feelings of discomfort when first introduced to spirituality. It was when I heard Debbie Friedman's *MiShebeirakh* sung during a prayer service. The rabbi announced that anyone in the congregation who wanted to publicly say the name of a person who was ill could stand and do so. This was shocking to me; I was used to the rabbi reciting Hebrew names submitted to the office by people who knew the secret of getting a name on the list. What made it so strange? The public sharing of a very private matter? The invitation for the congregation to stand up during the service, in place, and participate? The willingness of people to show emotion? The power of the music? Whatever it was, I recall my visceral reaction to it: a combination of shock and embarrassment. I even began to sweat, worrying that this just wasn't right. It was so different, so strange, so weird.

When I reflect on this experience now, I realize that displacement of accepted behavior is a kind of violation of an unspoken code. Synagogues—particularly liberal ones—were not the place for emotion or commotion; they were to be filled with intellectualism and prayer conducted in quiet decorum. Yet, clearly this code was not working anymore. Once a few pioneers began to skillfully introduce prayers of healing and other forms of spirituality into the synagogue service, it was as if everyone recognized that something new was needed, a radical overthrow of what was most definitely not working for people. Once the strangeness wore off, an enormous feeling of relief and liberation supplanted the often uptight atmosphere of the classical worship experience.

This small example reveals much about the challenge of creating the synagogue of the twenty-first century. The first lesson is the challenge of overcoming the natural hesitation of people about attempts to be spiritual. The second lesson is that the process of change, of introducing something new, is particularly vexing to an institution that, by definition, is rooted in tradition. "New" is anything that the people in the congregation are not used to doing, hearing, or saying. The challenge of change applies to all synagogues, in all denominations.

As I became more familiar with my colleagues in the Reform Movement, I was amazed to learn how challenging it was for their clergy to introduce changes into the worship services. In the mid-1990s, the transformation of the Classical Reform service was well under way, but there was still plenty of resistance from congregants who were comfortable with the old way, who worried that the changes were robbing them and their families. Suddenly, rabbis and cantors began introducing more Hebrew, more singing, more lay participation, and more spirituality—moments that broke through old conventions to make genuine contact with a twenty-first-century spirit, shaped and influenced by the culture in which we live, yet still maintaining authentic connection with tradition, so the spirit remains Jewishly grounded.

In the Conservative Movement, other changes were challenging congregants. Perhaps the most striking was the introduction of gender-neutral language into the English translations and the addition of the *imahot,* mention of the ancestral "mothers" of the Jewish people during the *Amidah.* Of course, the very presence of female rabbis on pulpits has been an enormous change and benefit to Conservative congregations. In my opinion, the sensitivities, understanding, and scholarship of female clergy have been an important stimulant to the introduction of spirituality into the synagogue. In the Reconstructionist Movement, the introduction of God into the service has been a radical change. Mordecai Kaplan, the founder of Reconstructionism, would be shocked to hear all the talk of God and spirituality in congregations that embrace his naturalist theology.

Even in the Orthodox Movement, changes in the *davenning* have been introduced. The enormous influence of Shlomo Carlebach and his Hasidic melodies led to the development of Carlebach-style services and the Happy *Minyan* phenomenon. I once asked an Orthodox friend who attends a Happy *Minyan* why it is called by that name. He simply smiled and replied, "When we leave the service, we're happy." What he implied is that because the music is so uplifting and the spirit so energizing, congregants are spiritually moved and emotionally elevated.

What's going on? As strange or different as these breakaway spiritual experiences feel to those who are new to them, it is my belief that just under the surface of most people, you will find a spiritual soul waiting to find expression. I have witnessed hardened businesspeople melt into tears when led expertly through a prayer service that is designed to tap into this reality. Why is it that Debbie Friedman, Craig Taubman, and Danny Maseng can bring a group to a spiritual high in a concert setting in a matter of minutes, while the typical Shabbat service in many congregations can mean hours of passive sitting with no discernable impact?

If emotionality in worship opens people up to the possibility of a new relationship to God and the synagogue, the next step is to understand what I call the "four questions of spirituality." The term is so elusive, I have asked many congregants to tell me what it is they are looking for when they say they want *spirituality* in their lives. They say they are looking for answers to these four questions:

### What Is the Meaning of My Life?

At the end of the day, or better, at the end of my days, when I look back over my life, what meaning has my presence had? What difference did I make in the lives of others? It is the question immortalized in the song "What's It All About, Alfie?" It is the story of George Bailey who discovers the meaning of his existence in the classic film *It's a Wonderful Life.* After I have worked my sixty-hour week, shuttled my kids back and forth to their endless activities, acquired the home of my dreams and everything that goes with it, what does it all *mean?*

### What Is the Purpose of My Life?

After considering the question of meaning, I am faced with the question of *purpose.* What am I here to do? To use spiritual language, what did God put me on earth to accomplish? Ask many people what they want to achieve in their career, they will answer "to make a difference." For what purpose can I use my talents and gifts to make the world a better place?

### Where Can I Connect to Community?

It is difficult, perhaps impossible to live alone. There is a deep-seated human need to belong, to *connect* to others. Where can I find a community to belong to, a community that will be there for me, a community that I care enough about to be there for its members?

### Where Is God's Presence in My Life?

However you define God, most of us believe, or want to believe, in a divinity that impacts our lives. But many of us need help in finding a *personal relationship with God.* Do you have to believe in God to be Jewish? No. But where can I look for God, discover God, find the godliness in others?

The seekers of spirituality come to the synagogue asking these questions. A spiritually centered synagogue, a *kehillah kedoshah,* a sacred community, will be a place to answer them.

## The Spirituality of Welcoming: The View from the Summit

My own research in Synagogue 2000 focused on the central issue raised in this book, namely, how synagogues can fashion a *kehillah kedoshah,* a sacred community, infused with the spirituality of welcoming leading to a deeper relationship with the congregation, with each member and guest, and with God. The three initial factors in creating such a spiritual community are (1) welcoming ambience (the A gate, ambience of welcome), (2) welcoming worship (the P gate, prayer), and (3) welcoming membership (the I gate, institutional deepening). Due to limitations of space, I will leave my reflections on the other PISGAH gates for another time. (Larry Hoffman's parallel book, *Rethinking Synagogues: A New Vocabulary for Congregational Life* [Jewish Lights], covers many of the details of the S2K story.)

Synagogues often do a fine job of offering a variety of opportunities to study Judaism, to participate in social action activities, and to provide comfort for those who are mourning or caring for someone who is ill. That is business as usual. The times, however, require synagogues to be much more. We need synagogues that can be on the front lines of growing the Jewish people—spiritually and physically. The best way to reach in and strengthen the relationship of synagogue members to each other and to the congregation and the best way to convince synagogue regulars to reach out to bring in seekers and the unaffiliated is to begin the process of synagogue transformation by changing the ambience of welcome (chapter 3), by creating spiritually uplifting prayer experiences (chapter 4), and by connecting members significantly to the congregation (chapter 5). These, then, will be the primary topics of this book. First, however, I will turn to a brief overview of the theory behind synagogue transformation, which is the subject of the chapter that follows.

# 2

# The Synagogue 2000 Theory of Synagogue Transformation

## How to Transform a Synagogue: Strategies for Effecting Change

During the first ten years of Synagogue 2000, Larry and I were challenged to explain our vision, create and manage expectations, and outline our evolving process of synagogue transformation. In short, we learned how to effect change successfully and realistically. The following strategies reflect our hard-earned wisdom.

### *Recognize the Challenge of Change*

It is extraordinarily important to point out that change is difficult. I recall a story told to me by a president of a synagogue who wanted to remove three rows of pews in the back of the sanctuary in order to create a stroller and play area for families with babies and toddlers who wanted to be in shul. "It took three years of contentious debate," he said, "but we finally got it done." In many synagogues, there is a saying inscribed above the holy ark that reads *Dah lifnei mi attah omeid,* or "Know before whom you stand," referring, of course, to God. I told our teams that the saying should be changed to "But we've always done it that way."

Ron Heifetz, cofounder of the Center for Leadership at Harvard University, teaches that people are actually *not* resistant to change; we resist the *loss* that inevitably accompanies the change. In fact, people welcome change when we know it is for the good, when the change is likely to improve matters. Nevertheless, in the midst of change, we try to hold on to what is important to us.

27

### Understand Why You Do What You Do

Many things are done in synagogues "because we've always done it that way." There are any number of humorous—and telling—stories to illustrate this. One of my favorites is about the synagogue where congregants would always take four steps to the left just as they approached the ark for an honor. There was no apparent reason for this little dance, but everyone did it. One day, a new member of the congregation was given the honor of returning a Torah scroll to the ark and was told to take the four steps to the left. She asked why. No one knew—not the rabbi, not the cantor, not the president. She suggested that, perhaps, one of the elders of the congregation would know why this was done. They approached Mr. Schwartz, nearly one hundred years old, and a member of the congregation forever.

"Mr. Schwartz, why do we take four steps to the left when approaching the ark?"

"Well," Schwartz said, "in the old shul downtown, we used to have hanging in front of the ark there a big chandelier, and you had to walk around it. So when we moved to this place, people kept doing it. I guess it's a tradition!"

### Be Aware of How Quickly the New Becomes Traditional

I was a witness to the creation at a synagogue of a Jewish "seeker" service that was an immediate hit with the congregation. Even though it was billed as an experiment, the service was so well-received that virtually everything about it became an instant tradition. When the service was offered again a month later, the leaders kept experimenting, and the people objected wildly: "What happened to the dancing? Why aren't we dancing with the Torah like we did the first time?"

### Tradition and Change

When I was growing up in the 1950s, one of the national leaders of the Conservative Movement, Rabbi Mordecai Waxman, wrote an influential book, offering an ideology for the middle-of-the-road position between Orthodoxy and Reform. He called it *Tradition and Change*. In the book, he argued that Judaism has always thrived because we hold these two seemingly competing ideas in a dialectical balance—

honoring tradition while embracing change. Change comes about for a variety of reasons—new understandings and insights, attempts to right an injustice, belated recognition of the rights and potential contributions of those who have been overlooked or left out.

Take the Conservative Movement itself. Over the last forty years, it has embraced a number of significant changes, most importantly the inclusion of women into the life of prayer—allowing women on the *bimah*, counting women in the *minyan*, and ordaining women at Conservative seminaries. Even the Modern Orthodox world has seen an incredible change in how women are included in the service in some congregations and *minyanim*. In the Reform Movement, perhaps the most significant change in the past ten years is a return to tradition with the use of more Hebrew, the option of wearing of *kippot* and *tallitot,* and spiritual practices within prayer such as turning to welcome the Shabbat Queen at the end of *L'cha Dodi* and raising oneself up on tiptoes during the singing of *"Kadosh, Kadosh, Kadosh"* in the *Kedusha.*

Judaism is an adaptive religion; change is nothing new.

Ron Heifetz makes the point that when faced with an adaptive challenge (as opposed to routine technical problems), the real work is in figuring out what is precious and essential and what is expendable; what is at the core and what is not; what can change and what must not.

### *"Don't Leave Sadie Behind"*

We once held a workshop on the S2K process of synagogue transformation at the Reform Biennial Convention. Hundreds of synagogue leaders packed the room to hear lessons learned from our first few years of work. Someone in the audience who was grappling with making the transition from one style of worship to another asked a key question: "Isn't there a huge risk in making a change in something as basic as the worship service of alienating the people who regularly come to temple in the hope of attracting the spiritual seekers who are not yet there?" One of the S2K rabbis gave a wise answer: "Don't leave Sadie behind." He continued, "I have a bunch of 'Sadies' in my congregation, several of them major supporters, who are very nervous about all this talk of changing the worship. One reason for their concern is that they like the current service, it's familiar to them. But there is a deeper reason. They don't want to go through the experience of loss. They don't want to feel disloyal to those who came before them. They need to understand *why* we're making the changes, how it will grow the congregation. So, I took Sadie out for a long lunch, and I explained what we were doing, that it was an experiment, and I looked forward to her being my partner in the process. Basically, Sadie didn't want to be left behind."

Heifetz calls this "having reverence for the pains of change." He would applaud the rabbi for sustaining Sadie through her experience of loss and for getting her support for the experiments that must be done if we are to meet an adaptive challenge.

### Listen to People and Adjust According to Their Feedback

I vividly recall the first day of the first S2K conference in California, to which each participating congregation had sent a team of people. Larry and I wanted to assault their understanding of what it meant to be a congregation and we began by piling the teams onto buses and taking them to church. We drove an hour south of Los Angeles to attend the Sunday seeker worship services at Saddleback Church. The experience was mind-blowing. On the ride back to the retreat center in Ojai, it became immediately clear that, for many in our group, the church visit was disturbing and raised questions about what Synagogue 2000 was *really* trying to do. These participants did not hesitate to voice their concern and reservations.

By Sunday night, we were deeper in trouble because of a welcome sign. We were committed to modeling the kind of culture of welcoming that we believed was an important gateway of spirituality. So, above the entrance of the chapel, our meeting room, we had placed a banner that read, in Hebrew and English, *Bruchim Ha-Ba'im B'Sheim Adonai*, "Blessed Are Those Who Come in the Name of God." It turned out that a fair number of the delegates didn't actually believe in God. Once again, there was an uproar.

The coup de grâce came when we handed out the curriculum we had written for the teams to study together, to guide their visioning process. We called it the Synagogue 2000 Itinerary for Change. *Change?* That did it. By Monday evening, we had a full-scale revolt on our hands. Several teams threatened to go home.

To be fair, Larry and I were new at this and no one really had much of an idea how to do "synagogue transformation" at the time. So, we stayed up most of Monday night rethinking our plan. On Tuesday morning, we had a heart-to-heart with the delegates, admitting our failure to be clear about our expectations, our failure to plan for a debrief of the church visit, and our failure to allow time for the teams to assimilate and react to the challenges we had put forth. We unveiled a completely revised agenda for the rest of the conference, revisions that were a direct response to the feedback we were hearing.

An amazing thing happened. We learned our first and possibly most important lesson about transformation: our responding, our *changing,* made the participants feel they had been *heard.* Their anger subsided. Their enthusiasm was renewed, especially after hearing a spectacular presentation on sacred space by Richard Vosko, singing with Merri Lovinger Arian, and experiencing several model worship services. Three days later, when the teams departed, one of the shuttle drivers who had made several trips to the airport stopped us and asked, "What did you *do* with these people? I have never seen such enthusiasm in my life. They are leaving here with stars in their eyes!"

### Recognize that Personal Transformation Precedes Institutional Transformation

The Ojai conference taught us another lesson as well. We realized that a project centered on spirituality could not just be about organizational life. In fact, most of the early presentations on organizational development at our conferences resulted in glazed-over eyes. I recall one of our clergy leaders, after listening to a two-hour PowerPoint lecture from a well-respected former partner with a top New York–based consulting firm, standing up and declaring: "All of this OD stuff is a bunch of endless navel-gazing. I am the Nike rabbi: *Just do it!*" Moreover, many of the synagogue leaders, particularly the laity, were overwhelmed by how moved they were by the music, the worship, and the learning. They left Ojai inspired, uplifted, personally changed by the experience—exactly the kind of outcome we hoped synagogues could achieve with their own efforts back home.

### Strive for Application, Not Replication

If there was a danger in exposing the teams to these superb experiences of worship, it was that some participants erroneously concluded that we were pushing certain models that seemed out of reach. In a candid moment, one of the rabbis said, "Listen, I am a good rabbi, but I can't do what so-and-so can do. Besides, what so-and-so does would never work in my congregation." Our response was clear: *think application, not replication.* We never counseled an S2K congregation to import, clone, or in any other way attempt to replicate a particular worship service. We urged the teams to debrief the experiences at the conferences, to tease out the *principles* that made them work, and to apply these principles to their own settings.

### Raise the Bar

I believe that the most significant outcome of the S2K conferences was what one of our S2K fellows, Rabbi Ed Feinstein, called "raising the bar" of what synagogues could be. It is difficult to overstate how much of an impact the conference presentations made on the S2K teams. Truly, once they saw what was possible, there was no turning back. They had experienced excellence, their hearts and minds had been opened, they now knew what spiritually welcoming worship and community felt like, and they wanted it in their home congregations. They left the S2K conferences recognizing that change must involve the ability to raise the bar, to experiment, to adapt, and to transform their congregations into sacred communities of moral and spiritual depth and meaning.

### Ask the Right Questions

For me, the most important contribution of the S2K process to the emerging field of synagogue transformation is that we sought to ask the right questions about congregational life. We were never as interested in sharing best practices as we were in asking the right questions. We were never as interested in promoting programs as we were in asking the right questions.

This insistence on asking questions frustrated some of the synagogue leaders in our cohorts. They wanted answers, not questions. They wanted solutions, not problems. They wanted product, not process. They wanted instant results, not years of deliberation, study, reflection, and experimentation.

In the end, we remained steadfast in our strategy of transformation, believing that achieving a number of short-term successes would sustain our teams as they did the more difficult work of creating a culture and a process that would permeate the entire congregational conversation centered on the question of its purpose, a purpose we called "becoming a *kehillah kedoshah,* a sacred community."

### *Create a Culture of Honor, Not a Culture of Blame*

One of the great pleasures in S2K was to learn of new colleagues who shared our vision of synagogues as spiritual communities. We learned about Rabbi Jonathan Rosenblatt, a Modern Orthodox rabbi from New York City, who was speaking out on a crucial topic for our work. We invited Rabbi Rosenblatt to speak at several S2K conferences. His talk was titled "A Culture of Honor, Not a Culture of Blame." It was the one talk we offered that had most of the conference participants squirming in their seats.

Rabbi Rosenblatt gave voice to the reality that everyone knew: Most synagogues are far from sacred communities when the individuals within them resort to blaming each other for perceived and real failures in the life of the congregation. Instead of creating a culture that honors every human being, many congregations are rife with dissension, fights, and arguments among the very people who are charged with leading a sacred community. Using examples far too close for comfort, he challenged the S2K teams to learn what Jewish sources have to say about honoring each human being, to realize that it is possible to confront shortcomings without ascribing blame, to build a community that is communally responsible for what happens within it. This no-fault synagogue is a place where the dignity of each human being "made in the image of God" is paramount, and failures, challenges, and problems are dealt with and solved by the group. It was—and is—an inspiring, deeply Jewish message.

## Engage the Clergy in the Process of Change

Change requires the partnership of the clergy and the laity. And it is a particular kind of rabbi, cantor, or executive director who can best facilitate the process of synagogue transformation.

The rabbi is the key factor in the success or failure of a synagogue transformation effort. For better or worse, the rabbi is the de facto chief executive officer of the congregation and is therefore responsible for the articulation and implementation of its mission and vision. In short, the rabbi could embrace the process or kill it. This is not about charisma. The most successful of the S2K teams were not led by charismatic rabbis. They were led by rabbis who were willing to empower their lay leadership, to work hand in hand with the cantor and other professional staff, and to support the process of transformation in any way possible. The more courageous rabbis welcomed the opportunity to study with and teach their congregants about the structure, purpose, and meaning of Jewish prayer and acted as the rightful authoritative resource and ultimate arbiter of the religious practices of the congregation. But they were also open to the dialogue and the often excellent suggestions that emerged from the deliberations of the S2K teams. For these rabbis, the S2K process created a group of partners who could share their vision, their hopes, and their ideas. As one rabbi put it, "I am no longer alone."

The cantors in S2K congregations were also challenged, perhaps even threatened, by the questions we were asking, particularly about the prayer experience. Those courageous cantors, like their rabbinic colleagues, welcomed the chance to teach a group of influential congregants about their work, to share their knowledge of *nusach* (traditional chants) and music, to engage them in a serious conversation about what the experience of prayer is like in the pews. But this was often not easy. Many cantors work in a congregational system where they are clearly second fiddle to the rabbi, except in matters of music. It is no wonder that some would go to great lengths to protect their turf. In short, to engage in a dialogue about prayer with the lay leadership, even with the rabbi, was seen by some as tantamount to inviting disaster.

The executive directors of congregations were also invited to participate in many of the local S2K processes. These professionals are responsible for the shaping of the ambience of the congregation, including the way guests are welcomed, the physical characteristics of the building, the financial relationship between the congregation and its members, and the way the frontline staff interact with people. These are critical functions in a synagogue that hopes to welcome in the stranger and to grow its membership. During the course of our work, I developed a workshop called The Front Line is the Bottom Line and invited S2K congregations to include every paid professional who worked for the congregation—custodians, administrative assistants, receptionists, bookkeepers, gift shop clerks, caterers, librarians, educators, teachers, school office staff, security guards, executive director, cantor, and rabbi because, as we will learn below, creating a spirituality of welcoming is the responsibility of everyone.

**Tips**

## *Strategies for Effecting Change*

Recognize the challenge of change

Understand why you do what you do

Be aware of how quickly the new becomes traditional

Tradition and change

"Don't leave Sadie behind"

Listen to people and adjust according to their feedback

Recognize that personal transformation precedes
institutional transformation

Strive for application, not replication

Raise the bar

Ask the right questions

Create a culture of honor, not a culture of blame

Engage the clergy in the process of change

## What Values Should Guide Us as We Seek to Change?

Our S2K staff realized early on that one of the most troubling aspects of synagogue life is the fact that, somehow, the crucial values of Judaism are rarely used as a guide for how synagogue business is conducted. So, we developed our own Statement of Values to help the S2K team literally change the way they encountered each other:

### L'shem Shamayim, For the Sake of Heaven

> All who labor for the community should do so for the sake of heaven.
>
> —*Pirke Avot 2:2*

> Committees are places where people keep minutes and waste hours.
>
> —*Milton Berle*

The essence of Synagogue 2000 work is done in collaborative teams, not litigious committees. We call our gatherings *meetings* in the sense that Martin Buber meant when he said that we often know God best in our meetings with each other.

### Sh'tikah, Silence/Listening: Reflection in silence while others are speaking

> All my life, I have been raised among the sages, and I have found nothing better for a person than silence.
>
> —*Pirke Avot 1:17*

Talmudic conclusions follow from assuming that the opposite positions from our own are no less arguable than our own beliefs.

**Dibbur, Speech: Speaking the truth as we see it, but carefully, lest we hurt others**

> Speak as if God were listening to everything you say.
> —Martin Buber

Talmudic debate is brief, even laconic. Each word is chosen with care. Martin Buber quotes a Hasidic master: "We learn a lesson from every modern invention. From the telegraph we learn that every word is counted and charged, and from the telephone we learn that every word said here is heard up there."

**Savlanut, Patience: Patient empathy with others**

> Menachem Mendel of Lubavitch would restrain his angry outburst until he had looked into the codes to learn whether anger was permissible on the occasion in question. But how much real anger could he feel after searching for the authority in the *Shulchan Arukh*?

The Hebrew word for *patience* comes from the root meaning "to bear, suffer, put up with." When team members begin to think that they no longer can put up with others and their opinions, they would do well to recall the following from a High Holy Day prayer in the *Machzor* of the Reform Movement of Great Britain: "I remember the times when I was able to put up with people who were irritating or ungrateful. I remember the times when they were able to put up with me."

**Elu v'elu, These ones . . . and these ones: Allowing for multiple perspectives**

> In debates between *Beit Shammai* and *Beit Hillel*, a heavenly voice was heard saying that since some decisions had to be made, the opinion of *Beit Hillel* would generally prevail, but nonetheless: *Elu v'elu divrei elohim chayim*—"Both *Beit Hillel* and *Beit Shammai* [teach the] words of the living God." No

one loses, regardless of whose judgment ultimately prevails. As long as the motive behind them is "for heaven's sake," all opinions honestly voiced at our meetings are "words of the living God."

—Larry Hoffman

When opinions become so divergent that it seems we will never reach agreement, the following advice from Nachman of Bratslav may be valuable:

The essence of peace is to join together two opposites. Do not be alarmed if you see someone whose way of thinking is completely opposite your own, so that you imagine that it is absolutely impossible that the two of you should ever be at peace. On the contrary. That is the essence of the wholeness of peace; to find peace between two opposites, just as God makes peace above between fire and water which are two opposites.

### B'yachad, Together: Progress emerges from collaboration

A favorite saying of the Rabbis at Yavneh was, "I am God's creature and others are God's creatures. My work is in town, theirs is in the country, I rise early to do my work, they rise early for theirs. They do not presume to do my work, and I do not presume to do theirs. Can you say that I do much and they do less? We have learned, one may do little or a lot; it is all the same as long as we direct our heart to heaven."

—Babylonian Talmud, Berakhot 17a

Talmudic study occurs not alone but in pairs. Even our prayers require *minyan*. But togetherness is not just physical proximity. It is the group attribute of harmony, as one of our favorite prayers implies: *Hinei mah tov umah na'im shevet achim gam yachad* (How good it is for brothers and sisters to dwell together). Rabbi Chalafta taught, "If two sit together working hard on Torah, the presence of God comes to rest among them."

### *Derekh eretz,* Decency toward others: Mutual respect

> Hillel used to say, "In a place where human decency is lacking, practice decency yourself."

American culture is increasingly brash, even litigious. People play to win, not to find truth together. Their concern is the bottom line, not each other. The end is all that matters, not the means to the end, the process of human interaction through which the deepest truths are revealed. If meetings lack evidence of our concern for each other and commitment to each other, they are not *l'shem shamayim,* but the opposite: *l'vatalah,* meetings held in vain.

### *Sofo shel davar,* When all is said and done

> Jewish spirituality is of two kinds: there is first and most obviously our relationship to God, which we call in Hebrew *bein adam l'Makom* (between individuals and God); there are also the relationships we build with each other, which the Jewish tradition calls *bein adam l'chaveiro* (between one person and another). The Mishnah teaches: "For transgressions between a human being and God, Yom Kippur atones. For transgressions between one human and another, Yom Kippur does not atone, unless the transgressor regains the good will of the one who is hurt" (*Yoma* 8:9). In a way, the hurt we do each other is a greater offense than the hurt we do God. God recovers; the men and women we ignore, dismiss, don't take seriously, or offend by our words and manner, may not.

## Features of the Synagogue 2000 Process of Synagogue Transformation

We quickly discovered that casting a vision of what the twenty-first-century synagogue would look like was insufficient information and direction for the synagogues in our cohorts. Rather, they required a specific process with which to engage in the visioning work. We knew that programmatic change could happen by fiat of the professional staff or lay leadership, but all of the experts we consulted advised against it, urging us to develop a process of transformation that recognized and valued the voices of all the "stakeholders" in the congregation and that sought to transform the very culture of synagogue life.

The S2K process evolved over several of the early cohorts into a sophisticated and elaborate model of transformation. It involved the following major features:

### Teams

We insisted that synagogues create an S2K team, consisting of the key clergy and professional staff, top lay leadership, and people from the congregation who could be called spiritual seekers, voices not normally integral to synagogue planning at the highest levels. This S2K team of ten to twenty people committed to a three-year program of meetings designed to elevate the conversation about the purposes and goals of the congregation as it envisioned itself in the twenty-first century.

The most radical idea embedded within the notion of "team" is that both clergy and laity are empowered to work together to implement change. In a staff-driven congregation, this was close to heresy. In fact, as we gathered the S2K teams for our initial kickoff conferences, we were constantly amazed at how many of the clergy who had been supportive of the project in the planning stages suddenly realized that the actual process they would be engaged in virtually demanded the empowerment of the laity. But as we have seen, this sort of collaboration is essential.

### Structured Meetings

We believed that the S2K team should reflect the kind of sacred community that we were advocating the congregation itself to become—a community that respected each individual as made in the image of God, a community that cared for each person's Jewish journey, a community that prayed and studied together, a community that, in its meetings, embodied the values of Judaism. We viewed these team meetings as a way to experiment with "doing synagogue differently"; spiritual, not corporate; adult, not pediatric. The structure of the meetings itself is quite unique:

1. An opening ritual, prayer, or song marks the gathering as a Jewish spiritual occasion and formally announces its beginning.
2. Check-in provides an opportunity for everyone to share a few words about what's happening in one's personal life; takes from a few minutes to more than half an hour.
3. Jewish study is combined with thematic material whenever possible.
4. Thematic material or work group activity occupies most of the meeting time and varies depending upon the nature of the group.
5. Reflection is an opportunity for participants to address their responses to the theme of the session, the structure or dynamics of the group, or other issues of process or content.
6. A closing ritual or prayer, with a quick go-around of last words, is an opportunity to hear how people are feeling and to create closure for that day's session. Follow the personal sharing with a simple closing circle, song, poem, or short prayer to help create a transition out of group time.
7. Food is an important component that encourages the forming of social connections; the sharing of food can be infused with Jewish meaning by including the appropriate blessings before and after eating.

## Conferences: A Glimpse of the Emerald City

Each cohort of congregations was invited to a series of conferences designed to bring the S2K teams together for cross-congregational sharing and learning from experts in key topic areas such as sacred space, membership, ambience of welcome, music, study, healing, social justice, and prayer. A highlight of each conference was the opportunity to showcase an innovative prayer service reflecting the best practice of each denominational movement. Led by the S2K fellows, these prayer services were the highlight of the conferences, allowing what we called a "glimpse of the Emerald City." In other words, we demonstrated to each cohort of congregations what was possible to achieve in prayer services that were engaging, uplifting, and spiritually satisfying. We knew that it was rare for synagogue leaders to have the opportunity to see how different synagogues and clergy lead services; at S2K conferences, we brought the best of the best to share their approaches. Although we intended these services to be demonstrations—we modeled Shabbat and High Holy Day services on weekday evenings!—the power of the services turned the modeling into moving spiritual experiences for nearly everyone in attendance.

### Low-Hanging Fruit

Another strategy that emerged in the S2K conferences was the idea of identifying and adopting "low-hanging fruit," small practical ideas that could be implemented easily back home. Like picking the low-hanging fruit on a tree, the harvesting of these ideas was relatively easy and their adoption fairly painless relative to larger, more systemic challenges that required much more deliberation before the change could occur. As we will see below, the best of the low-hanging fruit often came from the presentations on what I am calling here spiritually welcoming ambience, welcoming worship, and welcoming membership. Thus, throughout this book, you will find some of the best low-hanging fruit collected by our S2K congregations and highlighted with this icon:

### Consulting: Lending an Ear and a Hand

In every community in which we mounted a project, S2K hired a consultant to work with each synagogue as the process unfolded. These outstanding organizational development professionals lent indispensable assistance to the leadership of the teams as they negotiated the challenging process. The national S2K office also facilitated assistance to the teams through consulting offered by staff and S2K fellows.

### Curricula: A Road Map for the Journey

We knew that the S2K teams would need a "road map" to guide their studies and deliberations. We invested enormous energy and funding in developing highly sophisticated and jam-packed curriculum guides for nearly all of the PISGAH gates. Individual curriculum guides exist for sacred community (*kehillah kedoshah*), prayer (*tefillah*—Reform and Conservative versions), and study (*limud*). The early work in healing is integrated into the *tefillah* curriculum, while our work in Good Deeds is yet to be realized. Each of these curricula is infused with the S2K understanding of institutional deepening, reflecting much of the best thinking of organizational development applied to synagogue systems. We sought to create a vehicle that would encourage graduate-level study of Judaism and institutional development within the teams. These curricula were created by a collaboration of S2K staff and guest authors under the supervision of Dr. Adrianne Bank and Rabbi Yoel H. Kahn. They represent a rich resource of material for any congregation that wants to do the deep work of synagogue transformation.

## Synagogue 2000 Becomes Synagogue 3000

After ten years of action research into the process of synagogue transformation, the leadership of Synagogue 2000 spent a year reflecting on our achievements and planning how we could best serve the Jewish community. We decided our next iteration—Synagogue 3000—would focus on the crucial role of leadership in making change happen. To that end, our first decision was to make the S2K model of synagogue transformation, including all of our curricula, low-hanging fruit best practices, and other resources, available free of charge through a link to the S2K archives on the Synagogue 3000 website, www.synagogue3000.org. Since they are available there in their entirety, I have only included in this volume key concepts and ideas presented in the curricula, as well as specific pieces I authored. Complete directions on how to create a visioning team, organize and run meetings, and use the curricula are also available on the website.

## Adopting the Synagogue 2000 Transformation Process: You Can Do It!

All of this may sound incredibly challenging. It is. But it is also thrilling and inspiring.

You can do this.

You can envision the future of your congregation.

You can adopt the S2K transformation strategy, create a visioning team that studies and reflects on how the synagogue can deepen as a sacred community.

You can develop a relationship between the professional staff and the lay leadership that leads to a joint commitment to transforming your synagogue.

This is not rocket science; it is good social science. This is not make-work; it is sacred work. Most importantly, synagogue transformation expresses the fundamental Jewish value of *chadesh,* to "make new again."

When we return the Torah scrolls to the ark, the congregation raises its voice in a crescendo of music and heartfelt expression that never fails to move me:

> *It is a tree of life for those who grasp it,*
> *And all who uphold it are blessed.*
> *Its ways are pleasantness,*
> *And all its paths are peace.*
> *Help us turn to You,*
> *And we shall return.*
> *Renew our lives as in the days of old.*

**3**

# Welcoming Ambience

## What Does Jewish Tradition Teach Us About Hospitality?

### *Greeting Guests: The Model of Abraham and Sarah*

The first step in transforming a congregation into a sacred community is to create an ambience that overflows with the *spirituality of welcoming*, with radical hospitality. In the classical Jewish texts, the mitzvah of *hachnasat orchim*, the welcoming of guests, is ranked among the most important spiritual imperatives in Judaism.

Read carefully this text from Genesis about Abraham and Sarah:

> The Lord appeared to him by the terebinths of Mamre; he was sitting at the entrance of the tent as the day grew hot. Looking up, he saw three men standing near him. As soon as he saw them, he ran from the entrance of the tent to greet them and, bowing to the ground, he said, "My lords, if it please you, do not go on past your servant. Let a little water be brought; bathe your feet and recline under the tree. And let me fetch a morsel of bread that you may refresh yourselves; then go on—seeing that you have come your servant's way." They replied, "Do as you have said." Abraham hastened into the tent to Sarah, and said, "Quick, three seahs of choice flour! Knead and make cakes!" Then Abraham ran to the herd, took a calf, tender and choice, and gave it to a servant-boy, who hastened to prepare it. He took curds and milk and the calf that had been prepared and set these before them; and he waited on them under the tree as they ate.

> —*Genesis 18:1–8*

This is a text in a hurry. Look at the words used to describe Abraham's actions: he *ran,* he *hastened,* he *ran* again. The Hebrew verbs are even more dramatic: *vayaratz, vayimaheir, mahari!* The word for "run" is used twice, "rushed" three times, and "fetch" four times. The biblical commentators have a field day with the story. What was Abraham doing as he sat in the heat of the day at the entrance of his tent? The medieval commentator Rashi points out that he was healing; after all, at the conclusion of the previous chapter, Abraham circumcised himself at the age of ninety-nine! Another commentator suggests that Abraham was engaged in the morning prayers. And yet, when the three strangers come into view, Abraham overcomes his pain, interrupts his worship, and rushes to greet them.

Moreover, Abraham does not know anything at all about the strangers. They could be wealthy donors and community big shots, or they could just be beggars off the street. He has no idea that they are angels of God sent to visit the sick and to announce to Abraham and Sarah that they will, at long last, become parents. To Abraham, they were sojourners in need of respite and he implored them to enjoy the hospitality of his and Sarah's tent. From this example, the Talmud teaches this remarkable lesson: "*Hachnasat orchim,* welcoming strangers, is a greater mitzvah than welcoming the *Shechinah,* God's presence" (*Shabbat* 127a).

The spirituality of welcoming elevates both the guest and the host. A warm greeting eases the unspoken anxiety a guest feels at being a stranger and immediately answers the first question anyone in a strange place asks: Will I be welcome here? For the host, the act of hospitality is a gesture of spiritual generosity, uplifting the soul. It is an offering of oneself, an invitation for connection between human and human and, in that meeting, between human and God.

### In the Image of God

The spirituality of welcome is rooted in a core value of Judaism that is expressed in the very first chapter of the Bible:

> And God said: "Let us make humankind in our image, after our likeness".... And God created humankind in God's image; male and female God created them.
>
> —*Genesis 1:26–28*

This is a stunning statement: *Every human being is made in the image of God.* From this core value, we discover the ultimate purpose of a congregation. The task of a spiritual community is to help each human being made in the image of God recapture the knowledge of how to live a life filled with godliness, a life committed to becoming a partner with God in doing the ongoing work of creation and repair of the world.

Creating a culture in which every person who crosses the threshold of the congregation is treated as an image of God is the fundamental reason to become an enthusiastic practitioner of the spirituality of welcoming.

The synagogue can be a sacred community that offers everyone who steps into its midst a welcome infused with spirituality—with meaning, purpose, connection, and the presence of the Divine. For the core members of the congregation—the regulars and the leadership—the task of creating a community of welcome through the mitzvah of *hachnasat orchim,* the welcoming of guests, is filled with meaning and purpose. For the newcomer, encountering a warm welcome offers connectedness to community imbued with the presence of God—a sacred community. To create such a community requires an intention to transform the culture of the congregation into one in which the welcoming ambience is tangible, palpable, and unmistakable in every aspect of congregational life.

### Embracing the Stranger

The Torah teaches the importance of loving strangers and treating them like our own people:

> So you are to love the sojourner, for sojourners were you in the land of Egypt.
>
> —*Deuteronomy 10:19*

If Judaism is to flourish, if synagogues are to become spiritual centers for many more Jews, then we must become passionate about opening our doors, encouraging people to come in, and welcoming them once they step across our threshold, without preconceived ideas about what they should or should not be.

Here is a true story from Rabbi Rick Jacobs, an S2K fellow, and the senior rabbi of Westchester Reform Temple in New York:

> She was a little old lady in ragged clothes who came every day to the synagogue, probably because she had no place else to go. Her name was Ina, but most people didn't know that. She almost never spoke to anyone, preferring her privacy. People in the congregation hardly had a relationship with her, yet most would smile at her and wish her a *Shabbat Shalom,* even if there was never a return greeting. We thought she must have had some sort of mental illness or social insecurity. Each week, I would welcome her to the synagogue. She paid some dues to maintain her membership, but the way she dressed and acted, no one ever thought she was a person of means.
>
> When she died, I officiated at the funeral. There was no family to sit *shivah.* There were no memorial plaques. I thought I would never hear of her again. Yet one day, about two months after her death, I received a phone call out of the blue.
>
> "Rabbi Jacobs? This is Sam Adler, Ina's attorney. As you know, Ina was not one to talk much. I didn't know her well myself. But it turns out she had accumulated a substantial portfolio of stocks. She has left your congregation a bequest of $750,000. Why? She always felt welcomed at your synagogue."

We never know everything about everyone who comes through our doors, but we are obligated to welcome all who enter.

### A Welcoming Tent

What is the very first prayer said in most synagogues when the morning service begins?

It is this, from Numbers 24:5:

| | |
|---|---|
| *Mah tovu* | "How good are" |
| *Ohalekha* | "your tents" |
| *Ya'akov* | "(people of) Jacob" |
| *Mishkenotekha* | "your prayer houses" |
| *Yisrael* | "Israel." |

Why did the Rabbis choose this prayer to say when first entering a synagogue? Because when they thought of synagogues, they envisioned tents. In fact, the first "prayer houses" were undoubtedly tents.

**Exercise**

## *What Makes an Inviting Tent?*

Imagine what a tent looks like. How is a good synagogue like a good tent?

If you are doing this exercise with congregational leaders, turn to a colleague and come up with a list of answers to the question.

Here are some possible answers:

Provides shelter from elements such as rain, cold, sunlight

Offers protection

Portable; can move

Things inside can change

Comforting

A safe place

Place of refuge

A strong center holds it up

A gathering place

Often visitors are offered food and drink

Durable

The roof leaks

> Sense of belonging
>
> Can enter from all sides
>
> Place of rest
>
> Space for conversations we do not usually have
>
> Usually has an open door that implies "come on in"
>
> A good synagogue, like a good tent, should be all of these things to everyone who enters. What can you do to make your synagogue more like a good tent?

## Why Is Hospitality So Important for Synagogues?

We live in a time and a culture that seems to work against the very thing we hope to create: a synagogue of relationships. Relationships begin with a sincere greeting—a handshake, a smile, and a good word. Radical hospitality is the way to open the door to the possibility of spirituality.

We are in danger of losing the art of hospitality. We don't welcome strangers anymore—we are afraid of them. We don't invite people to our homes anymore—we entertain at restaurants or clubs. We don't greet people on the street—we avoid them. We don't even answer our phones without first checking caller ID to see if it is someone we know or want to talk with. What is happening to us? When we lose the art of hospitality, we lose a part of our souls. For kindness to others is not simply an imperative to improve the lives of those who seek welcome. The act of hospitality improves the lives of those who offer it. Welcoming, serving, and feeding others embody the value of generosity of spirit, of sharing what we have, of caring for others when they are in need.

The spirituality of welcoming begins with radical hospitality that brings people closer to each other, to community, to Judaism, and to God. The spiritually welcoming congregation has two objectives: *outreach* and *inreach*. We need to open our doors wide, put out the welcome mat, invite in the stranger, and extend hospitality to all who enter, to bring them *closer* to our spiritual communities. And we need to encourage our current congregation members to move from peripheral or occasional involvement into a *deeper* relationship with each other, with the community, with Judaism, and with God.

All too often, we fail at both of these tasks. We do not put out the welcome mat to the stranger, nor do we do enough to deepen the relationships we already have. Only to the regulars does the synagogue seem very friendly. For them, it is. They recognize each other, know each other, kiss each other Good *Shabbes,* and invite each other over for lunch. They are friendly to the people already there! The guests experience this as insular and off-putting. Some people in synagogues like it this way. They don't want the synagogue community to be too big; they like the intimacy of a small group. And, after all, integrating new people into an existing group is one of the more difficult challenges in social engineering. But this aversion to guests can keep a synagogue from growing.

The regulars have also forgotten what it feels like to enter an unfamiliar synagogue. Here is how one person described the experience of coming to a congregation as a newcomer:

> I parked in the lot. I walked into the building and immediately felt lost. There were no directional signs to the synagogue sanctuary. I had to ask someone "Where is the service?" They pointed me to the sanctuary. I walked by a table that had stacks of those prayer shawls and a pile of skullcaps. I hadn't put one on in years and it felt very awkward. The material of the shawl was polyester; it kept falling off my shoulders. The skullcap didn't fit very well and it felt weird on my head. The service had already begun; the cantor was singing. People were sitting in the pews holding open a prayer book. No one was at the door. I entered and found an empty seat. There were two books in the back of the pew in front of me: a small black book and a larger blue book. I looked around at the people nearby and noticed they were looking in the black book. I opened it up and tried to look like I knew what I was doing, but, once again, I felt lost. I listened for an announcement of the page, but the rabbi didn't say anything for at least twenty minutes. I tried to follow what was happening on the stage, but it was basically one long series of prayers sung

in Hebrew by the cantor or the Bar Mitzvah boy. There were some people who clearly knew what was going on; they responded to the prayers from the stage. They knew when to stand up even before the rabbi said anything. They even launched into a kind of swaying motion as they prayed. I had no clue what that was all about. At the very end of the service, someone said *Shabbat Shalom* to me. That was the first time all morning I felt welcomed.

Let's be honest—in some synagogues, guests are barely tolerated. The people in the constantly changing Bar and Bat Mitzvah crowd are viewed by many regulars as interlopers instead of as guests who are to be welcomed and valued. Changing this attitude toward guests is the first step in creating a welcoming ambience in the congregation.

How can a synagogue love guests? The single most important way is for the congregation members themselves to express their personal welcome when they see a stranger.

## The Radical Hospitality Experts: Chabad and the Megachurches

During the course of my research, I discovered two groups—one in the Jewish community and one in the Christian community—that understand the importance of radical hospitality. Chabad, a group of Orthodox Jews descended from a Hasidic rebbe from Lubavitch, Poland, and megachurches, very large, seeker-friendly, purpose-driven Christian congregations, view the welcoming of strangers as a core value. Consider what Chabad and the Christian megachurches do to encourage their regulars to become *shlichim* (messengers) and evangelists to others. There are several lessons to be learned from their practices.

The first lesson is the practice of welcoming. Walk into a Chabad house and you are immediately embraced by a warm and inviting culture. The Chabad rabbi will often offer visitors a meal on site or an invitation to someone's home for Shabbat lunch. The welcoming of guests is one of their highest priorities. The same is true for evangelical megachurches that were founded on the vision of being a church for the un-churched.

The second lesson to learn is the Chabad and megachurch approach to influencing people toward spiritual formation. Once on the Chabad rabbi's radar screen, prospects receive incredible levels of personal attention—phone calls of support and encouragement for taking on Jewish practices, home visits, step-by-step instruction—all offered in a nonjudgmental, progress-at-your-own-pace approach. They know very well that the people they are working with are uncomfortable with Jewish living and are not ready yet to commit to the kind of Jewish lifestyle they represent. Their strategy is to focus on the joys of Jewish celebration in the context of a deeply devoted community. In the megachurches, guests and new members alike are encouraged to ask questions, to take classes, and to join a small group.

The third and perhaps most interesting lesson is that the Chabad and megachurch regulars have been taught that the stranger, the guest, is no intrusion whatsoever. If anything, they represent lost souls who can be returned to the fold (or, in the megachurches, reborn as believers). Chabad represents an effective example of "evangelical" Jews who see the task of *keiruv*—bringing people closer to Judaism—as central to their mission. And the megachurches have redefined how churches reach the un-churched.

Moreover, both Chabad and the megachurches emphasize the imperative to welcome the stranger in their socialization process. In other words, once you become a regular, you are constantly reminded of the obligation of personal hospitality. The best example of how this becomes institutionalized is the commitment of both Chabad and the megachurches to literally give over the "prime time" of prayer to the newcomers. Chabad will offer High Holy Day services that are designed for spiritual seekers, those with little access to and knowledge of the worship service. When do the Chabad regulars pray? During early-morning prayers held *before* the seeker service. In the megachurches, the Sunday morning service is shaped with the seekers in mind; the regulars pray on Wednesday evening!

Finally, in Chabad and the megachurches, the greatest praise is lavished on those who do the work of *keiruv* and evangelism. Bringing the seeker closer is as important as one's own personal spiritual growth. In fact, bringing someone closer to God is considered a spiritual act of the highest order. Substantial funds and time are devoted to outreach in both organizations. Yet, both are among the fastest growing, most successful, and financially secure religious institutions in the American religious community.

## Emergent Congregations: Redefining Hospitality

The latest trend in American religious life is the establishment of small spiritual communities that have been called "emergent" congregations. A response to the corporate, results-driven megachurches, these emergent churches meet in homes, clubs, coffee shops, often over a communal meal. Hospitality is at the root of these communities, along with an emphasis on "relationality," social justice, and spiritual direction. New forms of synagogue have emerged—such as Panim Hadashot in Seattle, where the rabbi, Dov Gartenberg, invites people to his home for Shabbat meals and teaches Judaism in the Whole Foods grocery store—parallel to the Christian emergent phenomenon. Synagogue 3000 has termed this development "Jewish Emergent."

## How Synagogues Can Provide Quality Service: Learning from the Corporate World

While synagogues are known for offering religious services, synagogue leaders need to understand that they are also in the *service* business. We serve members and guests in all kinds of ways. *Avodah,* the Hebrew term for "prayer" is also the word for "service." A synagogue of the twenty-first century will serve its members and inspire them to serve God.

Ironically, there is much that sacred communities can learn from secular companies. The best companies in America are well known for their attention to customer service. Frankly, they inculcate their employees with the value of serving people much more effectively than many religious organizations. Their motivation is material profit and they saturate their culture with the belief that serving people well improves their bottom line.

The importance of quality service has transformed the way many institutions and companies conduct business. The customer or client—not the product—is thought of as the central focus of the organization. At first, the emphasis on quality service revolved around ambience issues, such as the way people are welcomed and how easy it is to use the product or service offered. More recently, the focus has been on two deeper concerns: the total *experience* of the encounter with the organization and cultivating a *relationship* between the individual and the company.

Congregations are not like for-profit businesses. They are spiritual communities rather than market communities. Nonetheless, there are many practices that businesses have adopted that are appropriate to the synagogue community when offered in the right spirit.

Here are descriptions of how several companies deliver quality service and some suggestions about their applicability to synagogue communities.

### Personal Attention

Nordstrom is a department store famous for the personal attention afforded its customers. Clerks are encouraged to establish personal relationships with their customers in order to engender loyalty. A personal profile that details each client's preferences for styles, colors, brand names, and so forth, is created in the company's database.

Most synagogues have a database on members that includes basic information collected during the initial membership process and updated each year in the annual membership renewal questionnaire. But what do we really know about our members? One synagogue has created a survey to develop a spiritual profile for each congregant in an effort they call Project Soul. Can you imagine implementing a similar program in your congregation? What sort of questions might you ask in your survey?

### Anticipating Needs

I do a good deal of traveling, and I often stay at a Marriott hotel. A couple of years ago, I noticed that the company did several things that improved the lodging experience, all based on the same principle of customer service: They anticipated my needs. I found an iron and ironing board in every single room I stayed in. This eliminated my need to call the front desk to see if I could borrow one when I had to iron a wrinkled shirt. They placed a sign in the bathroom with a simple question, "Forget Anything?" followed by an offer to provide a toothbrush, shaving kit, or other toiletries I may have left at home. In every Marriott hotel room, there is high-speed Internet access.

Synagogues anticipate some needs of congregants, but we can do better. How does the congregation—not just the clergy—respond when a member or a loved one of a member falls ill, suffers a loss, or experiences a setback? What sort of advice and support do we offer congregants when they prepare to celebrate a lifecycle event? How do we think about the educational, social, emotional, and spiritual needs of each individual within the community?

## Exceeding Expectations

The Disney Company challenges their employees to find a way to take five minutes per day to exceed the expectations of guests. For example, they train the housekeeping staff in their hotels to notify the front desk if a child in a family falls ill during their stay. The manager will then arrange to send the child a bowl of chicken soup from room service, often accompanied by a stuffed toy. Although this costs the company money, they have budgeted significant dollars to empower their staff to exceed expectations.

Synagogues often hear about someone who becomes ill, especially if they end up in the hospital. But usually only the clergy make hospital visits. One Synagogue 2000 congregation deployed a team of visitors to hospitals and elder care facilities, thereby exceeding the expectations of the sick hospital patients. Consider the expectations that exist in your synagogue community. In what ways can your synagogue work to exceed those expectations?

## Providing Ombudspeople

At the world-famous Mayo Clinic in Rochester, Minnesota, family members awaiting news on the progress of a surgery are linked to a nurse communicator who checks in at regular intervals with updates.

The waiting room is lined with educational brochures explaining the most common surgical procedures.

Many people who encounter Jewish practice only occasionally in their lives approach synagogues with some of the same fear and concern that people have about medical procedures and hospitals. How do we help demystify the experience of the synagogue? Do we provide explanations of our worship services and lifecycle events? Many congregations today do offer a guide to the synagogue experience. Some couples prepare explanations of the Jewish wedding ceremony at their celebrations. Valley Beth Shalom, a Conservative congregation in Encino, California, and Beth Am, a Reconstructionist synagogue in White Plains, New York, send a paraprofessional volunteer into the homes of families preparing for a Bar or Bat Mitzvah. Can you think of other ways to demystify the synagogue experience?

### Teaching People

Do you know what grout is? I didn't. But one day, my wife, Susie, said to me, "Ronnie, we need to grout the tile in our kitchen." So, off I went to The Home Depot to learn about grout. I walked in feeling somewhat anxious and embarrassed. The employee who greeted me at the front door directed me to the correct department, where I sought the help of another clerk. He immediately set me at ease by asking what project I was working on. The easy conversation enabled me to ask what I thought were stupid questions. "Oh," he said, "There's no such thing as a stupid question at our store." Later, when I met Bernie Marcus, the visionary entrepreneur who co-founded The Home Depot, he confirmed that all of the "associates" are given training in putting customers at ease and never, ever assuming they know how to do a task. Moreover, Bernie repeated a line from his book *Built from Scratch*, "If I ever saw an associate point a customer toward what they needed three aisles over, I would threaten to bite their finger. I would say, 'Don't ever let me see you point. You take the customer by the hand, and you bring them right where they need to be and you help them.'"

How many of our members are embarrassed to ask Jewish questions? Do our congregations offer family education and adult learning opportunities that meet the real, practical needs of those who are taking the Jewish journey? What can we do to create an atmosphere in our synagogues where people feel more comfortable asking? How can we convey the message that there are no stupid questions?

### Creating Great First Impressions

At the Outback Steakhouse, a greeter opens the front door of the building for you. The server introduces her/himself by name, bends down to get to eye level with the patrons, and asks, "Have you visited our restaurant before?" If the answer is no, guests are given an explanation of how the food is served. These first impressions create the climate for everything that transpires during the meal. It is in the first few seconds that a visitor senses a feeling of welcome or of indifference. In a moment, you feel glad you came or wish you had gone somewhere else.

What do visitors feel when they first enter your synagogue? Your sanctuary? How is the ambience of welcome created? What can you do to make your synagogue seem more welcoming?

### Customizing Service

Rather than building thousands of copies of the exact same machine, Dell Computer revolutionized the business by customizing each computer to the customer's specific needs. As it tracks orders, the company learns from its customers about their current needs and expectations.

Every person's Jewish journey is different. How do we individualize the synagogue experience for our members? What do we do when members join to assist them in assessing where they are on their Jewish journeys and what next steps they want to take? Are we ready with advice when our members need it? How do we learn from them what their needs are?

### Finding the Book

I once asked a clerk at an information desk at Barnes and Noble if they had a certain volume in stock. The clerk looked up the title on the computer and told me that, indeed, they had one copy and I could find it on the third floor in aisle five. Recently, when I asked a clerk at Barnes and Noble if they had a specific book, the clerk searched the computer and then physically led me to the shelf, found the book, and handed it to me. When I inquired about the difference, the clerk told me that the company had held new training seminars designed to elevate the level of service to customers.

How many times have you seen a guest lost in the prayer book? One level of quality service would be to tell the person, "We're on page sixteen." A completely different level of service would be to hand the person your prayer book turned to the correct page and pick up another one for yourself. Which would you prefer if you were the person who was lost?

### Coffee or Community?

Howard Schultz, the founder of Starbucks Coffee, makes a remarkable point in his book *Pour Your Heart Into It*: Starbucks is not in the coffee business; it is in the community business. He modeled Starbucks after the hundreds of neighborhood cafés he saw on a trip to Italy.

Congregations are spiritual communities, communities that would do well to offer a good cup of coffee. To encourage adults to come into the building after driving their children to Sunday School, a number of synagogues have instituted coffee bars. Some have clever names. My favorites are *Java Nagila* and *Mi Ka-Mocha*. Can you imagine a similar venture in your congregation? What effect might it have on your members?

### Honoring the Front Line

My mother once called me from Omaha to tell me that she had been to the best luncheon in the history of Beth El Synagogue. The social hall was packed and the love was palpable. Who was the honoree? The cook, Lucy White, an African American woman who for thirty years had baked the cookies and prepared the after-service receptions. And what did Lucy want as a gift from the congregation? A leaf on the Tree of Life plaque in the lobby of the synagogue. They gave her a branch!

How do congregations honor their staff? How many congregations list every member of the staff on their marquees and in their publications? And yet, the frontline people often have far more interaction with members and guests than the clergy and officers of the congregation. What can your congregation do to increase their visibility? What sort of message will this send?

## Getting the Name Right

Synagogues would do well to learn the lesson of the Mayo Clinic, where thousands of people visit the 1,800 physicians every day. I once took my father-in-law Abe to Mayo for a checkup. We sat in a large room with dozens of other patients, waiting for the receptionist to call his name. Abe comes from Poland, a Holocaust survivor who refused to let the U.S. immigration authorities change his name. "I've lost my family; I'm not going to lose my name," he would tell me. Living in the Midwest, most customer service people bungle his name, badly mispronouncing it. Abe's name is spelled K-U-K-A-W-K-A. When it came time for Abe's appointment, a lovely receptionist, who certainly had little experience with Polish Jewish names, strode to the microphone and announced, "Mr. Abram Kukawka," pronouncing his name absolutely perfectly! I could not believe my ears. As she took us back to the doctor's office, I asked her, "You said his name perfectly—how did you do that?" She pointed to the appointment card. Under the name *Kukawka* was a transliteration: *Koo-cough-kah*. When she saw how surprised I was, she explained, "Sir, we have guests from all corners of the world. We have a whole department of translators who transliterate foreign names so that we pronounce them correctly. It's important to the patient."

One of the greatest faux pas moments in the rabbinate is to mispronounce a name at a Bar or Bat Mitzvah, a wedding, a funeral, or in reading the names on the *Yahrtzeit* list. Is *Levine* pronounced *Leh-veen* or *Leh-vine*? I know of cases when family members were so appalled that the rabbi mispronounced a name at a crucial lifecycle moment, they dropped their membership from the synagogue. People want you to know their name.

**Exercise**

## *What's Your Experience with Service?*

Think about your own experiences with organizations and businesses that deal with the public—banks, grocery stores, shops, telephone and Internet service providers, bookstores, and so on. Recall examples of poor service you have experienced. (If you are doing this exercise with a colleague, each of you take three minutes to share experiences of poor service.) Think about what the problem was with the service. Here is a list culled from workshops I have conducted:

Poor attitude

Nobody is there to solve the problem

Nobody can answer a question

I'm given the runaround

Surly

Rude

No compassion

Employees chatting, ignoring me

Give me your money now!

Red tape

Lack of training

Poor communication

Not taking responsibility

Make the application to synagogues. Are there examples of poor service in your congregation? Don't blame—just name!

Now, think about experiences of great service. (In a group, turn to a different person and share these experiences. Take three minutes each.) Collect a list of what made the service great. Here are some of the characteristics of great service I have learned:

Can-do attitude

Individualized attention

Warm greeting

Eye contact

More concern for the individual than the system

Doing the unexpected

Exceeding expectations

A compassionate response in crisis

Initiated help

Anticipated needs

You know who is in charge

Prompt and speedy service

Pleasant tone of voice

Taking time to take care of the problem

Thanked for coming

Now, discuss how you can apply the principles of quality service to the congregation. An example of great service might be "The teller at the bank calls me by name during the transaction." The application to the synagogue could be "Anyone who speaks to a congregant or a prospective member on the phone refers to the person by name during the call." How many parallels can you find?

## Giving the Synagogue a More Welcoming Face: The Importance of Greeting

The congregant does not just exist in a customer relationship, but also in a spiritual relationship. The beginning of a spiritual relationship is often found in the moment of greeting a fellow human being who is made in the image of God. This requires a paradigm shift from the consumer relationship to an encounter that recognizes the oneness of us all. This is true not only for the way in which the synagogue sets up arrangements for greeting and hospitality but also for how people treat one another.

Interestingly, of the many low-hanging fruit—the easy-to-implement and immediate changes—that most Synagogue 2000 sites have "plucked," one of the most effective has been to have greeters in the synagogue during services. Synagogues report that the presence of the greeters has helped to fundamentally change the climate of the congregation, warming it up considerably.

### Greeters, Not Ushers

We know that most synagogues have ushers. But we also know that an usher is not necessarily a greeter. Ushers worry about decorum; greeters offer a warm welcome. Ushers hand out books; greeters introduce newcomers to regulars. There is a fine art to the act of greeting that can transform the culture of congregational life.

Why? Why has something so small, which on the surface appears so obvious and so simple, had such a major impact on the feeling of the place? Because greeting, in the context of synagogue life, is not just about improving quality service. Martin Buber taught that all life is meeting. Greeting is the basis for meeting, which is the first step toward creating a sacred community.

### Great Greeters

I have known a number of great greeters: people who instantly connect with others, who can "work the room," who know how to schmooze, who genuinely enjoy meeting others. My *zaydie*—my grandfather—Louie Paperny was a natural greeter. He built the first modern supermarket in the state of Nebraska, where just inside the front door, he created a place he called the courtesy counter. This is where you could cash a check, redeem soda bottles, and find Louie. This is where he hung out, at the very front of the store, greeting his customers. He knew each of them by name, he knew their family members, and he knew their stories. And they knew him. Every time we went out to dinner with Zaydie, at least a few of his customers stopped by his table to greet *him*. He was so popular in Omaha, I thought he was the mayor! Louie was not alone in his generation. In Indianapolis, Indiana, Sid Maurer, the owner of Atlas Market, created the same sort of courtesy counter at the front of his store where he could be found greeting his customers. He was so well known that when he died, a thousand people attended his funeral, including someone who as a young man had worked for Sid, David Letterman.

My father, Alan, is a gregarious Brooklyn-born soul. He is the kind of guy you get on an elevator with on the ground floor and, by the tenth floor, you know his story and he knows yours. He refuses to fly, so he'll take a two-day bus ride to visit us in Los Angeles, and when he gets off, complete strangers are saying heartfelt goodbyes. He is color blind and status blind; Alan treats every human being he ever met as someone made in the image of God.

## "Wolfsoning" a Room

Without even realizing it, I began my career in education by serving as a greeter. In my first classroom experience, I quickly discovered that class did not begin at the bell. It began with me hanging out near the door of my classroom, greeting my eighth-graders as they came in. Amazingly, I found that students who were inattentive during class were completely engaging during my conversations with them in the hall. We shared opinions about sports, movies, and current events. I asked them about their lives outside of school and they asked me about mine. In class, I was a teacher; in the hall, I was a real human being. The greeting at the door was the basis of a personal relationship with each and every student.

As I began to give lectures to large gatherings, I continued this practice, greeting my "students" as they entered a ballroom, an auditorium, a sanctuary. Often, people thought I was actually the greeter from the sponsoring organization. Inevitably, when introduced as the keynote speaker, many people were shocked that I—the speaker!—had greeted them with a handshake and a warm welcome.

One day, our daughter Havi told us about a Shabbat dinner she had enjoyed with a number of my graduate students. "Dad," she exclaimed, "you have become a verb! Your students were talking about how you taught them to greet their students at the door. They call this Wolfsoning a room!"

As a teacher, I "Wolfson a room" for several reasons:

- In order to teach, I need to *connect* with my students and audience.
- The personal greeting creates immediate warmth in the room.

- I "walk the talk," modeling the very practice of hospitality that I teach.
- By introducing myself, I bridge the divide between teacher and student, between speaker and audience.
- I invite people into a relationship with me as a fellow human being, made in the image of God.

### Everyone Must Be a Greeter

As the Synagogue 2000 project was launched, an experience in a shopping mall fueled my interest in the art of greeting. My wife, Susie, and I entered a Disney Store to buy a birthday present. Standing just inside the entrance was a delightful young woman wearing a name tag that identified her as Jackie. She greeted us warmly: "Welcome to the Disney Store. Good morning!" Susie began to explore the store while I watched as Jackie greeted every person who walked in, offering welcome, directions, and advice. After fifteen minutes, I approached her:

"May I ask you a question? Is this your job?" I asked.

"Yes, it is," Jackie responded proudly.

"Do you get training on how to do this?" I continued.

"Yes, I did," she replied.

"From whom?"

"From the Disney University!" Jackie said. "They sent trainers from Orlando."

I teach at a university and I graduated from a university, but I had never heard of the Disney University! I Googled the term and learned that the Walt Disney Company established the Disney University in Florida to coordinate all the internal training for their employees, and they had recently begun offering seminars to outside companies hoping to learn the secrets of Disney's success as a leading customer service organization.

Within a month, I was in Orlando, enrolled in the excellent Disney Approach to Quality Service five-day seminar. The most important lesson I learned began with a question: When you visit a Disney theme park, how many employees will you likely interact with before you get on the first ride?

The answer is seven: the parking gate person, the parking lot attendant, the tram operator who takes you to the front gate, the ticket seller, the ticket taker, the person who sells you a Coke or rents you a stroller, the person who guides you into line, and the person who puts you onto the ride. Every one of those interactions can be positive or negative. Their mission is clear: to make you happy. If any one of the employees is rude or unhelpful, your day is off to a terrible start. So every Disney "cast member" is trained to be a greeter. They know that the front line is the bottom line.

Is not the same thing true for a congregation? Who does a visitor or a congregant meet when entering a synagogue? A parking attendant, a security person, the custodian, the gift shop person, the front office receptionist, the staff secretaries, the kitchen crew, the caterer, the school office staff, the religious school teachers, the executive director, the cantor, the rabbi—every one of these people, professional or lay, represents the congregation. Every one has the potential to make each interaction with members and guests a positive experience—or not.

The rabbi and cantor have particularly important roles to play because of their high visibility. Typically, the rabbi and cantor in many synagogues greet congregants as they leave the sanctuary. Why not welcome people when they come *into* the sanctuary? In Synagogue 2000 congregations, a number of rabbis and cantors decided to greet people as they arrived for services. This has changed the entire atmosphere of the worship. By walking through the sanctuary and onto the pulpit instead of entering from the side of the pulpit, the clergy demonstrate that they are representatives of the congregation. Their welcoming serves as a welcoming on behalf of everyone in the room.

Remember the story of the man who kicked me out of his seat? There were greeters at the door of that sanctuary, but I still felt rejected. What could the man have said to me that would have gotten him his seat and welcomed me? How about *Shabbat Shalom*? He knew I was a stranger. What if he had said, "Welcome to our congregation. Would you like to sit with me? Please do, but we need to save a seat for my friend who will be here soon. My name is Sam. What's yours?" I would have warmly accepted the greeting and the invitation.

## *Successful Greeting*

Here are just a few examples of successful approaches to welcoming visitors that have emerged in S2K synagogues:

- *At Valley Beth Shalom in Encino, California, congregants volunteer to act as m'kablei panim (literally, "greeting faces"), positioned at the main entrance of the sanctuary throughout the services.*

- *At the library minyan of Temple Beth Am in Los Angeles, a designated individual or family stands at the end of the service to invite guests to a Shabbat or Yom Tov lunch.*

- *In a synagogue in Orlando, Florida, a lamppost with street signs has been erected in the social hall identifying the spot as kikar shalom, the "greeting square." Greeters and officers of the synagogue stand near the post immediately after the service, available to greet visitors.*

- *One of the first Synagogue 2000 pilot sites, Temple Ner Tamid in California, recruited a group of fifty volunteers from the congregation to act as greeters. This "shalom squad" takes up positions in the parking lot, at the front doors of the building, at the doors of the sanctuary, and inside the sanctuary, looking for ways to greet members and guests.*

- *Realizing that members would be standing in line to go through the security gauntlet installed in the synagogue since 9/11, the Synagogue 2000 team at Temple Israel of Hollywood offered trays of apples and honey to those inconvenienced by the wait. Several of the team brought guitars and led a festive sing-along as well.*

Why is it important that all members of the congregation, not just the greeters, learn how to be welcoming? If we are to create sacred communities, where each and every person—member and guest—is treated as a human being made in the image of God, then infusing a *spirituality of welcoming* in the culture of the congregation is everyone's responsibility.

## What Makes a Great Greeter?

What are the characteristics of a great greeter? See how many you can come up with. Feel free to look at the list below for ideas:

> Friendly
> Approachable
> Smiles
> Makes eye contact
> Likes people
> Uses humor
> Enthusiastic
> Authentic
> Sincere
> Loves meeting others
> Proud of organization
> Thanks people

### The Greeter of LAX

There is one more greeter I would like you to meet. His name is Randy Kramer and he is one of the greatest greeters I have ever encountered.

Randy is a retired pilot who spent thirty years flying for the late, great Trans World Airlines, *alav ha-shalom,* may it rest in peace. I flew TWA for years, departing out of Los Angeles International Airport, often on an early-morning flight to the East Coast. And every morning, I would encounter Captain Randy, who volunteered to greet passengers as they boarded their flights. He was so popular that the local ABC television station did a segment about Captain Randy, a video that captures his expertise at greeting. (You can download it from the Synagogue 3000 website, www.synagogue3000.org. If you are working in a congregational team, view the video and discuss what makes Captain Randy such a great greeter.) When asked where he acquired this special talent, with his characteristic modesty, Captain Randy says, "Well, you've got to know how to go up to people, smile, and shake hands. If that takes special talent, well, that's what I've got!" The truth is that Captain Randy embodies much of what makes for great greeting.

**Tips**

## Seven Tips for Great Greeting

Here are the seven most important tips for greeting another human being:

1. Acknowledge the presence of the other. Don't ignore anyone. Don't make anyone feel that they are less important than the conversation you are having, the task that you are completing, the other people in your life.

2. Approach people with an attitude of welcome. Be enthusiastically friendly. Make the first move. Have your body language match your words: Make eye contact, maintain eye contact, smile, nod, or show empathy in some other way.

3. Greet the other. In the synagogue, offer the appropriate greeting in addition to the usual *Hello, how are you?* Add: *Welcome, Shabbat Shalom,* the appropriate holiday greeting, or *Mazal Tov!* or *Congratulations.* Remember that some people come to the congregation in mourning; greet them with *I'm sorry for your loss.*

4. Offer assistance, guidance or directions. *May I help you? What can I do for you? Let me show you to the child-care room.* Don't point people down a hall laden with a complicated set of directions; offer to take them there.

5. Answer all questions with respect. There is no such thing as a stupid Jewish question. If you don't know the answer, promise to get the answer and follow through.
6. Introduce new people to others. Build community by connecting people who share a life stage, an affinity, or live in the same neighborhood.
7. Thank people for coming. The flip side of greeting is "waving," expressing gratitude to busy people for participating in community.

## How Can the Synagogue Be a More Welcoming Space?

The spirituality of welcoming is mainly carried by the relationships and communications of individuals. It is also transmitted very powerfully, although often subliminally, through the experience of coming onto the campus of the congregation and into its lobbies, offices, hallways, and sacred space.

### Signs of Welcome

During my visits to synagogues, I am constantly amazed by the signs that greet me. At one large congregation, the very first sign at the entrance of the property read:

Drop-Off Lane

with an arrow indicating where parents were to deposit their children for religious school. As someone who has devoted years of work to encouraging congregations to invite parents into the building for Jewish family education, the not-so-subtle message reinforces the very behavior we are fighting against, what Rabbi Jeff Salkin calls "carpool tunnel syndrome."

Inside synagogues I have seen signs that are mind-boggling:

This Is Not an Entrance

Do Not Enter While Service in Progress

Door Does Not Lead to the Sanctuary

We Accept Mastercard/Visa

Many synagogues have poor signage, making it virtually impossible for a guest to find important locations—the sanctuary, the office, the youth lounge, the school office, the library, the rabbi's study, the cantor's study, the restrooms—without asking someone. Why is it that I can visit the Mayo Clinic, which covers ten city blocks, and never once get lost? Good signage.

## *Temple Beth Abraham (Reform)*
## *Tarrytown, New York*

Consider this example of how an S2K team implemented a strategy to improve the ambience of welcome in their congregation:

*Temple Beth Abraham's S2K committee embarked on creating a warm and welcoming atmosphere. Initially we split into two groups. The first group dealt with the physical space. They inspected the lobby area and made some changes. They removed clutter and changed some wall coverings that made the overall appearance more attractive. They also added signs around the building. As you approach the building it was not clear to newcomers and delivery people which of our two entrances to choose, so a big sign was put up that says "Welcome to Temple Beth Abraham" and notes Main Entrance, with an arrow pointing the way. Upon entering our smallish lobby, there are six doors from which to choose. There were no signs. We installed a sign in the lobby pointing the way to the library, religious school, main offices, and the restrooms.*

## A Welcoming Parking Lot

Think of your synagogue parking lot. Who gets the spaces closest to the entrance? In most places, the first spaces are for the disabled, then there are spaces for the rabbi, the president, the cantor, the executive director, the principal, the caterer(!), and other staff.

Now, imagine a synagogue parking lot where the first spaces after the disabled parking were marked in green with signs reading *For First-Time Visitors.*

I saw this for the first time at Saddleback Church. When Larry Hoffman and I arrived there on a Sunday morning, we were shocked by what we found. There were five thousand people leaving the church property after the early service and five thousand people trying to get in for the second service. Picture six lanes of traffic: three lanes of exiting cars, three lanes of entering cars. As a first-time visitor, the traffic and parking lots were a nightmare. We might have turned around and left had we not seen a large sign at the very front of the property that said.

FIRST-TIME VISITORS TO SADDLEBACK
Please move into the far right lane and put on your
emergency blinkers. You will be directed by traffic monitors.

We immediately moved into the first-time visitors lane, which was not jammed with cars, whisked past the distant parking lots, and arrived at the visitors parking lot, right next to the entrance of the church sanctuary! When we emerged from the car, we were welcomed warmly by parking lot greeters. It became clear that the members, not to mention the staff and leadership, wanted the prime parking spots to go to guests; they parked in the faraway lots.

When I shared this example with a group of synagogue leaders, one man retorted, "It would never work in my congregation. Our members would take one look at the sign, move into that lane, and say, 'First time this week! First time this month! First time this year!'"

## A Welcoming Building

Have you ever really looked at your home as a guest might on a first visit? We are so used to our environment that it is difficult to see things that others see. The same is true of synagogue "homes." The leaders and regulars who have made the synagogue a second home rarely see the place as visitors, guests, and shul-shoppers see it. Take a group of leaders from your congregation and visit another synagogue, or even a church. Visit a mall, a museum, or any other public facility to see how welcoming it is. Then, return to your building and look at it with fresh eyes.

## Exercise

# *Conducting a Synagogue Walk-Through*

Here is an exercise to do at your own synagogue. Drive up to the property and ask yourself: If I were a guest on a first-time visit, how welcoming would I find the synagogue? Use this and the following questions as a guide to assess the spirituality of welcome in your space.

## The Campus

What are the signs of welcome? Is there a marquee in front of the building? Does it say *Welcome*? What information is listed there? Often, if there is a marquee, the names of the rabbi(s), cantor, and president are listed. The name of the upcoming Bar or Bat Mitzvah may be highlighted. The sermon topic may be announced. Is there room for a greeting? Is the name of the congregation visible from the street? Is the address visible from the street? What did you notice in the parking lot?

Do you have reserved spaces for the clergy, the president, the office staff? Are they the best spaces, located closest to the entrances? Are there parking spaces marked for visitors? Do you have sufficient spaces for disabled parking? Do you have a space reserved for someone deserving of special recognition? Are there any directional signs? Does this look like a place that welcomes your arrival? How do you find the entrance? Is it easy to find? What is the security like? Does the building look well cared for and clean? What protects people during inclement weather? Are umbrellas available in the lobby?

## Signs of Welcome

Upon entering the building, are there signs of greeting? For example, are there any fresh flowers, bowls of candy, resource materials? Can you find someone to assist you? Do the people you meet greet you and offer assistance? Are there good directional signs to the places you want to visit in the building? Can you find the restrooms easily? Are they clean and inviting? Is there a coatroom? Is it easy to find, with plenty of hangers? Is it clean or messy? Is there a greeting area outside the sanctuary? Is there a place to sit? Is there a place to get a cup of coffee?

## The Lobby

What is the message of your lobby? Is it festooned with plaques, fliers pasted on walls, and stacks of information? Are there photos or paintings of any people on the walls or in the halls? Who are they? Is there a gift shop? When is it open? Do the volunteers who staff it act as greeters?

## Directions and Information

Is there a directory of offices in the lobby? Is there an information desk? Is there a window into the receptionist's area? Are there directional signs to the most visited places: the sanctuary, the chapel, the main office, the school office, the rabbi's study, the cantor's study? Can you find information about what the synagogue does?

How is the information displayed? Is there a board listing the names, roles, and office location for the staff? Is there a listing of the officers of the congregation? How are donations recognized? How are upcoming programs advertised?

## Waiting Areas

Where are the seating areas when waiting to see someone? What is the ambience of the waiting area? Is there reading material of Jewish content? Is there information about the synagogue? Are visitors offered something to drink?

### Office Space

If you work in the building, how difficult was it to find your space? Once you found it, did you experience it as welcoming? If someone were visiting you for the first time, what would they learn about you and the congregation? Are there photos of you with your family, with the congregants, on vacation? Do you display mementos of your work with the congregation? Is there candy on the reception desk?

### The Sanctuary

Is there a transitional area between the business end of the congregation and the sacred space of the sanctuary? How can one find a *kippah,* tallit, prayer book, or Bible before entering the sanctuary? Is it easy to find a seat? Is there any message of welcome in the bulletin at the seat? Is there any explanation of the objects in the sanctuary? Is there a guide to the service?

### Public Restrooms

Are they easy to find? Is there a rack for a tallit near the door of both the women's and the men's restrooms? Is there a baby changing table in both? How do they smell? Are there any amenities offered on the counter?

## Welcoming Phone Calls

The first contact with a spiritual community is often on the telephone. Whoever answers the phone creates the first impression of the congregation in the mind of the caller. If that person sounds tired, irritated, interrupted, or is curt, a negative impression will be made. If, on the other hand, the phone is answered with a friendly, welcoming, cheerful voice, the caller understands that this is a place that cares about people.

## Tips

# *Phone Etiquette*

### Answering the Phone

Here is a basic guide to welcoming phone etiquette:

1. Greet the caller. Here the congregation faces choices. There are any number of greetings: *Shalom, Hello,* and so on. Some synagogues will use Hebrew on purpose; others will avoid it.
2. Identify the congregation. "Congregation B'nai Shalom."
3. Identify yourself. "This is Ellen."
4. Offer assistance. "How may I help you?"
5. If the person is not available, ask permission. "I'm sorry, but Rabbi Schwartz is in a meeting at the moment. May I put you through to his assistant?" Or, "May I put you through to his voice mail?" If the caller refuses, take a message and assure the caller that the party will return the call as soon as possible.
6. Thank the caller. "Thank you for calling Congregation B'nai Shalom. Have a great day!"

### Voice Mail Etiquette

Many synagogues have adopted an automated telephone answering system, arguing that it saves time and money. If your congregation has such a system, consider carefully how your callers encounter the congregation for the first time. Here are four important tips:

1. Be short. Callers get very frustrated very quickly with long-winded messages. If the member or prospective member is calling to talk to someone, they don't want to hear a long *shpiel* about what events are happening at the synagogue. If

they are calling for basic information, you can direct them to press a key that connects them to the location of the synagogue, upcoming events, and so on.
2. Be direct. If you have an extended message, offer a quick escape hatch to speak to a real person, or an option to skip the message entirely.
3. Be welcoming. It costs nothing to add a warm welcome to the beginning of your message.
4. On-hold music. Play music by the cantor and/or choir or other Jewish music. Be careful using unmonitored radio stations for this purpose.

### Unwelcoming Voice Mail

Here is an example of the kind of voice mail that is not welcoming of first-time callers:

Shalom. You have reached Congregation LoBabayit. We are located at 1111 Peaceful Lane. Shabbat services are held at 8:00 Friday nights and 9:00 Saturday mornings. Daily *minyan* is at 7:00, morning and evening. If this is an emergency, please call 999-8888. If you would like to reach the school office, dial 777-3333. If you know your party's extension, press it now. If you would like a directory, please press the pound key. (Press pound key) You have reached Congregation LoBabayit's phone directory. Using the letters on the phone pad, spell your party's last name and press the pound key. (Press *K, A, N*) Gene Kanner, executive director, extension 201. If this is correct, please press 1. If you would like to hear another name, please press the pound key. (Press pound key) Rabbi Kantor, extension 301. If this is correct, please press 1. If you would like to hear another name, please press the pound key. Shalom. You have reached Mrs. Ezra, Rabbi Kantor's administrative assistant. I am either on the phone or out of the office. If you would like to leave a message for Rabbi Kantor or me, please record it after the beep and we will return the call as soon as possible. *Beep.*

**Exercise**

## *Making the Call*

Imagine that you are calling your synagogue for the first time. How do you feel before you pick up the phone? What is the first thing you hear? Do you talk to a human being or to a recorded message? Is it easy to find the information you need? How do you feel when you hang up?

## The Art of Dealing with Difficult People

All the quality service training in the world cannot prevent the inevitable goof-up. When an institution makes a mistake, attempts must be made to recover a positive relationship with the constituent. The cost of fixing a wrong, making amends, making it right, is always less than the cost of an upset member who talks badly of the synagogue. Here are some tips from the Disney University on how to deal with people when a problem occurs. Remember them with the acronym LAST:

L—**Listen:** The most important thing to do when someone is upset is to listen to their story without interruption or an attempt to explain. Just listen.

A—**Acknowledge:** Say "I'm sorry." It does not matter whether the institution was wrong or the person is out of line. It costs absolutely nothing to express your concern.

S—**Solve:** As quickly as possible, solve the problem. If you can't solve the problem, connect the person with someone who can.

T—**Thank:** Thank the individual for bringing the issue to your attention. Assure them that steps will be taken to improve service. If it becomes clear that the synagogue was at fault, consider creating a memorable recovery by giving something unexpected to the member: a discount, an *aliyah*, a mention in the bulletin.

**Exercise**

## *Assessing Your Welcoming Ambience*

It is important to assess how welcoming your ambience truly is now and how it is after implementing some of the suggestions offered here. What is the best way to do this? Ask your guests. Ask your members. Create a focus group. Take a survey—you can find adaptable survey question-naires in George Gallup Jr. and D. Michael Lindsay's book *The Gallup Guide: Reality Check for 21st Century Churches*, or check out the many good resources from the Alban Institute. Send in "mystery shul-shoppers": invite friends who are not members of the synagogue to visit and tell about their experiences. You may be surprised, chagrined, or elated at what you hear from these feedback loops. The most important response is to be ever-vigilant at creating the kind of welcoming ambience envisioned here.

**Tips**

## *33 Great Ideas for Welcoming*

1. Post directional signs within one mile of the congregation inviting visitors to the site.
2. Make sure that the name (including translitera-tion) and address of the congregation is clearly visible from the street—from every approach.
3. Include a sign of greeting on the marquee or banner. Suggestions include *Welcome, Sinai Temple Welcomes You, Bruchim ha-Ba'im b'Sheim Adonai* (Blessed are Those Who Come in the Name of God).
4. Drape a banner in the front of the building dur-ing the months preceding the new year with a message like the following: *Beth Shalom Welcomes Your Membership—Open House, Sundays, 12–4 p.m.*

5. Keep visitor parking spaces reserved in the front of the lot.
6. Make sure that the entrance to the building is clearly identified. If the entrance is not through the main doors, there should be a sign clearly indicating how one enters the synagogue. If security requires keeping doors locked, make the procedure for identifying visitors a welcoming one.
7. The lobby should feature a directory of offices, a map of the building (complete with *You Are Here* symbols), clear directions to major locations, couches, and an array of drinks and snacks.
8. During service times, make sure that there are greeters in the lobby who can welcome and sit with a newcomer to explain the service or other programs.
9. Present informational brochures about synagogue programs on a bulletin board. Display uniform information cards in a case similar to those found in lobbies of hotels featuring area attractions.
10. Structure the office so that it has an open window into the lobby area. Make sure a receptionist is available to assist visitors to the building.
11. The synagogue library should be located off the office and should offer resources for learning.
12. Provide directional signs to the main sanctuary, clergy, office, chapel, school, and restrooms that are clearly visible throughout the building. Install maps of the campus at key locations.
14. Hang a bulletin board labeled *Our Community Cares* next to the main office listing the names of upcoming *B'nai Mitzvah,* weddings, anniversaries, *shivah* homes, *Yahrtzeits,* and those in the hospital.

15. Make sure that offices are clearly marked with the names of the occupants, along with a color photograph of the person(s) who works in the space. Office desks and work areas should feature family photos, personal touches, and bowls of candy.

16. Keep restrooms clean, fresh, and furnished with diaper decks in both men's and women's rooms. Hang a tallit rack outside both women's and men's restrooms. Put out potpourri and amenities such as hand lotion on Shabbat and holidays.

17. Designate a nursing room offering privacy for nursing mothers and a crying room for families with young children.

18. Don't let the coatroom double as a storage area.

19. Provide a greeting area outside the main sanctuary.

20. Check that signs are worded in a welcoming manner.

21. Provide a welcome booklet in each pew with a brief history of the congregation, a description of the sanctuary with explanations of the various symbols, a list of the people on the pulpit and their roles in the service, an outline of the prayer service, and an invitation to consider membership.

22. Offer visitors a postcard that they can use to give feedback.

23. Serve refreshments *before* the service.

24. Invite newcomers to an open house with the clergy.

25. Hand out chocolate Shabbat "kisses" after services.

26. Provide umbrellas and umbrella escorts when it rains.

27. Consider offering valet parking.

28. Offer to sit with guests.

29. Create a concierge desk.
30. Publish a face book of the membership.
31. Recruit volunteers to give everyone in the congregation a call before High Holidays just to say happy new year.
32. Display photos of current members engaged in the work of spiritual community: worship, social justice activities, studying, comforting, and so on.
33. Have a greeter in the religious school carpool line.

# 4

# Welcoming Worship

For the spiritual seeker, shul-shopper, and guest, the welcoming ambience is the first gateway into a sacred community. But once inside the doors of the sanctuary, it is the experience of worship that defines the culture of the congregation. The language, theology, and length of most Jewish prayer services in all the denominations can be intimidating for the novice. Which book do I use? What page are we on? How do I pronounce the Hebrew and Aramaic? Why am I constantly asked to stand up and sit down? Do I believe in a God who brings the dead back to life? Why is the service so long?

Even among synagogue members, attendance at worship services is weak. According to the 2000 National Jewish Population Survey, among the 46 percent of American Jews who belong to synagogues, the percentage of those who report attending services more than once a month is not high: Reform, 24 percent; Conservative, 31 percent; and Orthodox, 66 percent. Where is everybody?

When confronted with a thorny question, the Rabbis of the Talmud would say, "Go see what the people are doing." As we started our research in S2K, I followed that suggestion by asking why most synagogue members did not attend religious services on a regular basis. The vast majority of members only showed up for Rosh Hashanah and Yom Kippur (although many rabbis report increasing numbers of empty seats even on the High Holy Days), to say *Kaddish*, or to attend a Bar or Bat Mitzvah, wedding, or other lifecycle event. The people were voting with their feet.

If services were not attracting the members of synagogues, it is no wonder that the large numbers of so-called unaffiliated Jews were not coming. The spiritual seekers in the Jewish community were clearly seeking somewhere else.

I decided to seek out prayer experiences that were, in fact, drawing a crowd. I had heard about the seeker services fueling the phenomenal growth of the so-called megachurches. What were they doing that attracted the un-churched? And, in our own community, had anyone discovered a way to overcome the many obstacles for those synagogue members and guests with few or no access skills to engage in Jewish prayer, such as knowledge of Hebrew and an understanding of the order and structure of the service? Was there a model of *welcoming worship*?

## Researching Welcoming Worship in Churches

### Agape

It was a call from a complete stranger that shook me to my core. On a Saturday, the *Los Angeles Times* had published an article about our critique of synagogues and the plans for Synagogue 2000. On Monday, a woman called me in the office and caught me by surprise:

"Dr. Wolfson, you don't know me, but if you want to know where the Jewish seekers are, I can tell you. They are at Agape Church. Have you heard of Agape?"

"No, I can't say that I have."

"Well, there are about three hundred of us Jews who have found Agape and it has become our spiritual home. We tried synagogues, but none of them offer what we're looking for."

"What might that be?"

"A place that touches us in the heart, that speaks to the challenges in our lives, that offers us a connection to something higher, that isn't concerned with appearances and materialism, that welcomes everyone. You should see it."

"When do you meet?"

"There's a service every Sunday morning. This week is Choir Sunday. There is a seventy-voice volunteer choir and there will be a thousand people."

"A thousand people! If a thousand people are coming to a religious service, I want to know what's going on."

And so I arranged to meet this woman, let's call her Karen, in a parking lot near the church. It was a Sunday morning I will not soon forget.

As Karen predicted, there were a thousand people, maybe more, waiting in line to enter a nondescript building located in the middle of an industrial zone south of Culver City on the west side of Los Angeles. The people represented a United Nations of colors, nationalities, and religions. Many appeared to be nicely attired—an upscale crowd.

As we entered what can only be described as a warehouse converted into a church, greeters with name tags welcomed us warmly at the front door. Just past a tiny lobby, we walked into the "sanctuary," a large space filled with row upon row of folding chairs. At the front of the room was a low pulpit with no chairs. There was no cross and no altar—only a brightly lit back wall with what appeared to be some sort of symbolic artwork. To the left of the pulpit, the choir was positioned on portable risers. There was ambient music playing while Agape members greeted each other as they found their seats. Karen introduced me to five of her Jewish friends.

The service began with music—spectacular music—sung by the volunteer choir that I later learned was populated by a number of professional singers from the Hollywood area. The pastor, Michael Beckwith, an African American, came from the world of music, a Grammy Award–winning songwriter of rhythm and blues. The songs were about love, peace, and seeking the spirit. People rose from their seats almost immediately after the music began, singing at the top of their lungs, swaying to the beat. One could not help but be swept up in the joy of it all.

Beckwith ascended the pulpit and welcomed everyone. He said a few words about Agape that were clearly intended to put newcomers at ease: "Whatever God you grew up with—Yahweh, Jesus, Mohammed, Buddha—you are welcome here. We all share one God and we are all one people." Within a matter of minutes, he began to speak about the challenges of living in late-twentieth-century America, about the emptiness of routines, about the importance of finding meaning and community. He spoke personally, relating heart-wrenching stories of people in the Agape community who had come broken and had found healing. People began to cry, unabashedly, and ushers walked through the aisles offering boxes of tissues. Beckwith spoke for at least half an hour, and he held the crowd in the palm of his hand. At the conclusion of the message, the choir started up again, this time a fifteen-minute set of songs that raised the roof. Again, people sang along heartily, raising their hands in praise, dancing in the aisles.

After the service, members met their "prayer buddies" for private spiritual counseling sessions. Others met in small groups to plan social action activities. Newcomers were invited to learn how to join the church.

I huddled with Karen and a few of her Jewish friends. They all told me the same sad story. They had gone to synagogues in Los Angeles and felt unwelcomed and unmoved. They were not looking for intellectualism and they were not interested in studying the Bible. They were mostly twenty-, thirty-, and fortysomethings who were seeking *spirituality*, and they found it in abundance at Agape. There was nothing overtly Christian about the place; the ideology was universalism in the extreme. They raved about the personalized attention offered by the prayer buddy sessions. "Show me a synagogue where you get that!" one of Karen's friends challenged me.

### Saddleback

I learned about Saddleback Church from a colleague, Rabbi Elie Spitz. One of his congregants, Mel Malkoff, was consulting with the founding pastor, Rick Warren, who had set out to plant a new kind of church in a remote corner of Orange County. Today, Rick Warren is a world-renowned figure, second only to Billy Graham in surveys of influential religious leaders in America. But in 1995, he was virtually unknown, except to a growing legion of pastors who looked to him for guidance and inspiration in creating seeker-sensitive churches. Warren, a former youth pastor, had decided to come to an un-churched area of the country to start a congregation. He settled on the Saddleback Valley, a bedroom community an hour south of Los Angeles. With no assets and no knowledge of the community, Rick decided to create a church for people who don't go to church. He spent days going door-to-door asking people if they belonged to a church in the area. If they answered yes, he said "God bless you" and moved on. If they answered no, he asked a simple question: "Why don't you go to church?"

The answers were stunning:

The services are boring; All they want is my money; The sermons don't relate to my life; I hate getting all dressed up; I can't trust the childcare.

Saddleback Church was formed with the intention of reaching these people. The story of how Rick built the church from six people in a living room to one of the largest congregations in America today, with 82,000 members, is found in his book *The Purpose-Driven Church*.

The megachurch phenomenon was just about to burst on the scene of American religious life in 1995. Some articles describing these new churches in the lay press had appeared and a case study of Willow Creek Community Church in Barrington, Illinois, published in the *Harvard Business Review*, had received attention. Larry and I were determined to learn what we could about this new model of congregation.

One Sunday, Larry and I made the drive from Los Angeles to Saddleback Valley to attend church. It was a stimulating— jaw-dropping, actually—morning. It was immediately apparent that the church had been built to attract seekers. There was no visible iconography—no cross on the building, no altar on the pulpit, no denominational identification in the name, and no dress code. The welcoming ambience was extraordinary. Much of the sixty-acre campus had not been built yet. The sanctuary was nothing special—five thousand bleacher seats, a nondescript pulpit, and two huge screens on either end of the front of the hall. But, the minute the service began, it was clear we were witnessing something very different from regular church. A band played uplifting, easy-to-sing music, followed by a warm welcome from the pulpit. Then, Rick Warren walked out, a large man dressed in a floral print Hawaiian shirt. His message was direct and aimed at the heart. The topic was "Though I Walk Through the Valley of the Shadow of Death, I Will Fear No Evil." The congregation followed along using a printed outline of the talk, with spaces to fill in key points. Using illustrations and metaphors, Rick spoke plainly and to the point—a strategy he explains as "saying something on Sunday that you can use on Monday." He introduced a congregant who had "walked through the valley" and survived cancer. She spoke movingly about her journey through the ordeal and the power of her faith to sustain her. Warren's talk took up about forty-five minutes of the hour-long service. A plate was passed, but visitors and seekers were encouraged *not* to give money: "The collection is intended for our members."

At the conclusion of the service, Larry and I walked to the outdoor plaza where dozens of booths featured various small groups and opportunities to serve the community. It was a happening place. Parents retrieved their children from the elaborate childcare and educational programming (they had received beepers so they could be called if a child needed a parent). At one booth, it was possible to receive an instant audiotape of that morning's message to take home or share with a friend.

On the spot, Larry and I decided that the very first thing we would do at the first S2K conference was to take the pilot congregational teams to Saddleback on Sunday morning. The impact of that visit continues to ripple through the synagogue community to this day.

We learned early on from our research that one of the key strategies of the megachurches was their understanding that "the larger we get, the smaller we must be." The whole idea is counterintuitive, but these leaders realized that the answer to establishing an intimate connection with such a big community is to link every person to a small group. I traveled to Willow Creek Church for a seminar in creating small groups at the annual Willow Creek Association conference; it was outstanding. I joined a group of two hundred congregational leaders from across North America, all of whom were there to learn the secrets of Willow Creek. The seminar inspired the development of Jewish journey groups in Synagogue 2000.

# WIN A $100 GIFT CERTIFICATE!

Fill in this card and mail it to us—or fill it in online at

**jewishlights.com/feedback.html**

—to be eligible for a $100 gift certificate for Jewish Lights books.

JEWISH LIGHTS PUBLISHING
SUNSET FARM OFFICES RTE 4
PO BOX 237
WOODSTOCK VT 05091-0237

Place Stamp Here

Fill in this card and return it to us to be eligible for our quarterly drawing for a $100 gift certificate for Jewish Lights books.

*We hope that you will enjoy this book and find it useful in enriching your life.*

Book title: _____

Your comments: _____

How you learned of this book: _____

If purchased: Bookseller _____ City _____ State _____

Please send me a free JEWISH LIGHTS Publishing catalog. I am interested in: (check all that apply)

1. ☐ Spirituality
2. ☐ Mysticism/Kabbalah
3. ☐ Philosophy/Theology
4. ☐ History/Politics

5. ☐ Women's Interest
6. ☐ Environmental Interest
7. ☐ Healing/Recovery
8. ☐ Children's Books

9. ☐ Caregiving/Grieving
10. ☐ Ideas for Book Groups
11. ☐ Religious Education Resources
12. ☐ Interfaith Resources

Name (PRINT) _____

Street _____

City _____ State _____ Zip _____

E-MAIL (FOR SPECIAL OFFERS ONLY) _____

Please send a JEWISH LIGHTS Publishing catalog to my friend:

Name (PRINT) _____

Street _____

City _____ State _____ Zip _____

**JEWISH LIGHTS PUBLISHING**

Tel: (802) 457-4000 • Fax: (802) 457-4004

**Visit us online at www.jewishlights.com**

**Available at better booksellers.**

Ten years later, the continued growth and influence of the megachurch movement is truly stunning. *The New York Times Magazine* published a ten-page story of a disciple of Rick Warren who had "planted" a megachurch in an exurb of Phoenix and created the fastest-growing church in the state, virtually overnight. Warren has created networks of thousands of congregational leaders who are linked via the Internet, satellite broadcasts, and in-person conferences. More recently, Joel Osteen, a new breed of televangelist, brought his Lakewood megachurch to an expanded former basketball arena, the Compaq Center, in Houston, seating 18,000 people at each of three services per weekend.

There is plenty of criticism of critics of the megachurch phenomenon, fueled in part by the perceived emphasis on marketing and "dumbing down" of religion, not to mention a fair amount of envy. Moreover, there has been a backlash in today's younger generation, who dislike "church as a mall" and prefer the new "emergent" and "house" churches, which offer intimacy and engagement with traditional forms of religious practice. Yet, it is hard to deny that the megachurch leaders are onto something important. They are up front about their mission: to reach the un-churched, the people who would never walk into church, to help them discover their God-given talents and spiritual gifts, and to encourage their use to glorify God's kingdom. Whatever the critique, the ideas and methods of the megachurch have found broad acceptance in many congregations throughout the world.

## Researching Welcoming Worship in Synagogues

As our research continued, I began to hear of synagogues that were experimenting with new models of worship. Although the Havurah Movement of the late 1960s and 1970s did involve a highly participatory prayer experience, something that Jewish Renewal continued in the late twentieth century, most mainstream synagogues appeared unaffected by these fringe groups. Some congregations did add a "learner's *minyan*," a parallel Shabbat morning service where the pace was slowed and questions were welcomed, or a "family service" where children were tolerated. Small *minyanim* emerged within the context of larger synagogues, often meeting in the synagogue library or some smaller room. But, for the most part, these breakaway services were led by knowledgeable Jews, often rabbis and professors of Jewish studies, who could not tolerate the "Bar Mitzvah mill" service typical of many congregations on Shabbat morning. Shabbat eve, the "late" Friday night service that was so popular in the mid-twentieth century, lost much of its appeal, especially for families who valued staying at home to enjoy a leisurely Shabbat dinner.

When Rachel Cowan agreed to support a planning grant for Synagogue 2000, she asked me if I had heard of B'nai Jeshurun, a congregation in Manhattan. "There are more than a thousand young people coming to the Kabbalat Shabbat [Friday evening] service every week," she told me.

I gave her the same response I had given Karen from Agape, "When there are a thousand people waiting to get into a service, I want to know what's happening."

### B'nai Jeshurun

B'nai Jeshurun is a classic example of synagogue transformation—a transformation shaped by a visionary leader. I had met Rabbi Marshall Meyer, *zichrono livracha,* may his memory be a blessing, when he was recruited from Argentina to take a position as vice president of American Jewish University. We had a number of conversations when he was a colleague, and I could tell he was a man on *shpilches* (pins and needles) who could not wait to do something important in American Judaism. When he decided to move to New York to take over B'nai Jeshurun (BJ, as it is now widely known), the congregation was nearly dead. There was hardly a *minyan* on his first Shabbat as rabbi. For Marshall, this was an opportunity to create a congregation in his own image, to use the knowledge he had gained as head of the Seminario Rabinico Latinamerico in Buenos Aires where he had trained a whole generation of young rabbis. Informed by the prophetic vision of his spiritual hero, Abraham Joshua Heschel, driven by a passion for social justice, shaped by his intellectual pursuits, and infused with a blend of musical influences encompassing traditional *nusach,* neo-Hasidic *niggunim* (wordless tunes), and Latin-flavored Sephardic melodies, B'nai Jeshurun quickly became the most talked-about congregation in New York City.

Rabbi Meyer eventually invited two of his young protégées to join him in fashioning BJ: Rabbi Rolando Matalon and Rabbi Marcelo Bronstein. Along with them, Ari Priven was recruited to lead the music of the congregation. Together, they created a *davenning* experience that would dazzle the significant Jewish community of the Upper West Side. Within months, the Friday night Kabbalat Shabbat service at BJ was attracting hundreds of Jews—young Jews—the kind of Jews that did not usually go to synagogue. When the roof on the dilapidated building suddenly collapsed, the service was moved down the street to a neighboring church, and the crowd grew. After the building was renovated with important innovations, the clergy decided to offer two services on Friday night to handle the ever-growing throng of nearly fifteen hundred people every week.

Just after my initial meeting with Larry Hoffman in the Catskill Mountains, I returned to New York City to attend services at BJ—at church. The sanctuary had been transformed into a synagogue, with a huge banner that read *Shalom* covering the cross, and with a portable ark on the pulpit. Hundreds of people, mostly in their 20s and 30s, streamed into the place, many dressed in business suits, coming directly off the subways from work. There was not much in the way of greeting; a few laypeople handed out prayer books and a weekly bulletin.

Two rabbis stood behind a reading table and began the service. To one side sat the *hazzan* at an electronic keyboard. The first hymn, *D'ror Yikra,* was sung to a slow, lilting melody that created an atmosphere of calm and sanctity. Roly, as Rabbi Matalon is widely known, welcomed the assembled crowd in a soft, Latin-accented voice. The message was "It's Shabbat. Slow down. Catch your breath. You have come to a place of spirituality."

Amazingly, nearly the entire service at BJ is sung out loud, in Hebrew, to tunes that for most newcomers are unfamiliar. Yet, the sweep of the service is so moving, the tunes so easy to catch, the choreography of the prayer so inviting, that the same young professional Jewish adults who absent themselves from older models of Jewish prayer flock to this synagogue every week.

The Kabbalat Shabbat service I participated in that night was one of the most thrilling, moving, and satisfying religious experiences of my life. I had come as an ethnographer, ready to make observations as a dispassionate researcher. Instead, I was swept away by the beauty and spirit of the music and the expert choreography of the ritual. It is where I first identified many of the components of the kind of Jewish seeker worship I was seeking.

### *Friday Night Live*

Like most rabbis in North America, Rabbi David Wolpe of Sinai Temple in Los Angeles heard about the success of BJ. Rather than dismiss the phenomenon as peculiar to the Upper West Side of New York City, as many critics did, he made a visit to see why the Kabbalat Shabbat service in particular was attracting so many young professionals. Wolpe, a charismatic rabbi known for his oratory and writing who had recently taken on the pulpit of one of the largest congregations in the community, knew that there was a large population of Jewish twenty- and thirty-somethings in West Los Angeles, and he was interested in experimenting with a service designed for them. Friday night was the obvious choice, especially since the late Friday night service was a thing of the past for the regulars at Sinai Temple.

Wolpe knew that he needed a partner to provide music that would engage the target audience. He approached Craig Taubman, a popular composer and performer of contemporary Jewish music, with a commission to write new melodies for the Kabbalat Shabbat service that would resonate with the young professionals and create the spirit he was looking for in the sanctuary.

Together, Wolpe and Taubman gathered a focus group of young leadership in the community with whom to share their ideas and to help build a crowd. They called the service Friday Night Live, a takeoff of the popular television show *Saturday Night Live*. Young professionals would serve as greeters before the service and, instead of brownies and punch at the *Oneg Shabbat* afterward, the group suggested that their peers would hang around the synagogue if they were offered a light supper featuring Chinese chicken salad, Israeli dancing, a study opportunity, and coffee and conversation.

The first Friday Night Live service was held on June 15, 1997, and attracted several hundred young professionals. I was out of town visiting another synagogue that night, but from all accounts, the service worked and generated excitement and enthusiasm for all involved. Planned for the second Friday night of every month, I was able to attend the second FNL service. In fact, I had to be given a special dispensation by the leadership to do so; in a controversial move, anyone older than the target ages of 21 to 35 was not welcomed to the service.

As at BJ, I was amazed by the energy and anticipation evident in the hundreds of people gathering for the 7:30 p.m. service. A dozen attractive young professionals acted as greeters, offering a warm welcome to the throng. As soon as one entered the enormous sanctuary seating nearly a thousand people, it was clear this was not going to be your parents' service. A five-piece band was occupying one side of the high *bimah*, playing ambient music as people took their seats. Craig Taubman, informally dressed, guitar strapped around his neck, began the service with an upbeat melody that had the crowd on its feet. He bounded down the front stairs of the pulpit and into the crowd, whipping them into a frenzy of singing and clapping. The music Taubman composed specifically for FNL was infectious and instantly accessible. Using a variety of motifs—from Hasidic klezmer to Israeli folk song—the music propelled the service. Amazingly, the young people did not sit passively; they sang along, participating fully in the unfolding experience.

After the *Amidah*, David Wolpe offered his sermon—a seven-minute message that spoke directly to the lives of his congregants. He spoke with humor and understanding about the plight of young Jewish singles. He quoted famous authors of English literature. He referenced popular culture. The congregation laughed, gasped, and nodded in recognition. It was a tour de force of rabbinic oratory.

Once again, I was surprised at the receptivity of a group of people who did not know the Kabbalat Shabbat service, who did not know much Hebrew, and who most likely had not been in a synagogue for a long time. The crowd had grown from three hundred at the first FNL to five hundred at the second. When I met with Craig and David immediately after the hour-and-fifteen-minute service, I predicted that there would be one thousand the next month. I was correct. The word of mouth in the young professional community was electric. Groups of singles, young couples, and individuals looking to meet someone came in droves. At its peak, more than two thousand young professionals crowded into the sanctuary and social hall annex. It was like Kol Nidrei every month.

Nine years later, Friday Night Live continues to thrive.

## The Reform Movement

In 1999, Synagogue 2000 was invited to organize a worship service for the Board of Governors meeting of what was then known as the Union of American Hebrew Congregations (UAHC), now called the Union of Reform Judaism (URJ). We turned to our S2K director of music, Merri Arian, and three of our S2K fellows, Cantor Benjie Ellen Schiller, Rabbi Ramie Arian, and Liz Lerman to lead the service. The 150 members of the board had heard about Synagogue 2000; this was their chance to experience the evolving new Reform worship.

The service was held in a hotel ballroom. There was no *bimah*; the participants were on the same level as the officiants. Three of the leaders—Ramie, Benjie, and Merri—stood together in front of the congregation to lead the service. It began with the introduction of a *niggun* and a new candle-blessing melody. Ramie gave a brief introduction to that week's Torah portion, *Toldot,* which deals with generations and ancestors. He explained that the entire group would meet in small clusters of ten around the room, for about fifteen minutes, in order to share a brief remembrance of an ancestor who helped bring them to where they were today as Jews. Each participant was given a small card with the *Shehecheyanu* blessing, which they recited as they lit one Shabbat candle as a group. When it came time for the *V'ahavta,* Liz gathered stories about ancestors from several individuals and selected hand motions that each person used as he or she spoke. Then, in a miraculous combination of movement choreography and singing, the group experienced the prayer in a way that literally elicited gasps from the congregation. Words simply fail to convey the power of the moment.

The rest of the service was almost completely sung using a combination of melodies ranging from the neo-Hasidic to Debbie Friedman. Benjie sang a solo prayer after the *Amidah* in her angelic voice that riveted the group. A quartet of cantors offered another meditative moment of prayer. Merri, one of the most effective song leaders in the world, taught new melodies within the flow of the worship, a skill that is extraordinarily important—and the congregation participated in a deep and meaningful way.

What made the service so remarkable to me was that the people in the room represented the core leadership of Reform Judaism. They were fully aware of the revolution occurring in Reform worship. Abandoning the classical Reform style of prayer, which was highly dependent on responsive English readings, opting instead for rousing melodies of prayers sung mostly in Hebrew, building the energy in the room to the point of overflowing exuberance that led many to dance in the aisles—it was a validating moment in the emergence of a new style of Reform worship. It was clear to all present that the days of a docile crowd sitting through a call-and-response English service was near history. S2K had been effectively recruited to help along this important transformation.

### The Orthodox Psychiatrist-Hazzan of Riverdale

When we heard about Dr. Elli Kranzler, a practicing psychiatrist who fulfills the role of *hazzan* of the Orthodox congregation Hebrew Institute of Riverdale in New York, we invited him to offer a model Kabbalat Shabbat service during an S2K conference in Denver. A slight, bearded man with a twinkle in his eye, Elli took the *bimah* in front of 250 Reform, Conservative, Reconstructionist, and Modern Orthodox congregants from the fifteen synagogues in Denver and Boulder. A disciple of the late Shlomo Carlebach, Elli began with a classic Carlebach *niggun,* a catchy, wordless melody. Everyone joined in because Elli sang it over and over again *until* everyone was singing. Importantly, he never stopped singing, even as the congregation caught on to the melody. He explained the repetition by referring to the Baal Shem Tov's definition of a *niggun*: "a melody which takes us from where we are to where we want to be." The service continued apace until *L'cha Dodi*. It was then that Elli went into overdrive, singing loudly without the benefit of electrical amplification, something forbidden to Orthodox Jews on Shabbat. Of course, musical instruments would also be out of the question. But Elli found a way to transform the *bimah* itself into an instrument. He drummed incessantly on the Torah reading table, he clapped his hands, he bounced to the infectious rhythms of the melodies. For those of us in attendance, we could only imagine what it must be like at his home synagogue, which regularly attracts hundreds of congregants and visitors every Shabbat.

There are many more examples of worship renewal in our congregations. There is One Shabbat Morning, a seeker service at Adat Ari El in Valley Village, California, led jointly by Rabbi Moshe Rothblum, Cantor Ira Bigelisen, and Craig Taubman, which incorporates both traditional Shabbat *nusach* (prayer modes) and contemporary compositions. At Valley Beth Shalom, Rabbi Ed Feinstein and Craig Taubman lead The 25th Hour, a Shabbat afternoon service with upbeat music and stories that begins when a large hourglass is turned over and ends precisely when the last grain of sand runs out!

When I reflect on these very different prayer experiences, I am amazed by the similarities they share. Each of them is led by extraordinarily skilled worship leaders. The rabbis, *hazzanim,* and musical artists who are pushing the envelope to create new expressions of old forms are simply remarkable. This spiritually welcoming worship is indigenous to the Jewish experience in this country, not the old country. Even more stunning, however, is that each of them—to one degree or another—uses a number of strategies that make for an engaging and moving spiritual prayer service. The most important one of all is music.

## Using Music to Transform the Synagogue Experience

When I am asked the question "Is there any one thing that is essential to the creation of a spiritually moving prayer service?" I reply, "There are *three* things: music, music, music." As we will learn, the choice of music gives us the cues to follow the service, triggers our responses to the prayers, provides the beat of the choreography, and underscores the drama of the worship. To my mind, it is the most important component of the worship experience.

A congregation needs to give careful consideration to the function of Jewish liturgical music. It behooves the congregation to not only consider the talents and predilections of the cantor, the rabbi, and other clergy, but to assess where the congregants stand as well. Many of the seekers we want to attract to our worship services are those whose fondest Jewish memories are of songfests at Jewish summer camps or teenage youth groups. Hour upon hour of songs around campfires and Shabbat singing imbued this generation with a love of Jewish music. But, like so much of the camp atmosphere, we have failed to transfer the spirit of the camp songfest into the regular worship service. Few people have taken the time to figure out what works at camp that could work in the synagogue.

The key factor in a singing congregation is the presence of a musical leader who understands the importance of finding ways to teach and lead the community to a new level of participation. Music may be the most influential factor in determining who we reach and how we reach them. Music positions the synagogue in the community. There are still some congregations where the attraction is a great operatic cantorial voice, but they are likely to attract more traditional Jews or those, like me, who grew up appreciating *hazzanut* (cantorial solos). There are others where the majority of the congregants long for their youth group days when group singing was one of the peak moments of the experience. In *The Lord's Song in a Strange Land,* ethnomusicologist Rabbi Jeffrey Summit makes the central point that the musical style of a congregation is an expression of the core meaning of that particular sacred community: "Music is a deep vessel, a form of expressive culture that can combine and hold many expressions of identity."

I am not an expert in Jewish liturgical music, although I did sing in my synagogue volunteer choir from the time of my Bar Mitzvah through college. My observations about the power of music to move someone spiritually come from watching the *effect* of music on congregants, especially seekers. I offer these observations with the hope that those synagogue leaders who are experts will recognize and understand the experience of the congregant when shaping a prayer service and will choose the melodies that can make the difference between worship that soars and worship that deflates the spirit.

## The Value of New Melodies

In all my years of visiting many kinds of synagogues, I thought I knew most of the styles of *nusach* and most of the more popular melodies used for the Kabbalat Shabbat service. Some argue that the widespread use of the same musical themes makes it possible for any Jew to walk into any service anywhere in the world and participate. Perhaps. But at B'nai Jeshurun, I did not recognize 80 percent of the melodies, yet I was instantly engaged in the worship experience. Most of the unfamiliar melodies had been used in Argentina and imported to New York. Some were Sephardic in origin; others were adaptations of Shlomo Carlebach *niggunim*. I didn't know their *nusach,* but I was immediately able to catch on to the tunes.

There are some melodies that you hear that are easily learned; just watch how most teenagers can listen to a Top 40 pop song and learn it almost instantly. The same phenomenon is true for adults; some melodies are so easy to follow and beautiful to sing that, after hearing them just a few times, you can sing along. Clergy who realize this choose melodies that are easily learnable.

Music is an art form designed to stir our souls. The classic works of the great Jewish liturgical composers—Lewandowski, Helfman, Sulzer, Bloch—were written to invoke specific emotional reactions among the congregants. I will sit through hours of a Rosh Hashana service for the opportunity to hear and sing along with (I learned the second tenor part in choir) Lewandowski's inspiring *"Halleluya."* It sends chills up my spine. Bloch's *Sacred Service,* a beautiful setting of the Friday night liturgy, moves me to tears, especially the haunting *"Yi'hiyu l'ratzon imrei fi."*

At the same time, cantors are always searching for new melodies that can be taught to the congregation. Velvel Pasternak, an acknowledged expert in the development of Jewish music, points out that a variety of melodies that found their way into the liturgy were inspired by the popular music of their time. For example, the most familiar

*"Ein Keiloheinu"* melody is undoubtedly a takeoff of a famous German beer hall song. A number of melodies that are considered *mi'Sinai* (from Mt. Sinai) are actually winners of the annual Hasidic Song Festival in Israel. The nearly universal use of Nurit Hirsch's *"Oseh Shalom"* is a good example.

The B'nai Jeshurun clergy team is always on the lookout for new melodies they can introduce for specific purposes. Just before our first Synagogue 2000 conference for the original sixteen pilot congregations in 1995, Amichai Lau-Lavie, an S2K fellow, had heard a melody that he taught to the BJ rabbis and *hazzan*. It sounded Jewish, although it most definitely was not. But, together, they adapted the melody to a key prayer in the *Shacharit* liturgy—Psalm 150, *Halleluya*. They introduced it to the BJ community the week before the first S2K conference in 1995 and it was an immediate hit.

At that first conference, one of the most exciting features of the day was an extended song session with Merri Arian. On Monday evening, Roly Matalon told Merri about the new version of *Halleluya*, now called simply *Hallelu*. He suggested that Merri teach it to the group. Debbie Friedman, another S2K fellow, happened to overhear Roly teaching the tune to Merri. If anyone can recognize a great melody, it is Debbie. The next day, Merri taught *Hallelu* to the entire conference.

On Tuesday night, we had asked Roly and Ari Priven from BJ to model their Kabbalat Shabbat service for the conference participants. This modeling of welcoming worship services was part of our theory of transformation: Show the people a concrete demonstration of the vision of synagogue we were advocating. We literally pretended to make *Shabbes* on Tuesday night, installing greeters at the door of the camp synagogue who cheerfully welcomed the S2K team members with *Shabbat Shalom*. During the service, Roly and Ari wanted to use their new version of *Hallelu* as a closing prayer. The room was electric. In a matter of moments, the entire group was singing and clapping along. Within minutes, most of the people were dancing through the aisles of the sanctuary. The next week, Debbie added the *Hallelu* to her concert repertoire, most of the congregations began to sing it in their services back home, and the rest is history. What you may not know is that the melody discovered by Amichai and adapted by BJ and popularized by Debbie, Craig, Danny Maseng, and just about every other musical artist in the Jewish community is a Sufi song called *"Allah Hu"* by Nusrat Fateh Ali Khan.

In the synagogue of the twenty-first century, the congregation will know an ever-growing repertoire of melodies for the major prayers of the service. To be sure, each congregation is likely to have favorites, and my advice would be not to mess with whatever melody is sacrosanct in your community. But a healthy synagogue will never object to learning a new melody, especially if it works.

An important note about sound systems: When the goal is to get the congregation singing, it is important for the people to hear the voice of the prayer leader, for it provides the model to follow. It is perhaps even more critical for the congregants to hear each other as they raise their voices together in community. A good sound system fulfills both of these objectives. Don't forget those who have hearing loss; provide working audio assist devices for those who need them. An excellent sound system and/or excellent acoustics (especially in an Orthodox sanctuary where amplification on Shabbat and holidays is forbidden), are indispensable factors in helping build communal prayer.

### Can You Hear Me?

*When the sanctuary at BJ was renovated, the congregation installed a state-of-the-art surround-sound system, complete with speakers in the middle and rear sections of the lower floor and speakers in the balcony. The clergy report that the sound system vastly improved the level of participation of the congregation, now that they can hear, follow and join the davenning.*

### How to Teach New Melodies: Repetition and Slow to Rise

One strategy that enables the congregation to learn unfamiliar melodies is the skillful use of repetition. The constant repetition of a melody allows the congregation to catch the tune and begin to join in. For the uninitiated, this repetition can lead to expressions of "Enough, already!" Yet, our musical experts agree that it takes three repetitions for the typical layperson to get a melody, and another three repetitions to begin to pray with it. When a culture of participation is created and expected, objections fall by the wayside as the congregation raises its collective voice in song.

Another staple of Hasidic prayer, the strategy of beginning a *niggun* or melody at a deliberate pace during the first few refrains of the prayer and then gradually increasing the speed of the singing is known as "slow to rise." The combination of repetition and the steadily increasing pace leads to a kind of ecstatic prayer. Hasidim often get carried away with this; think of the fastest hora you ever danced at a wedding. The flip side of "slow to rise" is "rise to slow"; skillful worship leaders know how to slow down from the peak of the chanting, returning the congregation to a relative calm. A slow-to-rise repetition can be an exhilarating experience of prayer.

The use of slow to rise is an example of how the clergy can plan the emotional arc of the service. The structure of the traditional worship, the *matbe'a ha-tefillah,* has such an arc, but it is hardly perceptible to most seekers who know little about it. The blessings before and after the *Sh'ma,* for example, build to the *Mi Chamocha,* a reenactment of the "Song of the Sea," when the Israelites were miraculously saved by God from the Egyptians. The *Kedusha* contains several high points, including *Kadosh, Kadosh, Kadosh, Adonai Tzeva'ot, M'lo Kol Ha-aretz K'vodo* (Holy, holy, holy is the Lord of Hosts, the whole earth is filled with God's glory!). On the repetition of *Kadosh,* most congregations today, including Reform, have taught their congregants to move—to lift themselves up on the balls of their feet, the traditional movement to indicate the aspiration to be "a little lower than the angels" and a lot higher than our usual stance.

I was reminded of the importance of an emotional arc on a visit to the DreamWorks movie studio. Jeffrey Katzenberg was preparing his first animated feature for the new venture, *The Prince of Egypt,* and he invited hundreds of clergy and educators to preview the film as it was in development. When I arrived for a consultation, I was escorted through the hallways of the studio, upon which hung the storyboard of the film. The storyboard is a frame-by-frame illustration of each moment in the proposed film. Underneath each picture, I noticed a line had been drawn on a graph. When I inquired about it, I was told that the line was tracing the emotional arc of the film. For example, the opening features a chariot race between a young Moses and his Egyptian brother, Ramses. The emotional arc line was high on the graph, an indication to the musical composer and the director that the expected audience response would be edge-of-your-seat excitement. At another point on the storyboard, when Moses brings news to Pharaoh of the impending plagues, the emotional arc was drawn low on the graph, indicating a more serious, contemplative moment.

The leaders of welcoming worship use slow to rise, repetition, and other techniques to plan for and *move* the congregation to emotional highs, middles, and lows throughout the service.

## Thoughts on Musical Moods from Cantor Schiller

S2K fellow Cantor Benjie Ellen Schiller emphasizes the importance of choosing melodies that the congregation can easily pick up. Cantors should try to sing *with* their congregants, rather than *for* them. People wish to participate actively in services. They feel welcomed and accepted when they are invited to join in song. Moreover, singing prayers has become their entrance into Jewish ritual life as well as their gateway into learning Jewish sacred texts. Through singing Hebrew or English words, made possible either by soaring melody or simple *nusach*, they feel empowered to pray in a way that undeniably links them with the larger Jewish community and affirms their Jewish identity. Singing gives them the key that allows their access to Jewish sacred tradition.

As Cantor Schiller has taught us, there are musical settings designed to invoke five major feelings during prayer—majestic, meditative, meeting, moving along, and memory.

### 1. Majestic: A Sense of Awe and Grandeur

Our first mood is majestic—that which evokes within us a sense of awe and grandeur. A classic example is the music of the First and Second Temple periods. The Levites, with full choir and orchestra, assembled a magnificent offering suited only for God. What is our equivalent of majesty in musical prayer? Our liturgical texts certainly intend to inspire such passion on a regular basis. Look at the texts of the Torah service, *Kedusha, Adon Olam, Sh'ma,* or *Hashkiveinu,* not to mention our High Holy Day and festival liturgy. When are we ever so moved within our service as to sense the majesty implicit in so many of our prayers?

### 2. Meditative: Inward and Reflective

Our second mood is meditative—that which leads us inward, toward reflective, contemplative prayer. It is to know the "still, small voice" within ourselves, the one that often eludes us. Consider the silent prayer that precedes the *Amidah:* "Open my mouth, O Lord, and my lips will proclaim your praise." Or consider the *MiShebeirakh,* or even Kol Nidrei. Is our liturgical music conducive to moments of genuine meditation?

### 3. Meeting: Creating and Encountering Oneness

Our third mood is meeting—moments in which we become aware of the larger community and literally meet other souls through prayer. When all voices join to create a resounding chorus of prayer, when every voice contributes its sound to the whole, a new expression of prayer is born. Even among strangers, we sense both a personal and a spiritual connection with those with whom we pray. Imagine a seder table where everyone joins to sing a blessing or song. We have so many opportunities to create "meeting moments" within our liturgy: when the Torah is taken from the ark, at the beginning or end of a section of the service, or on Yom Kippur.

### 4. Moving Along: Creating Momentum

Of course, not every melody fits into one of these categories. Some music functions as the "connective tissue" of the liturgy, carrying the worship from one section to the next—the *Chatzi Kaddish* on Shabbat evening, for example, may not readily be identified as music of meeting, meditation, or majesty, although some of us no doubt experience it in each of these ways. Mostly, I think of it as the music of "moving along" or "momentum." In this case, the music is traditional and connects us to our musical history. Its familiarity is comforting; its specific melody, chant, or prayer mode is a reminder of where we are in Jewish sacred time. As an individual piece of music it is relatively neutral; its function is simply to punctuate one section of the service. But "connectors," such as the *Chatzi Kaddish,* fulfill an important task—they create momentum, so that one prayer flows smoothly into the next.

**5. Memory: Connecting to the Past**
Sometimes it is the associative connection that one's memory makes to a particular melody that moves people the most. In these situations, the melody and/or the words are symbols. The significance of these associations may be private—the melody that one's grandmother sang as she lit the Shabbat candles or the song always sung at a family seder—but if many people in the community have the same memory and bring similar associations, then the memory is a mood of shared prayer. If the music of meeting establishes connections with our community today, the music of memory creates continuity with our communal past. In Jewish tradition, particular musical themes serve as leitmotifs for corresponding Holy Days. Imagine Yom Kippur without the Kol Nidrei melody! While style and our own musical tastes have changed over time, we must nonetheless respect the power of the music of memory to evoke and embody the sacred. Memory is not a separate mood from the four Ms of meeting, majesty, meditation, and momentum; it is an overarching category that is often experienced simultaneously with the others.

Today, people call out to be included. They ask us to enrich their sense of meeting. Whether they know it or not, they do not wish to abandon either the majestic or the meditative moods of prayer. Ultimately these moods succeed when they complement and balance one another. When a part of the whole is not fulfilling our communal needs, however, we must examine the effectiveness of that part and its relationship to the whole. Do we offer an array of paths to God that all can appreciate? Does our music express the affective moods of our sacred texts? If we assess our meeting moments, both at specific times and within the entire service, perhaps we can determine how our music can encourage a sense of welcome and empowerment, even amidst a fully balanced range of moods and styles.

### Using Music to Set the Mood

Music is critical to setting the mood for any service, but it is of particular importance to a service designed to be spiritually welcoming. Silence is unsettling to visitors. If you were to walk into a large room with a large group of people sitting in silence, you would wonder what was happening. Many people grew up in a generation when entering a sanctuary was like entering a library—*Shhh! No talking!* There is a place for silence in worship, but it is not at the beginning of a seeker service. The atmosphere at the beginning of the service ought to be joyous, alive, contagious.

In most Conservative and Orthodox synagogues, this is not an issue because so few people are actually present when the service begins. This is especially the case on Shabbat morning when the only people likely to be present at the precise beginning of the service are the clergy, a few regulars, the Bar or Bat Mitzvah family, and their guests, who do not know that most people will not arrive for another hour. Friday night is a somewhat different story. Many people do find their way to services on time.

Think carefully about the beginning of the service. In some congregations, the strategy is to calm everyone with meditative music. At Valley Beth Shalom, the cantor literally warms up the crowd, leading the congregation in upbeat Shabbat *zemirot* for fifteen minutes before the actual service commences. People entering the sanctuary approach each other, not with whispers, but with hearty *Shabbat Shalom* greetings and kisses. The message is unmistakable: There is life in this place.

### Tips

## *Music as a Means for Creating Meaningful Worship*

*In addition to her role as director of music at S3K, Merri Arian has become a sought-after consultant and S3K lecturer in liturgical arts at the School of Sacred Music at Hebrew*

*Union College's New York campus, teaching a new genera-*
*tion of Reform clergy how to engage the congregation's voice.*
*She understands the importance of the function of music in*
*prayer. Below, she offers some thoughts on the power of music*
*to transform worship.*

For the traditional Jew, prayer is a commandment. One
comes to the synagogue to pray because one is commanded to do so. Music can heighten that prayer experience and enhance the text in such ways as to bring deeper
meaning to the ancient words. The *nusach* chanted
during the worship service sets the tone of the service,
signaling a particular time in the Jewish calendar, connecting the prayer with all the history and meaning of that
particular time. Melodies of old connect the person praying to a tradition and a long history—an understanding
that the sacred act that he or she is involved in is a link in
a long chain. Those melodies intensify the prayer experience as they bring to mind parents and grandparents
who came before, uttering these very same words and
melodies, hundreds of years before. These melodies serve
as touchstones—a guidepost—as one proceeds through
the prayer experience.

For the less traditional Jew though, prayer services can
be somewhat daunting—the language foreign and difficult to pronounce, and the customs unfamiliar and awkward. Often it is the music that can help ease these people
into the prayer experience. After all, music is the universal language, and music can help level the "praying field"!

**Beginnings**
How we begin the prayer experience is important. We
need to recognize where the congregants are coming
from—a missed train, a late babysitter, a hassled week at
work, a week of being indoors with a sick child. They

need to be welcomed into the prayer experience. I was reminded recently about how important this Kabbalat Shabbat experience can be. At Congregation Kol Hanishama, a Reform congregation in Jerusalem, Rabbi Levi Kelman takes this warm-up time, this welcoming of the Shabbat, very seriously. Taking time is important. It needs to be inviting and *not* intimidating.

We need to be cognizant of who plans our worship services. The Jewish professionals of the congregation plan our worship—those who do this "religion thing" as a profession. Getting into prayer is something that most probably comes easily to them! But not true for the layperson, who needs to be nurtured and guided into the experience. The opening music is our first chance! The music needs to be relatively easy to access and familiar. I do not want the congregant to be focused on an awkward rhythm or difficult melody. I want him or her to be looking inward and focusing on prayer. When carefully planned, the music at the beginning of the service can help the congregant do just that.

### Transitions

How one transitions from one part of the service to another greatly affects the prayer experience. The music that one selects during these transitional times needs to support the feeling that one is creating. For example, how one moves in and out of silence is terribly important. There needs to be a sense of quieting down, a slowing of the pace. Silence is not a familiar space for many of us whose lives are usually accompanied by a din of competing calls for our attention. Yet, the silent prayer is often cited as the part of the service that people most look forward to. When we select music that precedes the silent prayer, we need to help guide people to this special place. Similarly, when we come out of this silence, we want to help people hold on to the calm that they have just experienced, and so we select music that matches that quietude, gradually increasing the dynamics and tempo as we proceed onward through the liturgy.

It was not until the death of my father that I understood the importance of the transition that was needed following the Mourners' *Kaddish*. In most congregations, the next moment is filled with either announcements or a closing hymn. For the first time, I understood as a mourner how jolting that closing hymn or congregational announcement could be, coming on the heels of that prayer. Attention needs to be given to that transition in such a way as to provide closure for the person saying *Kaddish*. In some congregations, that transition is accomplished by the rabbi reciting something in English, acknowledging how we as a congregation take the names of all of these people into our hearts. This transition can also be handled musically, with the insertion of an a cappella refrain that is appropriately contemplative in nature, possibly using the text of *Oseh Shalom*. We ask people to open their hearts and be present in prayer, and we need to be sensitive and respectful of their needs and their vulnerabilities.

### Enhancing the Text

The music that we use in our worship services need to reflect the texts that they are accompanying. Surely we understand that our liturgical texts are sacred and enduring, yet sometimes we say the words without really thinking about their meaning. Music is an opportunity to check in on the meaning of the text. When chosen sensitively, music can enhance and sometimes even bring new or deeper meaning to these age-old prayers. Think about that time in our service when we ask God to grant peace to us and our people. Think of all the beautiful melodies that have been written for *Sim Shalom, Shalom Rav,* and *Oseh Shalom,* to name just a few prayers. Those melodies that you remember are the ones that truly gave extra meaning to those moments. What about the joy of the Israelites crossing the Red Sea as they spoke those ancient words: *Mi chamocha ba-eylim Adonai*? Again, we can almost hear the joyful, triumphant melodies that have been composed expressly for that moment. And what about all of the new melodies that have been written to support the healing moments that congregations are now creating within their regular worship settings? These melodies capture the urgency of people's prayers for healing for loved ones in a way that the text alone simply cannot do.

Our worship is made ever more meaningful by the inclusion of music that helps guide people into prayer, helps them make transitions within the service, and enhances and deepens the meaning of the text.

### Choirs, Organs, CDs, and Podcasting

I loved singing in a volunteer choir, but, quite frankly, I am not sure how much the congregation loved our singing. We were often flat, out of synch, and out of tune. We were volunteers, after all, and though there were some truly magnificent voices, most of us were pretty average. With one hour of rehearsal a week (maybe), we were amateur at best. Done correctly, however, use of a choir in a congregation can encourage congregational singing rather than usurping it.

Many older congregations feature what is known as a choir loft. This is a place, usually situated above or to the side of the pulpit, where the choir sits, often behind a lattice, out of sight of the congregation. The result: disembodied voices flowing over a congregation that often sits wondering, Where did that come from? Some congregations have liberated the choir members and placed them on the pulpit or nearby in the first few rows, creating a more intimate connection between choir and congregation.

Then there is the issue of using musical instruments during worship. Although Orthodox and most Conservative congregations have traditionally not allowed the use of instruments on Shabbat (lest it break and one is tempted to repair it—a category of work forbidden by traditional Jewish law), today, more and more do. (The Rabbinical Assembly Committee on Law and Standards is considering a ruling on the use of instruments.) Many Reform congregations have abandoned the organ for other instruments—guitar, flute, even soft rock bands. We can learn from the megachurches, which ask, What kind of music does our target audience listen to? It's doubtful that many people listen to organ music anymore.

One of the best teaching devices for developing the musical expertise of the congregation is to make CDs of the most popular melodies and make them available to the congregation. Encourage them to turn their cars into liturgical classrooms on wheels. Play the CD on your synagogue's telephone answering system so congregants hear it when put on hold. Podcast the music through the Internet to congregants' MP3 players.

## Temple Sinai (Reform) Summit, New Jersey

Here is a wonderful idea from an S2K team:

> We created an intergenerational choir. Prior to this effort only the adult and junior choir existed. This effort brought together congregants of all ages and enriched the experience for the participants and congregation alike. The cantor consulted choir members and invited adults to join junior choir for several performances. The response was very positive.

## The Spiritual Message

In addition to the music used during worship, another key component of the synagogue experience is the spiritual message transmitted from the pulpit. In the synagogue of the twentieth century, many innovative approaches to Torah study during or before the Shabbat morning service were offered. These opportunities to engage in the intellectual pursuit of wisdom were attractive to many, particularly when the rabbi engaged in dialogue with congregants.

In the synagogue of the twenty-first century, the seekers of spiritual wisdom want to know what Judaism has to say about the challenges of their lives. To paraphrase Rick Warren, "Teach them something on Shabbat they can use in their lives."

If the synagogue is to be a spiritual center where people find answers to the questions of meaning and purpose, then the message from the pulpit needs to be at the nexus of where Torah meets life.

The word *communication* comes from the Latin word *communis,* which means "common." Communication comes from finding something in common with the other. What do we have in common with most of our congregants, who have little or no understanding of biblical texts? The subjects of those texts: our common needs, hurts, interests, and stories of human existence. This is the way to capture the attention of people: Start with a need, a hurt, an interest, a story about being human, and then lead to what the biblical text and other Jewish sources say about it. How can I better my life? Relationships? Family? Community? What will happen to me as I get older? Speak to people's felt needs, hurts, and interests, and they will respond.

This is not a new phenomenon. Have you ever wondered why our ancestors developed so many names for God? Each name is a reflection of how God meets our felt needs. God as merciful, God as judge, God as teacher. God is revealed to us in a variety of ways, all meant to respond to our point of need. What does Judaism say about the challenges we all face? By starting with people's real concerns and needs, we capture the attention of our congregants. Part of the attraction of the healing movement is the recognition that virtually everyone who comes to the synagogue has some need to heal herself or himself or to ask for healing for another. What more basic need is there? Certainly, a major motivation to attend synagogue services is the need to celebrate—a lifecycle moment, an achievement, a holiday. But there might sometimes be a pain just under the surface, that, when addressed in the context of a religious service, can be healing.

People seem to be looking for answers to life's challenges. Answers, not questions. A famous minister, well known for brilliant sermons, once remarked, "Offer certainties, not doubts." We often err on the side of emphasizing the freedom to question in Judaism. Yet, what some people want is a sense of direction, a guide: "Tell me what to do. How can I live my life with a sense of purpose?" This is the comfort of orthodoxy—there is a right and wrong; God commands us to live our lives in certain ways. There is a place for doubts, and there is a place for giving people the wisdom of Jewish responses to the questions of life.

### The Value of Personal Testimonies

Synagogues can be safe places to share your Jewish journey story. The idea of giving testimony comes from Jewish tradition. Certainly, the Jewish prophets were not shy about sharing their views. Moreover, in the ancient Jewish legal system, certain acts required witnesses, or *edim,* in order to be prosecuted. Even the concept of confession is deeply rooted in Jewish liturgy and ritual; the High Holy Days feature the "great confessional" of *Al Chet* and *Ashamnu,* while the *Vi'dui* is the deathbed confession. The Christian community successfully took these Jewish concepts and made them a centerpiece of their spiritual work. We need to reclaim them as our own.

Personal testimony can be riveting and powerful. It is a power born not only of the intellect, but also of emotion. It is a way to touch people in their hearts.

Our clergy will need to learn how to feel comfortable offering testimony from the pulpit. Rabbis are trained in seminaries that value the intellectual, the academic, and the scholarly. As a "people of the book," we love to study, to learn, to gain new insight into biblical texts or rabbinic codes. Yet, there is an emotional intelligence in each of us that rabbis and synagogues rarely reach. Certainly, at a funeral, a wedding, a Bar or Bat Mitzvah, tears of joy and sadness often appear. But, by and large, the service itself is bereft of passion and emotion. We need to find ways to reintroduce the emotional into the worship experience.

Rabbis need to continue exploring how to teach Torah in engaging ways. Certainly, a well-crafted sermon can move people to think and to do; there is something magnificent about a good preacher delivering a powerful message. But frontal presentation is only one delivery system. Some rabbis have transformed the sermon time into a combination presentation/dialogue with the congregation. These Torah discussions transform the sanctuary into a classroom, with the rabbi soliciting questions, ideas, comments, even debate. It can be a dynamic and interactive format, requiring rabbis to bridge the gap between the pulpit and the pew.

## Ways of Bridging the Gap

I recommend that clergy find ways to get off the pulpit and connect with people. When Jay Leno took over for Johnny Carson as host of *The Tonight Show*, he inherited the set, blue curtain and all. Leno followed Carson's model, standing in front of the curtain to do his monologue. In the first month, he was bombing; he almost lost the job. Why? It turns out that Leno was shaped by his experiences in the comedy clubs, intimate settings where the performer stood just inches away from the audience. So, they junked Carson's old set and built a new one for Leno, complete with a stage thrust into the first rows. To this day, Leno begins the show by coming out onto that stage, shaking hands with the people, and launching into his routine.

Another example of bridging the gap is the "Lambeau leap." When a Green Bay Packer wide receiver scores a touchdown, he celebrates by jumping into the first rows of the crowd at Lambeau Field. The people slap him on the rear end, congratulating him and the team on their success. Why is this so unusual? Because the people in Lambeau Field are more than spectators; they are owners. The football team is actually owned by the people of Green Bay, and their pride of ownership is evident in the spectacle of the Lambeau leap.

Rabbis and cantors would be well served to jump off the *bimah* into the embrace of the congregation. Witness how congregants love the Torah *hakafah* (parade), many leaving their seats to touch, even kiss, the Torah scroll. When the rabbi and cantor accompany the Torah on its round through the sanctuary, it is a terrific opportunity for the clergy to bridge the gap and greet the people.

## Harnessing the Spiritual Power of the Pulpit

*There is great spiritual power on the* bimah. *For many, the simple act of walking onto the pulpit is an awe-inspiring experience. Imagine, then, the impact of standing before the Holy Ark during* Neilah, *the closing service of the Yom Kippur holiday. A number of S2K congregations have adopted this idea: The rabbi invites anyone who wants to approach the ark in order to offer private prayers the opportunity to do so during the long Amidah when the Aron ha-Kodesh remains open and the congregation stands. One S2K rabbi told me, "We started this a few years ago, and only a handful of people came up. This last year, we must have had three hundred people— individuals and entire families—stand in front of the ark. Most of them left the* bimah *in tears, visibly moved by the experience."*

### Storahtelling

Early in the Synagogue 2000 project, we heard of a young man from Israel who was experimenting with a traditional, yet revolutionary method for the public reading of Torah. Amichai Lau-Lavie called his new approach "Storahtelling." Citing the ancient custom of simultaneous translation of the Torah text into the vernacular language of the people who listened to it, Amichai developed a unique and compelling mixture of translation, storytelling, dramatic reenactment, improvisation, and contemporary midrashic commentary. We invited Amichai to bring Storahtelling to the second S2K conference in Ojai, and the response from the participants was nothing short of phenomenal. Fortunately, Amichai has trained a cadre of Storahtellers who have learned this approach. Once again, our goal was to demonstrate the "art of the possible" in synagogue.

### Spiritual Goose Bumps

How are the Olympic Games like an uplifting experience of worship?

I am a huge fan of the Olympics. Not because I am such a big sports fan, but because they *move* me. Along with millions of people, I have watched in awe as the finest athletes in the world compete for themselves and their countries in a spectacular display of discipline, hard work, and courage. I find myself having what I can only call "goose bump moments," times when my skin literally tingles and my eyes grow watery with emotion as I witness their achievements. What is it about the Olympics that turns me, night after night, into a blithering mushball?

It turns out that the Olympics are hardly about sports at all. An executive at NBC, which broadcasts the Games, put it succinctly: "The Olympics are a human drama played out on the stage of sports." That explains why there are as many stories about the athletes as human beings—their travails and triumphs, the obstacles they had to overcome, their families—as there is coverage of the events. These stories turn the athletes into people, people we can identify with, people who represent the best in what we hope we all can be.

There are many goose bump moments during the Olympics. Watching the reactions of the families of the athletes as they perform, anyone who has been a parent can identify with the tension and then the joy of family members celebrating the triumph of their children. When the athletes enter the Olympic Stadium to celebrate the youth of the world in the pageantry and ritual of the Opening and Closing Ceremonies, how can one help but be moved? When "The Star-Spangled Banner" is played and the athletes (and most of America) well up with tears, who can resist the emotion of the moment?

Is there such a thing as a spiritual goose bump moment?

My colleague and eminent professor of philosophy, Rabbi Elliot Dorff, talks about "hitting a home run in prayer." Sometimes, the combination of the service, the moment, and the place you are at results in a moving worship experience. Sometimes, prayer does not result in goose bump moments; it is more of a regular experience—a "single," in Elliot's conception—and this is important, too. Yet, I wonder why I can be touched emotionally night after night for two weeks during the Olympics, and I can count on one hand the times I have been truly moved during a worship service. And I have been attending services my whole life; imagine how much more difficult it must be for someone who is setting foot into a synagogue for the first time.

And yet, in the hands of innovative and skilled worship leaders, I have witnessed and felt spiritual goose bumps during the Synagogue 2000 model services and in many of the seeker services that have been developed during these past ten years. More importantly, I have seen newcomers and regulars moved by a Jewish prayer experience that touches the heart and stirs the soul. This is a marvelous and important development in American synagogue life.

## Welcoming During Worship

### Welcoming Newcomers

How are new people welcomed during the worship experience?

The first time I attended services at Valley Beth Shalom in 1974, I was shocked when Rabbi Harold Schulweis, just before *Shalom Aleichem,* asked everyone to stand up, turn to someone they did not know, and greet them with *Shabbat Shalom.* Amazingly, everyone in the congregation did it, and instantly, the atmosphere in the congregation was transformed. Since then, many rabbis have learned the importance of this moment of greeting within the service itself. I have witnessed this on a Shabbat morning just before the Torah service in anticipation of the large-scale communal greeting that happens during the Torah *hakafah* in many congregations. In one congregation, the rabbi invited anyone who was new to introduce himself or herself during the announcements.

While these gestures are well-meaning and often effective, it is important to proceed with caution. In the megachurches, focus groups revealed that first-time visitors do not like being singled out in front of the congregation. So, even though it might feel appropriate to ask newcomers to stand and be identified, this may put the person on the spot. Some newcomers like to hide in the crowd. Think of how you feel when you go to a party where you don't know anyone. Most people hate to speak in front of a crowd of strangers, so to ask a visitor to introduce herself or himself can be threatening and uncomfortable. Many times, newcomers attend with someone who belongs to the congregation. At the end of the service, anyone who has brought someone new to the service is invited to stand and introduce their guest.

Another way to acknowledge guests, especially the family of the Bar or Bat Mitzvah, is to have one of the officiants name each person who receives an honor on the pulpit. For example, in addition to calling someone for an *aliyah* with a Hebrew name, the English name and relationship to the Bar or Bat Mitzvah is announced. Some congregations prepare a printed program, welcoming all guests and identifying who has been given each honor. The same can be done for a couple blessing the Torah reading before a wedding, for a family celebrating a babynaming, an adult Bar or Bat Mitzvah, or any other occasion to be on the *bimah*.

## Welcoming Those with Honors

Keep in mind that many guests, particularly those celebrating a Bar or Bat Mitzvah, who are honored by the family and the congregation with an invitation to participate in the service, are unfamiliar with the rituals and behaviors of worship. This can be a nerve-wracking experience for anyone, especially in front of family and friends. Most congregations are aware of this challenge and offer a variety of ways to prepare the honoree for the occasion. But the help varies widely. In some synagogues, those honored with an *aliyah*—blessing the Torah reading—are given a small card with the number indicating which blessing they will be called to do. The card may or may not have the Hebrew and transliterated blessing on it so that the honoree can rehearse. One congregation gives each honoree a larger laminated sheet with a full explanation of the process: where to stand, what to do, what to say, how to respond to the congratulations; it reminded me of the laminated safety instruction card in every airplane seat pocket. At IKAR, a new emergent congregation in Los Angeles, these instructions come with a sensitive and humorous introduction designed to disarm and calm the already nervous:

Mazal tov! You have been given the honor of reciting the blessings before and after the Torah reading *(aliyah)*.

You may notice that everyone will praise and honor you for receiving this *aliyah*, which is, after all, a bit unfair, considering the person reading the Torah—who spent the past week preparing—will barely get a *yasher koach* (congrats). This may or may not lead you to think of other unfair things in the world, like the fact that over 42 million Americans don't have health insurance …

When the *gabbai* (person who calls people up) says *"Ya'amod"* or *"Ta'amod"* ("Arise!"), please come forward, wearing a tallit (prayer shawl) and head covering. Tell the *gabbai* your Hebrew name (i.e., *Yosef ben Ya'akov v'Rahel* or *Dina bat Ya'akov v'Leah*). Let the Torah reader show you where s/he will begin the reading. Touch your *tzitzit* (the fringes of your tallit) to the place where the reading begins, kiss the *tzitzit*, then close the Torah. Holding on to both *eitzim* (wooden handles), recite the blessing. (The blessings are on page 400 and 402, if you want to practice. There will be a transliteration of the blessings up there, too, just in case.) While the Torah is being recited, follow along in the scroll. After the Torah reading, again touch the place in the Torah where the reader stopped with your *tzitzit*, kiss the *tzitzit*, then close the Torah and recite the final blessing. When you have finished, please remain standing on the other side of the reader throughout the next *aliyah*, then return to your seat, knowing that your grandparents would *kvell* (be proud) over what you just did.

Even with these aids, the experience of being called onto the *bimah* for an honor can be intimidating. So it is important to have a sensitive officiant who can gently guide the unfamiliar participants through the process.

### Using Welcome Cards to Track Attendance

Depending on the time of the service or the religious practices of the congregation, a welcome card or other type of registration can be used to track who comes to the welcoming worship services.

Saddleback has learned that when everyone who attends a service fills out a welcome card, the visitors are not singled out. Their welcome card is an indispensable communication tool. On it is recorded the name, address, phone number, number of times the person has visited, name of the congregant who brought them, age group, marital status, names of children and birthdates, and a checklist of information about the church that can be requested, along with prayer requests and any other special messages to the leadership of the congregation. Orthodox and Conservative synagogues would not allow this writing on Shabbat and *Yom Tov*, but they could at a weekday service, on Hanukkah, Purim, and other minor holidays. At a young professionals service, consider asking the attendees to put a business card in a bowl.

### *Developing a Visitor's Guide to the Service*

Most congregants and nearly all guests to services have little or no understanding of the prayer service, the synagogue, and Jewish ritual. When people do not know what to expect, it makes them anxious. As much as we might encourage congregants to attend a learner's *minyan* or take a class in Jewish liturgy, the majority of visitors to a service need a guide to what's happening. Such guides are beginning to appear at Jewish services, particularly at lifecycle events. Guests at weddings are often given a program containing explanations of the ritual and listing the participants who are standing up.

Some synagogues do print a simple order of the service in the weekly handout. This alerts people to what will occur. But be careful of the language. Words like *invocation, benediction,* and *hymn* are foreign to most people. *Opening prayer, call to worship,* and simply *song* are likely to be more understandable. Include explanatory notes about the structure of the service. Like program notes at a classical music concert or an opera, most people need a guide. It is also helpful for visitors to have a brief explanation of the architecture of the sacred space. People are often curious about the ark, the Torah scroll, and other aspects of the pulpit. During holidays, explanations of various ritual tools (for example, *lulav, etrog, hanukkiyah*) used in the service are helpful.

## Staying On the Same Page

Many guests have a difficult time keeping up with the pace of the worship, particularly in more traditional services. They literally lose their place in the siddur and must wait for the rabbi's next announcement of page numbers or, if brave, ask a neighbor, "What page are we on?" In some Orthodox synagogues, a tall device with mechanical (as opposed to electronic) numbers (think old baseball scoreboards) displays the page number; a lay leader from the congregation changes the number at regular intervals throughout the service. Some S2K congregations have greeters at the door of the sanctuary handing out prayerbooks already opened to the correct page to latecomers. On the opposite end of the spectrum, at Sinai Temple's Friday Night Live, there have been experiments with projecting the words of prayers onto large video screens, freeing the congregation from depending on the book altogether. Rabbi Sharon Brous and her team at IKAR published a spectacular "map" detailing the spiritual journey of the High Holy Days, a step-by-step guide for the worship experience. For Yizkor, IKAR created a published booklet of personal reflections by congregants about the loved ones who were being remembered.

## Using Multiple Minyanim to Add Variety to Worship

One of the critical challenges for a synagogue in the twenty-first century that wants to offer spiritually welcoming worship is to learn that when it comes to prayer, it is most definitely different strokes for different folks. Some people prefer a service featuring *hazzanut*, some prefer meditation, some prefer participatory singing.

This trend toward offering a menu of alternative worship services, multiple *minyanim*, is gaining popularity in many synagogues. For example, at Valley Beth Shalom on a typical Saturday morning, in addition to the main Shabbat morning service that centers predominately on the celebration of a Bar or Bat Mitzvah, there is a service that features straight-through Hebrew *davenning* and a short *d'var Torah* from a layperson; a family service that lasts just one hour and features sing-along *davenning* and a short story; a monthly women's *minyan*; a junior congregation that acts as "basic training" in worship for children in the religious school; a tot Shabbat for toddlers and their parents and grandparents; a learner's *minyan* offering instruction in the basics of worship; and an early-morning Torah study for an hour preceding all the services. Congregants can choose from this variety of styles of worship, with everyone gathering for the kiddush afterward.

The concern most often expressed about this approach is that it will inhibit the sense of community in the congregation; all these different groups literally making *Shabbes* for themselves! Some congregations solve the problem by turning the *Oneg Shabbat* into a major sit-down luncheon each week, an hourlong affair during which members who have attended the different *minyanim* can come together to eat, sing, and sometimes hear a brief talk from a guest speaker.

Part of the challenge is to convince the leadership of the synagogue that a stand-alone welcoming worship service can be just as engaging for the regulars as well. But it is just as likely that dynamic synagogues in the twenty-first century will need to explore offering special seeker services or multiple *minyanim* to meet the worship needs of a broad constituency.

### Welcoming Children in Services

*Oy, kinderlach!* The subject of children in services is complicated. Most decisions about children will revolve around the philosophy of the shul. Is the service for adults? Then children with their inevitable questions and restlessness can be distractions. Is the service for families? Then children are not only tolerated, they are welcome and central to the experience. If the decision is made to welcome children into the service, it could help to offer parents advice on appropriate behavior in shul. Instruct parents that if (when) a child is too antsy to sit in the service or is making disturbing noise, it is preferable to take the child out to the hallway than to disrupt the service. The problem here is that some parents misjudge what is disruptive and let children sit in the service, putting ushers and often the rabbi in the uncomfortable position of either grinning and bearing it or saying something. Most rabbis will not embarrass a parent by asking a child to leave, even though the other adults in the congregation may be seething at the disruption. Rather than not saying anything at all, perhaps a small message in the weekly bulletin or in a guide to the service about the appropriate behavior of children in the synagogue would be helpful. In some congregations, this whole issue is moot: The presence (and noise) of children is not only welcomed, it is encouraged.

### Tips

## *Strategies for Welcoming Children*

Here are some ideas to consider for welcoming children in services:

- Encourage parents to prepare a "shul bag" to bring to the service. In it should be some reading or picture books, a quiet toy, a favorite stuffed animal, a snack and a drink (to be eaten in the hallway), extra diapers, fresh wipes, a pretend tallit, and a *kippah*.
- Create a children's area in the rear of the shul by taking out a few pews and establishing a play space for babies and toddlers while parents and grandparents participate in the service. Proximity to the door allows for a quick getaway.
- Offer children a basket of appropriate Shabbat toys to play with at the entrance of the sanctuary.

- Keep a cart of Jewish children's books for parents to share with children during the service.
- Encourage parents to take the children to babysitting and youth services, clearly sending a message that the main service is geared for adults. The babysitting is first rate, offered in a clean, well-stocked nursery.
- Take a strategy from the megachurches and establish a family room, sometimes called a crying room, in the congregation: a closed-off space constructed of glass where families can make noise, but still hear the service. At Saddleback, young children are most definitely not encouraged in the main sanctuary. But families can use the four family rooms in the building that receive live televised broadcasts of the service or sit just outside the glass walls of the sanctuary where speakers allow the adults to hear the service.

## Other Ways to Enhance Worship

### Jewish Meditation

Meditation is another misunderstood and underused skill of prayer that can be attractive to people. Of course, in the traditional service, there is opportunity for silent prayer, particularly during the recitation of the *Amidah*. Yet most congregants are not well equipped to use this time for meditation. Thankfully, talented teachers of meditation (see the Institute for Jewish Spirituality website, www.ijs-online.org) are beginning to instruct congregations in its use. In a rat race world, the opportunity to stop completely, to relax, and to meditate can be a great gift.

## Hebrew Institute of White Plains (Orthodox) White Plains, New York

*"Shhh." S2K team members collectively agreed to take an unofficial tefillah "vow of silence." All twenty-two members agreed to make every effort not to have conversations during tefillah on Shabbat, and to respectfully let others know that speaking during worship distracts one from the purpose of tefillah and detracts from the sacredness of the space. One of our S2K team members who now sits on the Religious Services committee has helped to create signage for the Days of Awe in the sanctuary reminding people of our objective. Sample signs include, "Praying is hard work. Quiet helps" and "Quiet please, Sacred Space."*

### Healing Community

A staple of spiritually welcoming services has been the inclusion of public prayers for healing. Stimulated by the wide acceptance of Debbie Friedman's *MiShebeirakh*, a number of other composers have written treatments for this prayer for healing. S2K published a compilation of a number of these melodies called *R'fuah Shleimah* (available through the S3K website, www.synagogue3000.org).

A number of different strategies for inserting a healing moment into the service have evolved:

- The rabbi asks congregants who wish to say the name of a person in need of healing to stand, then indicate with a nod or extended hand whose turn it is to say a name aloud.
- The rabbi asks those who are thinking of someone in need of healing to hold their names "in their hearts," eliminating the public announcement.
- The rabbi invites people to come up to the *bimah* and whisper the name to the *gabbai*, who then repeats the name.

Any of these options are certainly better than what used to happen: the quick reading of names in Hebrew that were submitted by those who knew enough to call the synagogue office during the week to get a name on the list.

It is important to note that "healing" should be interpreted not just as being cured of illness, but as "completeness." Most people are not complete, for example, when they are unemployed. At BJ, the last page of the weekly bulletin is a community job listing.

### Incorporating Movement

In the prayer service of the twentieth century, the only movement during prayer was standing up and sitting down. Up and down, up and down, up and down, all while most people in the service had no clue why they were asked to stand up during certain prayers. The only time of the year that dancing broke out during the service was on *Simchat Torah*.

In the prayer service of the twenty-first century, congregations have experimented with the use of movement to enhance the prayer experience. This initiative was pioneered by an S2K pilot site, Temple Micah, a Reform congregation in Washington, D.C. At Temple Micah, the senior rabbi, Danny Zemel, has partnered with choreographer, congregant, and S2K fellow Liz Lerman, a MacArthur "genius" fellow, to introduce new movements into the *davenning* experience.

In the prayer service of the twenty-first century, dancing in the synagogue is not limited to *Simchat Torah*. Spontaneous outbursts of dancing are regular occurrences during many spiritually welcoming services. At many seeker services, the dancing breaks out during *L'cha Dodi*. During One Shabbat Morning, the Torah *hakafah* is turned into an opportunity for the congregation to dance in the aisles. At Carlebach-influenced services in the Modern Orthodox world, it is not at all unusual for the congregation to erupt in ecstatic dancing.

In short, there is a new level of comfort with dancing and movement in many worship services.

## *Rethinking Space*

The need for space to dance is only one factor leading to a complete rethinking of the structure of sacred space in synagogues. The trend away from the "cathedral" synagogue of the twentieth century is well under way. Instead, congregations are renovating sanctuaries to enable people to be closer to the clergy, closer to the pulpit, and closer to each other, creating a closer spiritual community. Some congregations are returning to the first model of synagogue space by placing the Torah reading table in the center of the sanctuary instead of on the high *bimah* at the front. Even if it means losing some seats, imagine the dramatic difference such a setting would create.

Pews are passé. People today expect to have individual chairs. Movable seats offer maximum flexibility for congregations that want to experiment with different seating arrangements for worship. Set them up so each person can see someone else's face. It enhances the feeling of intimacy in the service. Set up fewer chairs than you think you need. It is always better to add chairs than to have a service in which a few people are scattered around a huge room. We also need to encourage congregants to sit closer to each other. Where is it written that everyone who enters a sanctuary from the rear needs to sit in the back rows? Have you ever wondered why people are so anxious to sit as far away as possible? I realize people often have their favorite seats, especially the regulars. But we should find ways of asking people to come closer together for worship. For example, consider blocking off the back rows with a sign that says "Reserved."

We have built huge sanctuaries that function fully only three days a year. There is nothing quite as discouraging as fifty people scattered in a room with five hundred seats. Some congregations move the service to smaller chapels when anticipating a low turnout. If faced with a small crowd in a large room, it is even more important to come down off the high *bimah* and gather the people in the front of the room.

If people are too hot or too cold, they stop participating in the service and begin wondering how long they have to suffer. Heat is the major culprit. A common miscalculation is to set a thermostat for a

## Temple Israel (Reform)
## Omaha, Nebraska

*One of our original S2K pilot sites, Temple Israel is the last of the synagogues in Omaha to "move west" in the city where the Jewish community has migrated. Currently housed in a small 1950s-era building, the congregation recently received a large donated piece of property in this newer Omaha neighborhood. Many of the original S2K team members now serve in leadership roles in the congregation and they are spearheading the exciting effort to plan a twenty-first-century synagogue building and campus. When I asked one of my Omaha cousins how he felt about this change, he was not happy.*

*"Why do we have to move out there?" he asked. "Besides, when I walk into this building, there are so many memories that well up in me. We'll lose all that."*

*I replied, "First of all, put yourself in the shoes of the parents of young children in the religious school who complain about the shlep to the old building. Second, figure out what is precious and essential and what is expendable. Perhaps you'll keep key components of the bimah—the ark, the eternal light—and integrate them into the new design; that will give you the visual cues to remind you of the past, yet enable the congregation to build a much more flexible, usable, and attractive space."*

*My cousin had to agree intellectually; he came to accept that his real issues are coming to grips with the emotions of nostalgia and loss. He has since become a big supporter of the move.*

*Think about the power of expanding the use of existing space. Rabbi Murray Ezring of Temple Israel in Charlotte, North Carolina, trains fifty members of his congregation to blow the shofar on the High Holy Days. He then positions them strategically throughout the sanctuary. The effect: surround shofar blowing! The congregation is moved to goose bump moments with the thrilling sound.*

## *Congregation Beth Evergreen (Reform)*
## *Evergreen, Colorado*

Several S2K congregations undertook building and renovation projects. Here is a report from one successful effort:

*Synagogue 2000 greatly influenced the design of our new synagogue. We had engaged an architect who was consulting with an architectural firm that specializes in synagogue design. Soon after our architect presented us with the initial design for our approval, we met with the S2K sacred space maven, Richard Vosko, who was pleased with our design, but made quite a few wonderful suggestions to make the building more spiritually compelling. Some of his suggestions included a shofar-shaped path to enter the main sanctuary/social hall space. Our architect was in attendance at the time of the meeting and was anxious to meet the challenges presented to her. In addition, we toured some of the Denver synagogues, pointing out to each other the elements that we felt contributed to the feeling of inclusiveness and spirituality emphasized by S2K. We are now in the process of building our sacred home and anticipate a place of warmth, togetherness, and deep spirituality.*

reasonable temperature but forget to factor in the body heat a large crowd produces. It is best to cool off the room, even if you hear some kvetching at the beginning of the service. The heat will rise quickly once the room is filled. Heat puts people to sleep; keep it cool.

Lighten up the place. Replace the light bulbs with double the wattage. Take the curtains off windows. Bring in extra lighting. Paint the walls a brighter color. Valley Beth Shalom painted over red brick because it was simply too dark. Here's a heresy: Rethink the necessity of stained-glass windows, especially those that darken the space. Be sure the lighting on the pulpit is good so people can actually see the clergy as they lead the service.

It is common for congregations to have *bimah* flowers, often fresh-cut bouquets. They add beauty to the pulpit and festivity to the celebration, but they die. Consider green plants and small trees as decoration. Of course, on certain festivals, vegetation can greatly enhance the atmosphere of the service: fall foliage for Sukkot and greens for Shavuot.

### *Meet Market*

It is quite moving to see hundreds of young people attracted to a religious service. Some have criticized the BJ Kabbalat Shabbat and Friday Night Live services for being "meat markets," attracting single Jewish men and women who are trying to find their soul mates.

What exactly is wrong with that?

With a declining population and an intermarriage rate well above 50 percent among young Jewish professionals, the need for young Jews to meet each other is more important than ever.

Moreover, the young professional community is notoriously fickle and difficult to attract to any programming. If the prayer services were not compelling, if the worship experience was not spiritually uplifting, there is no way that these young people would attend consistently. It would be much easier to meet at Starbucks.

As for older folks, they too need to meet together in community.

The secret is in the skill of the worship leader to create a sense of spiritual community out of a diverse group of strangers. Craig Taubman is extraordinarily gifted at this, coming off the *bimah*, standing in the middle of a cavernous sanctuary, instructing the crowd to turn in their seats to face him, instantly creating a circle in the room. He and his talented colleagues can transform an awful place into an *awe-full* space in a matter of moments—goose bump moments.

### *Rethinking a Dress Code in an Era of Informality*

Dress is another issue to consider in creating atmosphere. Many baby boomers who spent summers in Jewish camps recall with fondness the special clothing of Shabbat—white shirts and blouses, no ties, no jackets. Informal dress, yet lovely and dignified. The same is true in most synagogues in Israel—formal dress is almost never seen. Somehow in America, we have adopted the dress common in churches. Yet, in places like Saddleback, a conscious decision to dress informally has removed a huge obstacle to participation in services. Even the pastors dress casually, sending the message that what you wear doesn't matter. Most people do not like to dress up, particularly on weekends. Even in the workplace, the dressing down of work clothes is an unmistakable trend. What would happen if Jewish religious services were "come as you are"? Would more people come? Some synagogues have experimented with informal dress codes during family services. I know of one congregation that held a PJ Shabbat family service on Friday nights geared to young children who came dressed in pajamas! Why? Children who fell asleep before the end of the service could easily be carried home and put straight to bed. The PJ service attracted a huge crowd!

Informality can be another way to attract those who are put off by the stuffiness of high church religious services. Avoid pretentiousness in favor of an informal, relaxed, and friendly atmosphere. The use of doctoral robes and tall cantor's *kippot* (head coverings) are incongruous in such a setting.

Of course, there are moments in the holiday cycle when dressing more formally in order to stand in the presence of the Holy One is quite appropriate.

### Announcements: Short and Sweet

Announcements are a necessary evil of synagogue life. No one I know likes them. The larger the synagogue, the more announcements there are. And then, each sponsoring organization wants to make sure its announcement is announced. What to do? Here are several suggestions:

- Ask congregants to read the bulletin. Say something like, "There are many wonderful activities coming up listed in the bulletin. Please be sure to read it and take it home with you."
- Announce only events that apply to everyone.

- Do not conduct synagogue business from the *bimah*.
- Do thank everyone who participated in the service.

Think about when to interrupt the service for announcements. I have always thought the typical placement at the very end of the service just before the closing prayer interrupts the pace and emotional climax of the worship. Megachurches do their announcements at the beginning of the service; of course, they can count on everyone being there on time!

Appeals are another source of irritation in synagogue services, especially at High Holy Days. On the one hand, the thinking goes, this is our shot at a maximum audience and it does give congregants the opportunity to fulfill the mitzvah of *tzedakah*. On the other hand, asking people for money during the holiest day of the year can be a huge turn-off, especially to first-timers.

### *Refreshments as a Means of Building Community*

The kiddush or *Oneg Shabbat* is one of the most important elements of a service. Actually, the time a person spends in the synagogue can be extended by the length and elaborateness of the refreshments. Cookies and grape juice will often keep people for a few minutes—an extended kiddush of light foods may keep people around for another hour, socializing, enjoying each other's company, creating community. Some synagogues combine the refreshments with other incentives to stick around. Israeli dancing is a favorite option, and some congregations love to sit and sing Shabbat table songs. I once visited a congregation where refreshments were served before *and* after the service. On a Friday evening, the congregants gathered for appetizers before the service. This added to the feeling of welcome in the synagogue before anyone entered the sanctuary.

### *Social Justice*

The concern for social justice is evident in many of the emerging synagogues of the twenty-first century, and Shabbat services provide a weekly springboard for motivating the congregation to action.

## Larchmont Temple (Reform)
## Larchmont, New York

The S2K team decided to offer a wine and cheese Kabbalat Shabbat once a month on Friday night at 7:00. People arrive to find the lobby of the congregation full of beautifully decorated tables laden with trays featuring all sorts of exotic cheeses, along with vegetable crudités, dips, and crackers. Excellent wines from Israel are offered. The gathering is festive and builds a sense of community. The service itself is of the "family" variety, exactly one hour, filled with singing, a short story from the rabbi, and a prayer for healing.

A cautionary tale. In many Orthodox and some Conservative congregations, a group of men, usually the regulars and machers, will leave the sanctuary during the Torah reading to enjoy a schnapps and a piece of cake in another part of the building. These "Kiddush clubs" are exclusionary, elitist, and disruptive to the sense of community that most congregations hope to establish. I know of one such congregation where the rabbi outlawed the practice, and members resigned over the issue! Here's an idea: At IKAR in Los Angeles, a snack of honey cake and juice was offered to the entire congregation during the long Rosh Hashana morning service.

In many congregations, the call to social justice remains strong and constant. To cite just one example from our S2K congregations, Rabbi Joel Soffin of Temple Shalom in Succasunna, New Jersey, regularly takes groups of synagogue members and others to places around the country and the world to build houses for the indigent poor. This is not new, but the way Rabbi Soffin organizes the typical day is an excellent example of how to combine the spirituality and social justice agendas into a seamless whole. The day commences with a prayer service before the actual labor begins. When the work is completed, the group studies Jewish texts detailing the imperative for social justice and repair of the world. By the end of the day, congregants report a feeling of spiritual uplift, despite their physical exhaustion.

In the mid-1950s, my mother, Bernice, established one of the first Braille groups in a congregation by recruiting her friends to learn how to transcribe books into Braille. The synagogue dedicated a small room in which equipment was installed, and, together, they produced the first Braille Hebrew-English edition of the Passover Haggadah.

Danny Siegel, a dynamic Jewish educator, has spent his entire career visiting synagogues to teach the young and the old how to be "mitzvah heroes." A favorite example of his is the Giraffe Project, where people are taught to "stick their necks out"!

One warning: There is a difference between social justice and social action. Some synagogues mount a once-a-year mitzvah day to enable members to do a social action project. Social justice, however, requires a return to our roots as a people unafraid of prophecy, unafraid to cry out against injustice wherever it is found, unafraid to take up our mantle as a "light unto the nations." Our tradition implores us to take a stand, to right the wrong, to repair the world. The nexus of social justice and spirituality is contained in the words of the *Aleinu* prayer: *l'takein olam b'malchut Shaddai,* "[we are] to repair the world in order to bring God's presence [literally, 'Kingdom']." We do not simply repair the world because it is a good thing to do; we do the work of social justice in order to bring godliness into the world and into our lives.

The call to social justice needs to be a constant refrain in the welcoming worship of the twenty-first-century synagogue.

## Empowering the Worship Team

During our ten years of research, I have come to appreciate the value of a worship team for the planning and implementation of welcoming worship. In many traditional Orthodox and Conservative synagogues, the idea of planning a service is a foreign concept. The respective roles with regard to the prayer experience are well defined: The rabbi offers a sermon or *d'var Torah,* the cantor leads the prayers according to the appropriate *nusach* and/or chooses the melodies to be sung, and the laity participate—period. As one clergyperson told me, "It's pretty much automatic. The only thing we discuss together is whether we'll conclude the service with *Adon Olam* or *Yigdal.*"

## Shared Leadership

The development of an effective welcoming worship service demands a collaborative effort. This is clearly evident in every one of the successful services cited above.

The clergy in each congregation reject the idea of a bifurcated leadership. In each congregation, the rabbi and the cantor and/or musical leader recognize and respect each other's expertise. They are on the same page, sharing a vision of what a welcoming worship experience can be.

On many pulpits in synagogues, there are two lecterns: one for the rabbi and one for the cantor. This has led one wag to comment on the inevitability of the "battle of the *bimah,*" and in more than one congregation, such a battle for control of the service and sometimes the synagogue itself is reflected in this bifurcated leadership. Years ago, many Reform synagogues abandoned the dual-lectern *bimah* in favor of the clergy standing together at the central reading table.

At BJ, this notion of shared leadership is not just in the physical placement of the clergy. At various times during the service, the rabbi and *hazzan* take turns leading the singing. The partnership speaks to the congregation, and it says, "We are not leading; we are *davenning.*" The fact that it is absolutely clear to all that the clergy are not performing, but are rather in the midst of their own spiritual experience, is a powerful model for the participants in the service. Moreover, the congregation knows that there is a clergy team at work and they are all, literally, on the same page.

After working with nearly one hundred congregations, we saw our share of success—and conflict, especially when the topic was worship. When the clergy team joined with the lay leadership to study the issues raised in the S2K curriculum on prayer—to honestly assess the effectiveness of the prayer services in place at the time and to envision strategies for creating a more welcoming worship experience—real progress was made. On the other hand, when there was no such sense of shared purpose, real conflict erupted. In some cases, the laity advocated for major changes that were resisted by the rabbi and/or the cantor. In other congregations, the rabbi and cantor failed to come to agreement. In one congregation, I was called in for an emergency visit to mediate a brewing conflict over these issues. As I entered the sanctuary, I noticed two different prayer books were in each pew—one published by the Conservative Movement and one published by an Orthodox-affiliated press. When I asked about this, the president told me that the congregation could not come to an agreement about which prayer book to use, so it decided to offer both. They were literally not "on the same page"!

### *Rabbis and Cantors: Overcoming the Resistance to Change*

Rabbis often view themselves as the ultimate religious authority of the congregation. However, when it comes to the music of worship, the cantor is the resident expert. She or he has spent years of study, exploring the deep reservoir of Jewish liturgical music. Cantors rightly see themselves as guardians of this legacy and the shapers of the future of liturgical music.

Earlier in this book, I spoke about the resistance to change among certain rabbis in our S2K congregations. We certainly found some congregations where the cantor was the force for transforming the service but met with strong objection from the rabbi. We also encountered the opposite. One thing is certain: The importance of music as the key component of welcoming worship places the cantor center stage in the ongoing evolution of these services. In our Synagogue 2000 work, we emphasized the enormous opportunity for leadership this affords the cantor, but only if the cantor is willing to be open, flexible, even enthusiastic about the challenges of creating services that are engaging and uplifting for the congregation or specific target audience.

Cantors are justifiably nervous about all of this. I recall being invited to speak at a national convention of cantors who wanted to hear from me directly about what Synagogue 2000 was advocating with regard to worship renewal. As I walked through the lobby of the hotel, one of the cantors, an old friend, approached me. He was wearing a button on his shirt depicting a cartoon figure of what appeared to be a dragon. But it wasn't a dragon. Underneath the illustration was the word *Hazzanasaurus*. It was not meant to be funny; it was a sign of nervousness among the cantorate that their expertise was being dismissed, that their sphere of influence in congregations was under attack, that their jobs were at stake. My friend said, "We can't wait to hear what you have to say."

Here is what I said:

> You have a choice. You can stonewall the development of Jewish seeker services, refusing to participate. Or, you can seize the opportunity you have to be the musical leader of the congregation. I don't have to remind this group that the meaning of the word *hazzan* is "visionary." No one, certainly none of us in Synagogue 2000, is suggesting that we throw out *nusach*. No one, certainly none of us in Synagogue 2000, is advocating replacing cantors with "song leaders." But I am saying that, while there is a time and place for solos, we have found that congregations want an opportunity to sing *with* you; that music is the window to the soul and the engine of spirituality; that no one hums the sermon on the way to kiddush; that this can be your moment, if you only seize it.

There was another, barely whispered, reason that the cantors were nervous. The skills of leading a congregation in welcoming worship, of engaging their voice, of planning the emotional arc of a service were hardly taught at their seminaries and schools of sacred music. As one cantor told me in an honest moment, "Even if I wanted to do this kind of service, I was never trained to do it."

All of this is also true of rabbis. There is some teaching in the rabbinic seminaries about the structure and content of the liturgy but precious little preparation in the art of creating what I have called here welcoming worship. Some rabbis "get it" or learn it on the job; most simply mimic what they grew up with or were taught. Where do rabbis learn the difference between preaching and teaching, learn how to come off the *bimah* and engage the congregation, learn how to build the pace and choreography of the service, learn when to introduce creative liturgy and ritual? To be fair, the newest generation of rabbis and cantors are receiving much better preparation for the new demand for welcoming worship and some of the seminaries are beginning to respond to this emergent spirituality in mainstream congregations. They had better be prepared, because the train has left the station.

Today, ten years after beginning our work in Synagogue 2000, the explosion of welcoming worship in congregations across the country in every denomination is testament to the adaptability of those cantors and rabbis who are willing to experiment, to change, and to be visionary. In some congregations, seeker services are held occasionally and in the social hall, while the main service continues in the traditional mode of the congregation. But there is mounting evidence that even the most obstinate clergy have learned that congregants expect an engaging spiritual worship experience in the sanctuary.

### How the Worship Team Can Evaluate Worship

It is quite amazing how little time in synagogues is devoted to evaluating services. In many places, there is so little variety in what happens from week to week that the planning is automatic. Even less time is spent soliciting feedback from congregants and engaging in serious evaluation.

Yet, how can a synagogue improve its services without consideration of whether or not the worship is meeting the mission or goal you are trying to reach? Do you have a vision of what you hope the worship will achieve—Hebrew literacy, meditative contemplation, ecstatic prayer, sense of community, study? Do you strive for a musical balance between listening and vocal participation by the congregation? Is there a time for the head as well as a time for the heart? When there is a vision or goal for worship, you can ask for feedback that specifically tracks what worked, instead of the usual critique that clergy and lay leaders often get: "I didn't like such-and-such ... "

Courageous synagogue leaders should always be asking the question: How can we do it better? Here are some ideas on how to evaluate for improvement:

- Solicit feedback from first-time guests. A "first impression" card asking for feedback can be distributed at welcoming worship services.
- Form focus groups. Invite a small group of newcomers to meet with the professionals or a lay committee for a discussion of their impressions of the services.
- Establish a "feedback phone," a phone line with an answering machine dedicated to one purpose: hearing feedback. Members can call anytime to offer suggestions, ask questions, or express concerns about any issue. Someone monitors the comments and informs staff and leadership. A congregation from Boston set up such a line during the process of searching for a new rabbi: Congregants could call and leave feedback about the candidates, knowing that their voice would be heard, even though they could remain anonymous.
- Solicit feedback from the professional staff. Take time on a regular basis to "post mortem" services. Ask for suggestions about how things can be done better. Look at everything from the music to the bulletins to the sermon.

Many people fear evaluation because it is done irregularly and sometimes masks other agendas. The key to evaluation is to do it often. Make it a regular expectation of congregants and staff. Don't call it "evaluation." Call it "feedback." Find a way to build this important process into the life of the congregation.

## The Transformation of Synagogue Worship

When we began the work of Synagogue 2000 in 1995, there were precious few spiritually welcoming worship services as I have defined them here. B'nai Jeshurun's Kabbalat Shabbat service was the shining exception and news of it sparked a steady stream of visitors curious about what was attracting hundreds of people. While admitting that the service clearly worked for the seekers in attendance, the critics dismissed it as coffeehouse Judaism, *tefillah*-lite, or "a performance." Moreover, they claimed, the phenomenon was unique to the Upper West Side of New York City with its heavy concentration of young Jewish professionals: "This would never work in Omaha."

Nonsense.

I knew then and I certainly know now, ten years later, that the basic principles of a spiritually welcoming worship service are applicable to virtually any synagogue. Of course, it would be nearly impossible to clone the BJ service or transplant it into another setting. That is not the goal. Synagogue 2000 never advocated that all synagogues should look like BJ—or any other congregation. But the principles of spiritually welcoming worship can be used by a worship team to shape a service that works for your community.

Synagogue 2000 provided the stimulus, the motivation, and the models for the evolution of spiritually welcoming worship in American Judaism. Never before had the cutting-edge clergy and artists from across the denominational spectrum been brought together to watch each other do their work. It was an opportunity for synagogue leadership to experience what was *possible* in prayer. It was eye-opening—and soul-opening. It forced everyone to ask tough questions about the efficacy of the worship services that each synagogue offered. Armed with a substantive graduate-level curriculum about Jewish prayer that was primarily based on Larry Hoffman's classic book *The Art of Public Prayer,* 2nd edition: *Not for Clergy Only* (SkyLight Paths), S2K teams went home from our conferences uplifted by the spiritually welcoming worship they had themselves experienced, ready to reconsider ways to infuse their own services with new energy and meaning.

Synagogue 2000 enabled us to identify and convene some of the most creative leaders of Jewish worship in the world. These S2K fellows—rabbis, cantors, musical artists, choreographers, and teachers—represented the full spectrum of religious ideology. When we asked them to lead our conference attendees in prayer, we told them to break the mold, to experiment, to try new ideas.

The result was thrilling. Not just for the participants, but for the S2K fellows themselves. The lasting image in my mind is of Ed

Feinstein, a Conservative rabbi, literally sitting on the edge of his seat, watching Rick Jacobs, a Reform rabbi, lead services. I could see that Ed was taking reams of mental notes as he watched Rick work. The next day, the roles were reversed: Rick watched Ed lead a group in prayer, slack-jawed by his brilliance. Each of them took away dozens of ideas that found expression in their rabbinate.

How often does one rabbi get to observe another rabbi lead a service? Almost never, except when attending a relative's Bar or Bat Mitzvah. When does a cantor have the opportunity to hear how a colleague engages a congregation? Almost never. I believe synagogues should give their clergy time off every year to visit congregations where their peers are doing amazing work.

These S2K fellows reveled at being in each other's presence. It is the reason Synagogue 3000, the successor organization to the Synagogue 2000 project, is beginning its work by creating the S3K Leadership Network, a group of courageous synagogue leaders who embrace the vision of a spiritually welcoming sacred community and are creating a vibrant American Jewish spiritual renaissance.

Some Synagogue 2000 fellows hit the road, invited to communities and congregations to share their expertise and model these new services. Craig Taubman visited dozens of synagogues to model Friday Night Live, working closely with the local cantor and rabbi to include them in the service itself, but more importantly to encourage them to learn the organizing principles and strategies for application to the congregation's own worship. Merri Lovinger Arian, the spectacular S2K director of music, was invited to share her expertise in how to engage the congregation's voice. Richard Vosko, one of the world's leading experts on sacred space, a Roman Catholic priest, responded to the many requests from S2K congregations to consult on the renovation or construction of their sanctuaries and buildings. Liz Lerman brought her extraordinary talent to congregations willing to experiment with the nexus of prayer and movement. Amichai Lau-Lavie transformed the experience of reading Torah through his fusion of improvisational storytelling and text commentary. Cantor Ellen Dreskin was invited to bring her superb skills in leading worship to a variety of congregations and conferences. The list goes on and on; in fact, a complete list of the S2K fellows can be found in the final pages of this volume. Their contribution to this work is incalculable.

The result of ten years of this experiment in synagogue transformation is an explosion of creative, spiritually welcoming services across the country. In some congregations, like Shabbat Unplugged at Congregation Emanuel in Denver, Colorado, these services are specific, time-limited offerings targeted for particular groups. New Jewish Emergent spiritual communities are blossoming, each offering a version of these welcoming services: IKAR in Los Angeles, RitualLab, Brooklyn Jews, and Hadar in New York. And many synagogues have transitioned their weekly former worship model to a new, more spiritually alive experience. My favorite example is Temple Israel in Boston, which began offering an alternative service in the social hall as an option to the classical Reform worship held in the main sanctuary. Within a year, the people had voted with their feet and the alternative became the regular.

And, in Omaha, in the shul of my youth, a new rabbi and cantor (both from Argentina—what *is* in the water down there?) took the bold step of introducing musical instruments into the Kabbalat Shabbat service in the Conservative synagogue. Weekly attendance grew from 25 or 30 to an average of 150. More importantly, the people who come, including the regulars, marvel at the infusion of spirit. Not because of the instruments, but because the congregation is engaged, uplifted, and spiritually satisfied.

This spiritually welcoming worship is nothing less than what Rabbi Les Bronstein first called "a new American *nusach*," an expression of authentic Jewish prayer, rooted in traditional forms and renewed by the culture in which we live. This is hardly a new phenomenon; Jews have always borrowed from the sounds and rhythms that surround us. It is worship indigenous to America; it is ours. *V'nomar l'fanav shira hadasha—Halleluya!*—We will sing before God a new song—*Halleluya!*

# 5

# Welcoming Membership

## Rethinking Membership

The transformation of a congregation into a sacred community begins with creating a welcoming ambience imbued with radical hospitality and welcoming worship that is spiritually uplifting. Done well, the congregation is poised to concentrate on the next step: encouraging seekers and guests to consider affiliation with the sacred community—welcoming membership. Then, once a person joins the congregation, establishing a meaningful connection between the individual and the community poses another significant challenge.

In the twentieth-century synagogue, "membership" became the economic model of congregations. This required attracting a number of individuals and family units willing to pay dues in order to receive the services of the organization: worship experiences, religious school, adult education, and attention from the clergy. The result was congregations of various sizes, almost all based on a fee-for-service relationship with the member in the context of a limited-liability community.

As mentioned earlier, the entrance of many synagogues is a revolving door. Each year, a number of new members come in and a number of members leave. Often, these numbers even out, resulting in no growth whatsoever. We know why people join; most members sign up when they need the services the congregation offers. We need to ask the tough question: Why do members quit?

The answer should not be a surprise. People leave synagogues when they no longer need the services they signed up for in the first place. There is no reliable research on this topic, but my informal, anecdotal survey reveals that most members who quit do so shortly after their youngest child becomes a Bar or Bat Mitzvah. The failure to engage the adults in a serious relationship with the congregation is the most serious indictment of the synagogue of the twentieth century.

This is maddening. Many parents of young children look to join a synagogue in order to ensure their children get a Jewish education. Some families sign up if the synagogue offers a preschool; others join when the oldest child reaches the age of eight or so. Assuming a family with two children, spaced several years apart, the synagogue will likely have the membership "unit" in the congregation for at least twelve to fifteen years. The question we usually hear is, How can we keep the kids involved in the synagogue after the Bar or Bat Mitzvah? But I am asking, What can we do during the twelve to fifteen years of membership to ensure that the parents continue their affiliation with the congregation?

This will require a complete rethinking of every aspect of what it means to belong to a congregation. To do this thinking, synagogue leaders need to do something quite radical: analyze the entire experience of membership—from shul-shopping to joining a congregation to connecting with each person in a meaningful way—from the point of view of the prospective member, not from the point of view of the synagogue office.

While it is of course important to recruit new members, I am as concerned with deepening the relationship between the members we already have as I am with recruiting new members into our congregations. We must think carefully about how to do inreach even as we develop strategies for outreach. Otherwise, the door will keep on revolving and neither our congregations nor our members will grow, physically or spiritually.

## Rethinking the Purpose of Synagogue

What is the purpose of a synagogue? What is it in business to do?

If the answer to this question is to provide a religious school for children, a place to pray, and a rabbi on call, then most of the synagogues of the twentieth century serve these purposes well.

If, however, the purpose of a synagogue is to be a sacred community of people whose lives are enriched with meaning, purpose, connectedness, and a relationship with God through prayer, study, acts of social justice, healing, and loving-kindness, then we must redefine what it means to be a member of a synagogue in the twenty-first century.

Our goal can be simply stated, though it is challenging to achieve: to transform "membership" into a covenantal relationship between the individual and the spiritual community and to deepen the commitment of the member to the community, to Judaism, and to God.

Most synagogue membership can be categorized by their level of commitment. Typically, we think of the regulars, those for whom the congregation is like a second home; the involved, those who have some contact with the congregation through attendance at services or programs and serving as leaders (at least for a while) or volunteers; and the peripherals, the members who come for the High Holy Days, when they are invited to an event or a celebration, or to say *Kaddish* for loved ones.

The synagogue leadership, drawn from the ranks of regulars or involved members, often think of the congregation from inside out. Once inside, it is difficult to remember what it felt like to be new or on the periphery. And yet that is precisely where we need to start our exploration of how the process of deepening membership might happen.

### Circles of Commitment: A Model for Thinking about Membership

In the twenty-first-century synagogue—a synagogue that wants to reach spiritual seekers and grow the Jewish people—the old model of membership is turned on its head. The most important group is the *outer* circle, not the inner circle. It is the task of the core of the inner circle to consider the outer circle as essential, not peripheral, to the future of the congregation.

This is precisely how Rick Warren built the largest congregation in America, as he outlines in his book, *The Purpose-Driven Church.*

Warren envisioned the congregation as a series of concentric circles, beginning with those who are not involved in church at all. He called this outermost circle the Community. His goal was to attract a Crowd (next circle toward the center) of unchurched in the Community to a seeker-sensitive worship service. When some members of this Crowd make a decision to join the Congregation (next circle in), they begin the process of membership induction. Through it, members become Committed (next circle) to the works of the church and, ultimately, a percentage of these become the Core (center circle) of the congregation.

Borrowing Warren's model, let's examine each of these concentric circles as they apply to Jewish congregations:

**Community**
Community is the starting point. There is a pool of unaffiliated, under-affiliated, or once-affiliated people who have no commitment to any congregation. This is the largest circle of people in many communities. They are the people who rarely find themselves in the synagogue, except as guests at an occasional lifecycle celebration. They are the hottest prospects for spiritually welcoming services and other outreach activities. They are the singles, the young professional couples, the parents of preschool children, the intermarrieds who feel unwelcomed, and the empty nesters. We want to move them from the Community into the Crowd.

**Crowd**
The Crowd is everyone who shows up for services and programs. They may or may not have much commitment, but there is potential because they come. In fact, they may be people sociologist Steven M. Cohen calls "engaged, but unaffiliated." These are Jews who are very engaged with Judaism and Jewish living; they just are not affiliated with a synagogue. They may be shopping for a synagogue. Or, they may be shul-hoppers, going from service to service, synagogue to synagogue, searching for a place to call their spiritual home. When they show up as a guest, the goal is to warmly welcome them, engage them in an uplifting prayer experience, and perhaps even get their name so they may be put on a

prospect list. We want to move them from the Crowd to the Congregation.

**Congregation**

These are the people who belong to the synagogue—the official membership. They join the Congregation and pay membership dues. They are members of the limited-liability community, using the programs of the synagogue for their purposes. They may or may not be regular attendees at worship services. Steven Cohen calls them "affiliated, but not engaged." In fact, as with HMOs, the synagogue would likely not be able to handle the needs of all its members if they all used the programs at one time. Most congregations in North America are like this: They may have five hundred membership units representing two thousand adults and children, but see only fifty to two hundred people on a regular basis in the synagogue for Shabbat services.

**Committed**

The Committed are those people for whom Judaism is a serious business. These are the people who are dedicated to growing spiritually, to taking the Jewish journey. They attend services at least once per month, they study, they may even volunteer their time. These are Jews who have found their purpose in being a member of the congregation.

**Core**

These are the most devoted members of a congregation. They are the Core—the leadership, the people for whom the synagogue is a central part of their lives. They attend services every week, even every day in some communities. They are the paraprofessional rabbinics, the lay leaders of worship, the Torah readers, the teachers, and the youth leaders. When they reach the Core, they go back to the Community to recruit people into the Crowd. They start where people are, but never leave them there. They do not use the same approach with everyone, but tailor their outreach to specific target audiences. These are the messengers who go out and create interest in Jewish living and Jewish spirituality.

This model provides for both outreach and inreach. Outreach occurs when the Core membership reaches out into the Community to bring people into the Crowd. Inreach is the work of moving people in the Crowd into membership of the Congregation, deeper into the Committed, and finally into the Core.

The goal is to move people into the ever-deeper circle of commitment. In essence, we are growing the synagogue from the outside in, not the inside out. The starting point is with the Community and the Core simultaneously. The members of the Core become the *shlichim* (messengers-recruiters) to the Community.

## Recruiting New Members

How can congregations recruit prospective members? What are the best strategies for outreach? What does shul-shopping look like from the point of view of the shopper? Let us turn now to these issues.

### Evangelical Jews

The synagogue of the twenty-first century needs evangelical Jews. We need Jews who take seriously the imperative to welcome the stranger, to bring people closer to Judaism, to support Jewish spiritual journeys.

Of course, there are evangelical Jews. They are called Chabad, and they are the fastest-growing religious group in the Jewish community. Why?

In order to answer this question, I spent time with one of the most effective Chabad leaders in Southern California, Rabbi Moshe Bryski. From virtually nothing, Rabbi Bryski has built an impressive synagogue community, outstanding adult education programming, and attracted a fair number of liberal Jews who can hardly believe that they are involved with a brand of Orthodox Judaism. Meeting in his office in Agoura, California, an affluent northern suburb of Los Angeles, I asked him why people are attracted to Chabad.

"It begins with *Ha-Shem*'s instruction to us to welcome the stranger," Rabbi Bryski responded. "We believe the greatest mitzvah is *hachnasas orchim*. These people are strangers to Judaism, and we welcome them warmly, to our homes, to our *davenning*, to our classes. We don't ask questions about who they are, what they can pay, or what they know. We invite them in, give them a *Shabbes* meal, and treat them with respect. This was the Rebbe's genius; he taught us *shlichim* to be messengers from *Ha-Shem*. Our goal is to reach as many Jews as we can and introduce them to their heritage, their values, their Torah."

This process of bringing people from the Community to the Core takes time. At Saddleback, it was a four-year campaign. In the first year, the congregation concentrated on developing a seeker service that attracted a Crowd from the Community. The service was centered on uplifting music and a sermon about the human problems everyone faces. In the second year, the focus was on turning the believers in the Crowd into a Congregation. The third year challenged members to new levels of Commitment, to become spiritual disciples. Then the pastor encouraged the members to reach out to others. The slogan was *Every member a minister.* The message was that spiritual maturity was not an end in and of itself. The search for spirituality is not only an inward activity; it must lead to reaching out.

As we will discuss later, the only way outreach to the Community and inreach to the Congregation can truly happen is if the clergy is willing to empower the laity. The Core members of the congregation can be trained as paraprofessionals who are empowered to identify and fulfill their purpose. Our great mistake in the synagogue community is that we hire professional staff to do the programs rather than add staff to empower the laypeople to do the programs with us.

Can this really be done? In an article for *The New Yorker,* Rick Warren reveals how he can pastor 82,000 members of Saddleback Church. He doesn't. He pastors five colleagues who work with 9,200 lay ministers empowered to do the work of the congregation.

### *Targeting the Crowd*

In his book *The Purpose-Driven Church*, Rick Warren recalls a famous *Peanuts* cartoon that shows Charlie Brown shooting an arrow at a blank wall, then drawing a circle around the arrow, creating what appears to be a perfect bull's-eye. When Lucy asks him why he does it, he replies, "This way, I never miss!"

Synagogues do the same thing. We rarely specify a target population. We want to reach everybody: families, singles, youth, elderly, empty nesters. The truth is no single synagogue can reach all kinds of people, just as one *minyan* cannot satisfy the variety of *davenners* in a shul. Rick Warren cites this illustration to make the point: Imagine a radio station that played all kinds of music—rock, classical, easy listening, jazz, rap. No one would listen because it is not targeted to a specific audience.

Who is your audience? Who is your main target? The smaller the synagogue, the more important this is. A larger synagogue can have multiple targets because it is likely to have the resources to do so.

There are a variety of ways to target a market: geographically, demographically, culturally, and spiritually. Here, then, are the key strategies suggested by Rick Warren in his book *The Purpose-Driven Church* to target an audience, applied to synagogues:

### Geography

Identify where the people live that you want to reach. Take a map of the city and mark where the synagogue is located. In a fifteen- to twenty-minute drive in each direction, you will find your primary geographic area. Use ZIP codes to tell you the number of people in the area.

There are three rules about geography and synagogue attendance:

1. People will only drive a reasonable distance—Warren's rule of thumb is a dozen stop lights between a person's house and the congregation. Certainly, in more traditional communities, the ideal is for people to live close enough to walk to shul. But most liberal Jews will be driving.
2. People will drive past three other synagogues to come to yours if yours is the best "fit."
3. The larger the synagogue, the more resources you can deploy to recruit new people.

### Demographics

What type of people live in your geographic area? Are they single or married? College-educated? Affluent? Conduct a formal survey. You can collect information during the annual renewal of membership, or even hire a professional firm to get this vital information. Know who lives in your neighborhood.

### Culture

Do you really know the lifestyle of those who live in your area? Harold Schulweis, rabbi of Valley Beth Shalom in Encino, California, is brilliant at this. He often acts as a mirror, reflecting back to the congregation an image of who they are, what they think, how they live, what movies they see, where they shop, and what they drive. When the congregation laughs in recognition, he will say "I know you ... ," and he does. He knows because he listens to them—in his office, at services, in private conversations, and in group meetings. He is totally aware of the lives they lead, their fashions; their tastes in music, literature, and art—and he uses this information to reach, teach, and touch his congregants.

### Spirituality

What do your members believe? Do they question God's existence? Are they searching for spirituality? What do they think about life after death? What do people celebrate? Which holidays are widely observed, which are not? When do people show up?

Remember, the unaffiliated may very well have been the *once-affiliated*. There are different kinds of unaffiliated. There are those who have never belonged to a synagogue, those who belong to another institution in the Jewish community, and those who once belonged and dropped out for one reason or another. There are those who are shul-shopping for the first time, those who are unhappy where they are, and those looking for specific programs to meet their needs or the needs of their children.

## *Personalizing Your Target*

It is helpful to create a composite profile of the typical unaffiliated person you want to reach. Saddleback calls theirs "Saddleback Sam," a mythological person who looks like the neighbor next door. Adapting this profile for our purposes—identifying the target for the spiritually welcoming service—"Synagogue Sam" or "Synagogue Samantha" might look like this:

- Early thirties to early forties
- Married five to ten years
- Young children, with the oldest under thirteen
- College educated, often with advanced degree
- Successful, earning six figures, but carries lots of debt
- Lives his or her job, enjoys life, self-satisfied
- Health and fitness are important
- Likes to dress casually
- Very busy
- Carries baggage from previous synagogue experiences
- Listens to pop/folk/oldies music
- Remembers Jewish summer camp with fondness

Once you have identified key characteristics of the target, certain decisions can be made. For example, the preference for casual might lead to an informal dress code in the spiritually welcoming service or the learner's *minyan*. If dressing up is an obstacle to participation, encourage casual dress. The time of the welcoming worship service might be adjusted to allow for babysitting of children: 6:00 p.m. is better than 8:00 p.m.

### Identifying Your Current Demographic

You are unlikely to attract people different from those you have already got. Warren points out that the first question someone asks when they walk into a congregation is not a religious question; it's a cultural question: *Is there anyone here like me?* Young couples will look to see if other young couples are there. Retirees will look for more senior folk. The hip crowd will size up the audience in terms of their status or perceived coolness factor. If the congregation is populated with people who seem nerdy, they will likely not stick around. If visitors find other people like them, they are more likely to come back.

### The Face of the Leadership

Leaders can attract or repel seekers. What do the clergy look like? A young rabbi might attract young families. A woman president might send a message to the congregation that women have access to power. Who sits on the pulpit, makes announcements, participates in the service in your synagogue? If it is always men, or predominantly men, that sends a message, too.

The rabbi is, of course, critical. The rabbi may not be the attraction for first-time visitors but may be a major reason visitors come back. Who is the rabbi? Is he or she like the laypeople? Entrepreneurial, nice clothes, informal, likes sports, can talk about popular culture? Or is the rabbi so unlike them that there seems no basis on which to develop a relationship? Rabbis best reach those to whom they relate, people who are most like themselves. Once again, Rick Warren's insight is spot on: As leaders, clergy often attract who they are, not who they want. In larger congregations, the addition of staff to attract younger families, singles, and other target groups may balance this. Try to reach first those with whom you have something in common. Go for those you are most likely to reach. The best indicator of success is when seekers move from calling you "the rabbi" to "my rabbi."

## Tips

### *What to Do If Your Synagogue Does Not Match the Community*

- Rick Warren warns: "Don't try to be something you are not." On the other hand, if you've done your homework well, you can assess your strengths and experiment with ways to reach the seekers you have targeted.
- Start alternative services. Add another worship service with a different style targeted to a new group. The rapid development of alternative *minyanim* is an indication of this phenomenon. In recent years, the Reform

Movement has seen the introduction of parallel services, something that has been common in Conservative and Orthodox synagogues.

• Start a satellite congregation. Often, older congregations that have buildings in parts of towns from which the Jewish community has fled establish satellite operations in new neighborhoods. This is an area ripe for development in the Jewish community of the twenty-first century—"synagogue planting." There is precious little funding for this, yet the need to establish smaller, emergent sacred communities, often meeting in homes or even coffee shops and other public areas, is a trend to watch in the coming years. Large synagogues that cede this territory to others do so at their own risk.

### Shul-Shopping

The rush to enroll members in synagogues reaches a peak in the weeks before the High Holy Days. The local Jewish press is filled with advertisements from congregations trolling for new recruits. The tag lines of the ads are very interesting:

Join a warm, caring community.

Join us for life.

We're singing your song.

Bottle of Manischewitz Wine—$8.00
Lunch for two at Cantor's Deli—$28.00
Shabbat Candlesticks—$100.00
Being a part of our caring community—Priceless.

Catch the next wave of Judaism.

A Reform congregation where ritual rings true, learning runs deep, members matter, compassion counts, and where love and care are real!

The "Haimish" Synagogue by the Sea.

People. Prayer. Possibility.

*Bruchim Ha-Ba'im* (in Hebrew)

How are you going to continue your child's Jewish education? We have the answer!

I am not an advertising expert, but I do wonder how effective these ads are in reaching the target audience. Would the unaffiliated know the meaning of the Yiddish word *haimish?* Can they read Hebrew? If I join "for life," will it be a life sentence?

Most of these ads feature invitations to an open house at the synagogue. This is a standard way for many synagogues to invite prospective members to visit the congregation and learn about its mission and activities. Open houses can vary from weekly opportunities in August and September to tour the building and talk with volunteer lay leaders to more formal events featuring greetings from the rabbi and president. Most synagogues offer snacks, typically the old standards: synagogue brownies and mandel bread, while a few feature entertainment. Unless the open house is held in connection with a Shabbat service, there is rarely any activity of a spiritual nature. Yet, for many prospective members, the open house is one of the few opportunities they have to get a true feeling for the congregation. In some ways, it is a kind of test drive to see how the congregation meets the prospective members' needs.

Think hard about the substance of the open house experience. Ask the question: What does the prospective member really want to know about this sacred community? Instead of an open house, consider offering get-to-know-us gatherings in people's homes, Shabbat dinners and services, "*Havdalah* under the stars," barbecues and picnics for families, social justice projects, workshops on the spirituality of the High Holy Days, and other such opportunities for shul-shoppers to experience.

### Improving the Quality of Membership Information

When someone calls to inquire about membership in the synagogue, there is usually a short conversation in which the caller provides his or her name and address and the person at the synagogue promises to send out a membership packet. Typically, membership packets include a description of the congregation; the history of the congregation; a collection of fliers and brochures describing the programs of the congregation; messages and fliers from the affiliated arms of the congregation, such as sisterhood, brotherhood or men's clubs, and youth group; material describing the religious school and its programs; a calendar of activities; and dues information.

During our S2K research, we collected dozens of membership packets. As with advertisements, these membership packets ranged from slick, professional presentations to amateurish pieces of paper run off on copying machines. I took special note of the very first "message" from the congregation to the prospective member. Several featured a warm note from the rabbi and/or president of the congregation. One synagogue, however, stuck a computerized dues form in the very front of the packet that made all sorts of assumptions about the people applying for membership!

Many synagogues put membership information and brochures out on tables and in the lobby of the building, but usually there is nobody there to answer a question. Contrast this with the approach of the megachurches. They have mastered the use of the lobby as an information center. Most have large spaces featuring a concierge information desk in the center, surrounded by designated spaces for the various groups, ministries, and activities of the church. The spaces are laden with information about the many support groups, educational activities, and other services of the congregation. Each is identified with a large sign, volunteers (wearing name badges to facilitate conversation) are ready to answer questions, and opportunities to enroll in groups are offered.

Pay attention to your communications. Ask if they truly represent the congregation—its purpose and mission, its expectations, its values—not just its programming. What do you learn by reading the material? Is there any attention to the spiritual needs and motivations of prospective members? Does it talk about the benefits of membership? Do you feel drawn to it? Does it feature photos of the clergy? The lay leadership? Children? Teenagers? Elderly? What's the message you are sending with photos and graphics? Do you identify the denomination of the congregation? Do you think it matters to your target audience?

**Tips**

## *Ways to Welcome and Inform Guests*

- Use name tags to identify key members of the board, greeters, and membership outreach people.
- Create a place for guests to interact with representatives of the congregation.
- If you have a receiving line at the end of the service, announce that guests should look for the president or other greeters and encourage them to identify themselves.
- Set up an information table to distribute publicity about the congregation, membership, and upcoming events. Be sure a volunteer staffs the table to answer questions.
- Identify a member as a Shabbat host who is willing to invite strangers home for a meal. Rotate the responsibility among members.
- If lunch is served, invite newcomers to sit with members of the congregation at a special table reserved for them.

- Collect business cards or, if religious practice allows, ask guests to write their names and contact information on a sign-up sheet for follow-up.
- Encourage the regulars to move beyond their cliques and seek out strangers to welcome.
- Have greeters hand out cards that say, "My name is————. My phone number is————. Please call me if I can be of service to you. Check out our website: ————. Our synagogue strives to be a sacred community where people care about people."

## The Culture of Dues

What does it mean to "belong" to a synagogue?

In the synagogue of the twentieth century, people joined by paying dues and using its services. In the synagogue of the twenty-first century, people are so grateful to belong to a spiritual community that nourishes and encourages Jewish journeys that they support the congregation with annual contributions.

Pipe dream? Perhaps. The culture of dues is so ingrained in synagogue life that it is difficult to imagine how it can be transformed. Yet, this same fee-for-service culture presents an enormous obstacle to many of the seekers we seek. They tell me that the cost of being Jewish, including the high cost of synagogue dues, is the number-one barrier to affiliation.

Let's begin with a caveat: Synagogues are expensive institutions to run. The budget of even a mid-sized congregation can approach a million dollars annually. Clergy and staff demand and deserve decent salaries and benefits. Synagogue campuses are costly to build and maintain. Large-scale events such as the High Holy Days incur additional costs. In these days of terrorist threat, security is essential, adding to the budget burden. Schools are a major motivation for families to join, and excellence in Jewish education cannot be expected without recruiting and paying the best teachers. All of these initiatives require money.

### Dues: A Historical Development

So, how does the synagogue collect the money it needs to exist? Membership dues provide the bulk of the revenue; donations and fundraising fills in the rest. But was it always this way?

No.

Let's return to the biblical account of how the spiritual community was supported.

> Each shall give a half-shekel.
>
> —*Exodus 30:13*

The attractiveness of the biblical model is that everyone in the community contributes. Of course, as the Jewish people spread through the Diaspora and became citizens of national economies, some got rich while others were poor. Even in Jerusalem at the turn of the last millennium, some of the citizens were wealthy, others not.

In the European capitals, there were two sources of money to support synagogues: the *kehillah*, or community, and the rich. Both did their part to ensure that synagogues existed. Even in America, the earliest synagogues were mainly supported by wealthy merchants who paid for rabbis and later cantors to come over from Europe to serve the growing Jewish population.

As synagogues proliferated in America, the idea of one or two wealthy individuals funding a congregation seemed undemocratic and fraught with the potential for conflict between the funders and the clergy or the people themselves who frequented the synagogue. Although synagogues borrowed many ideas from churches, including styles of architecture, "passing the plate" would not work, even in Reform congregations. Thus, the idea of paying membership dues gained popularity.

Most congregations operate on one of two models for collecting revenue: flat-rate dues for specific categories of members (young couples, family units, singles, and so on) or a fair-share dues system, requiring members to pay between 1 and 3 percent of their annual gross income. If prospective members cannot pay the expected dues, there are procedures to enable a review of relevant financial information on a confidential basis and dues relief may be offered.

On top of annual dues, of course, most synagogues find other ways to raise money: fundraisers, charges for *Yahrtzeit* listings in memorial books and for memorial plaques, a Yom Kippur appeal (a sure turn-off for the masses of members who only show up once or twice a year), and even extra fees for religious schools in some communities. Most synagogues also invite board members and patrons who believe the synagogue is an important institution to give far more than the basic dues.

## Dues ... and Don'ts

> When I found out it costs over $1,000 to join a synagogue, I didn't even investigate it further! I am a single mother and just can't afford that much. It's just too expensive to be Jewish!

> We don't want to hear from people only when organizations need money. I know that it costs money to keep these organizations going, but I want to feel committed to where I give my money. I want it to come, as an act of giving, from me. I just don't feel that you can ask for money first.

> Why can't there be something like an affiliate membership? I would be willing to pay a nominal fee so that I can be on an organization mailing list and receive some benefits of membership. Then, I could figure out if it is a place I want to be part of.

Synagogue membership is widely criticized for being too expensive. Despite a variety of efforts to send the message that no one is turned away, the perception persists that synagogue dues policies restrict membership, particularly among the underserved populations of the young and the elderly. Even if financial assistance is offered, there is the fear that to qualify for aid or exemptions, a prospective member will be taken through a humiliating process by a committee, asked to produce tax returns and otherwise make a case for dues relief.

Some synagogues have developed innovative membership dues policies to counteract these impressions. Ohev Shalom, a Conservative congregation in Wallingford, Pennsylvania, offers free membership in the first year. Temple Emanu-El, a Reform congregation in San Francisco, has devised a voluntary membership dues program that offers a first-year affiliation with the synagogue for whatever fee the member wishes to pay. In both congregations, the synagogue works hard during the first year to connect the new member to the congregation in a significant way, so that when the time is up, many of the members will decide to continue their membership at regular dues levels.

B'nai Jeshurun looked at its membership and discovered that many people join the congregation to use the most basic services it offers: High Holy Day seats. They offer a *bereishit* membership, a kind of trial run. For a greatly reduced fee, the member can participate in synagogue activities, including special High Holy Day seating. During the initial year, the member is invited to participate in the new members orientation detailed below. If the person chooses to continue their affiliation, they are asked to pay dues as a full member of the congregation.

A number of Reconstructionist congregations offer *Tishrei* memberships—the opportunity to join the congregation for the Hebrew month of *Tishrei,* which encompasses the High Holy Days and Sukkot. For one reduced fee, *Tishrei* Members are entitled not just to High Holy Day tickets, but they are invited to a whole month full of activities designed to introduce the individual or family to the life of the congregation.

Many congregations offer a greatly reduced dues rate for young professionals (usually ages 21 to 35), young couples, or young families. Some have reduced rates for seniors.

Other synagogues have experimented with variations of the voluntary dues policy. One congregation has offered families with children up to third grade the opportunity to participate in religious school for one year without formally joining the congregation. Some synagogues offer preschool programs that do not require synagogue membership. The key to these programs is making the first-year experience so wonderful that there is an incentive to continue the membership at regular dues rates. Personal counseling, orientation sessions, and personal invitations from key members of the staff and laity are crucial in translating trial members into regular members.

## The Spirituality of Money

As we looked at membership packets and procedures, we found that every synagogue has a dues policy, but very few tackle the spirituality of money. There is precious little explanation of the need to collect dues and virtually no discussion of the meaning of money dedicated to the support of a sacred community.

Contrast this with the approach of the savvy churches that, in truth, must work harder to collect money than synagogues. There are no annual dues in most churches; they depend on weekly collections. To motivate this kind of giving, the congregations know that the amount of money that will be given is not just a factor of household income, or the fair-share concept. Rather, giving is directly related to how important the church is in the life of the individual. If the congregation has established a meaningful relationship with me, I will feel a deep sense of obligation to ensure that the sacred community thrives.

Thus, a tremendous educational effort is made to teach members about the spiritual stewardship of money. Many churches offer courses in personal financial management that teach basic principles of dealing with money but also give guidance for how to structure household finances to be able to tithe 10 percent of gross income to the church. Once again, the megachurches have this down pat. From the very first membership orientation sessions, giving of oneself is couched in terms of spirituality: giving of one's God-given talents and spiritual gifts, giving of one's time, giving of one's financial resources.

The truth is that giving to Christian institutions is widely regarded as philanthropic, while synagogues suffer from the resentment, the resistance, and the consumerist mentality that can result from obligatory dues. Giving is different from paying. When one gives, there is a deep satisfaction of knowing that the contribution matters. When one gives, knowing that a whole community of people is also giving, there is a feeling of belonging to a sacred enterprise.

The synagogue of the twenty-first century will strive to develop a meaningful relationship with each individual in the congregation that will lead to a desire to financially support the sacred community. It will not shy away from discussing issues of money. Rather, it will be transparent about the finances of the congregation, explain the need for support, and offer accurate information about how the membership contributes.

We need a theology of money—a real conversation about what it means to have a financial covenant between an individual and the institution. Rabbis complain that their congregants will kid them, "Rabbi, you're always asking for money." Well, certainly, most synagogues need money for the new initiatives they develop. If a synagogue never asks for money, it is not growing. Businesses need capital; synagogues need financial capital as well as social capital. And let's be honest—there are plenty of people who drive up to synagogues in $50,000-plus cars but complain about contributing a couple of thousand dollars a year to ensure that the synagogue is there for them when they need it.

The spirituality of money conversation would be well-informed by a basic understanding that we live in a time of abundance, not a time of scarcity. Communal activist Lynne Twist writes in her book *The Soul of Money* that, although most of us are surrounded by overwhelming abundance, we constantly complain (even the wealthiest of us) that we don't have enough: We don't have enough time, rest, exercise, work, profits, power, wilderness, weekends, and, of course, we don't have enough money—ever. This leads us to living constantly with what Twist calls the "myths of scarcity," the debilitating feeling that we will never have enough.

Judaism teaches us just the opposite. The most famous refrain of the Passover Haggadah says it all: *Dayenu!* "It would have been enough!" We would have been satisfied if all God did was take us out of slavery and into freedom, but God gave us the Torah, Shabbat, and brought us to the Promised Land. *Dayenu!* Our tradition emphasizes the abundance that surrounds us and teaches us to be grateful for it.

It also teaches us to give. The biblical injunction to give a half-shekel was incumbent on everyone. Everyone must give: "Even a poor person who is kept alive by *tzedakah* funds must give *tzedakah* from what they receive" (*Shulchan Aruch, Yoreh Deah,* 251:12). Rabbi Shawn Israel Zevit details the Jewish texts on money and values in faith communities in his volume *Offerings of the Heart.*

Contributing money for sustaining synagogue communities is a sacred obligation and we need much more conversation about it with our members, especially our young members when they first join congregations. Many in the younger crowd have always assumed that *someone* would pay for the synagogue to be there. But, as a famous rabbinic axiom in *Pirke Avot* (Ethics of the Ancestors) 3:17 teaches, "*Im ein kemach, ein Torah,*" "When there is no flour [money], there is no Torah [teaching]." A whole generation needs education in the meaning of *tzedakah,* the spiritual practice of giving dollars to support the Jewish community. On the other hand, those who understand the joy of giving also reap the knowledge that when they give to support a congregation, it is making the statement that "this is our sacred community." Being generous does wondrous things for the soul; giving is far more rewarding than taking.

### Dues in Emergent Congregations

The membership dues system has worked well for synagogues and it is part of the expectation of families and individuals who have children ready to enroll in religious school to prepare for Bar or Bat Mitzvah. But for the seekers we are targeting for the synagogue of the twenty-first century, the system is a turnoff and an obstacle to membership.

In the newest development of spiritual communities, Jewish Emergent synagogues, this issue of membership is challenging. In the church world, the emergence of small spiritual communities is, in some ways, the antithesis of the megachurch phenomenon. These emergent churches are not interested in tens of thousands coming to form a Crowd. They are pleased to be smaller communities, often with a focus on some issue of importance. The same is true for some of the Jewish Emergent communities.

One of the first of these Jewish Emergent spiritual communities is called IKAR (the essence). Founded by Rabbi Sharon Brous, a gradu-

ate of the B'nai Jeshurun Fellowship Program in New York, Sharon
came to Los Angeles as a teacher at the Milken Community High
School and quickly made a name for herself. Within a year, three couples who had initially approached her about tutoring their children
heard Sharon's dream of creating a vision-centered spiritual community and signed on to help. A dynamic teacher, tutored in the tradition
of Rabbi Marshall Meyer, Sharon weighed the risk of leaving her well-
established position at the school and starting something completely
new. In the summer of 2004, she decided to take the plunge and begin.

Sharon consulted with me early in the development of IKAR, hoping to glean ideas from the lessons learned in S2K. I will never forget our first meeting. She handed me two documents: one was a
"service theme" statement, a beautifully crafted vision of the kind of
spiritual community she hoped IKAR would be; the other document
was a business plan, written by the laypeople who were backing the
effort. It called for a dues structure that characterizes most synagogues,
although it did allow for a sliding scale.

I read the two documents and turned to Sharon.

"These are from two different planets," I said.

"I know," Sharon frowned. "I have this vision that IKAR should
not be a dues-driven synagogue. I don't even want to call it a synagogue. It's a spiritual community. And my hope is that the people who
will come and gain strength from it will support it with money."

We talked about different options that I knew of to deal with this:
voluntary dues, philanthropists, and the megachurch model. Sharon
was intrigued, looking for a solution to the complete disconnect
between the culture she wanted to create and the need for dues, an
idea that was anathema to her.

After researching a variety of approaches, Sharon and her board
deliberated on the idea of asking people to "pay what they will." It
didn't work. The culture of dues was so strong that without them no
one could imagine being able to collect enough money to pay the
expenses. Some of the board members stepped forward with generous contributions, but when Sharon began to talk about "doing dues
differently" at the weekly gatherings of IKAR, the plea fell on deaf ears.
Instead, the board convinced Sharon that it would be impossible

to sustain the community without dues, although they agreed that anyone could come to IKAR without officially joining for as long as they wished. As enthusiasm has grown for IKAR's combination of moving spiritual services, Sharon's superb teaching, and a strong commitment to social justice, the community has attracted significant support from a key philanthropist and several others who have stepped forward to ensure the financial foundation of this interesting twenty-first-century (un)synagogue.

Sharon is frustrated by the seemingly intractable conclusion that the membership model is diametrically opposed to the outreach model. She's right. We agreed that we need to study models of raising money to support spiritual communities. She does not want to sell tickets or demand membership dues, but she wonders how to support the growing demands for expanding the spiritual community.

## Beyond Dues: Alternative Models of Support

There are several ways in which a synagogue can raise money without membership dues:

### The Philanthropist Approach
A wealthy person pledges to provide all or most of the money for the synagogue. In some synagogues, several wealthy people contribute the lion's share of the resources.

### Grants
More and more foundations are interested in supporting innovative ideas and start-ups, and certainly, these new emergent synagogues are exciting and appealing models.

### Voluntary Dues
Some large synagogues can afford to ask new members to pay whatever they are comfortable with in the first year, after which they are expected to pay dues according to a sliding scale, usually dependent on age or fair share.

### Megachurch Model
Visitors may come as long and as often as they wish and are encouraged *not* to give until they are ready to consider membership. Then

these prospective members enroll in a series of induction courses that lead along a spiritual growth path, including instruction in what the church stands for, what each individual's spiritual gifts are, finding one's ministry, and stewardship of one's finances, including tithing. This model assumes that the deeper the commitment, the sooner the newcomer moves from the Community to the Crowd to the Congregation to the Core, the more he or she will give.

**Federation**

As noted before, in Europe, the community *kuppah* model collected money from everyone—a kind of community tax—and some of the money was used to pay for rabbis, teachers, etc. As I will argue below, federations should fund synagogues directly and in a major way.

The one synagogue I know of that does not charge dues, that is totally pay what you will, has resulted in enough money to support the congregation for seventeen years. According to Stuart M. Matlins, publisher of Jewish Lights and cofounder with his wife, Antoinette, of the Woodstock Area Jewish Community congregation Shir Shalom in Vermont, "They said it couldn't be done, but we've done it." Critics would point out that until this year, the congregation did not have a resident rabbi, relying on Stuart as lay spiritual leader and occasional visits by rabbinic students from Hebrew Union College in New York. However, when the time came to ask the congregation to increase voluntary donations to cover the cost of a rabbi in advance of recruiting, there was no problem "because participants value the community and its style and want to see it thrive." In fall 2005, the Reform Movement planned to devote the next two years to the issue of membership. In response to an e-mail from Rabbi Eric Yoffie, president of the Union of Reform Judaism, Stuart wrote the following:

> As you may know, our congregation has no dues, never asks anyone personally for money (although we certainly ask in general and often), never charges for any religious event, and provides religious education for children (including free books) without fee. The congregation has always depended upon "gifts of the heart" to provide the support we need. We have

raised approximately $2 million that way, including over $1 million for physical plant. We have no debt (that will end next week as we have to buy the property next door to the shul) and currently are raising a fund (two-thirds already done) to hire a half-time resident rabbi by July 2006.

This approach—combined with a welcoming congregational style, particularly to interfaith families—has allowed many people who no longer participated in synagogue life, and many among them who had the usual complaints about dues/pay to pray, to get over their hurt and hostility and join in our congregation. This approach deprived many people of their excuse for not participating in the synagogue—and, as a result, when they tried it, often they liked it and were willing to support the congregation financially. It has worked for us, and may work for others. While I realize that there are some unique circumstances at work here in Woodstock, the general approach will still be valid for some others.

There is no easy answer to the membership dues dilemma. The bottom line is that synagogues simply cannot exist without significant support from their members. Yet, if we hope to attract the seekers and unaffiliated in the community, we will need to be more aggressive about making the membership invitation without money becoming a high barrier. Moreover, is it impossible to think that the synagogue of the twenty-first century could develop the kind of deep, meaningful relationship with its members that they would voluntarily pay dues or make significant contributions on their own volition? If this model can work in megachurches, why can't it work in synagogues? I believe it can; but it will take a radical transformation of the culture of funding and a complete rethinking of how we induct new people into our sacred communities, how we establish synagogues of relationships that are so important, so valuable, so indispensable to members that they run to do the mitzvah of supporting synagogues.

### "But You're Not a Member"

Sometimes, we shoot ourselves in the foot. I was talking recently with Michael Brooks, the innovative director of the Hillel Foundation at the University of Michigan and a much sought-after community consultant, and the conversation turned to the problem of reaching unaffiliated Jews, especially young people of college age. I wondered why synagogues have such a hard time thinking differently about this population, which by and large doesn't *join* anything. Michael agreed and told me the following story:

> Two of my graduate students decided to get married and they asked me if I would be their *m'sadair kiddushin* (officiant of the wedding). But I was scheduled to be out of the country on the date they chose. So, I recommended a rabbi friend in their local community. The students called the rabbi, told him that I had sent them, and asked if he would do the wedding. The rabbi replied: "Oh, I am so sorry. I'd love to do it for you, but I can't." "Why not?" the students asked. "Because the synagogue policy is that I can only do weddings for members of the congregation." My students were devastated. When they told me about this response, I called my friend the rabbi. "I can't believe you turned these bright young people away," I said. "But I can't go against the policy of the synagogue," he protested. "*Chochem!* [The word means "wise one" but it is said sarcastically to indicate just the opposite meaning.] So don't go against the policy of the synagogue," I told him. "Offer them a free one-year membership to the congregation, they'll become members, and you can do the wedding! This will give you and the synagogue a year to convince them that it's a privilege to be a dues-paying member of your synagogue."

**Tips**

## Guidelines for Reviewing Your Dues Policies

- What do you know about your membership's demographics? On average, how many new members join the synagogue each year? Who are they? What is their geographic/age/family profile? How many members leave the synagogue each year? Who are they? What are their reasons? Can you discern a pattern that offers insight into how your congregation is doing with regard to membership recruitment and retention?

• What are the values that shape your dues policy? For example, do you believe that everyone should pay a "fair share"?

• Does the dues amount adjust through time? What assumptions guide the adjustments?

• Are your dues "all-inclusive"? If not, what services are offered for extra cost? What is included in the basic dues? What costs extra?

• What is your policy for handling dues adjustments? What must the members do to apply for reduced dues? Who makes the decision?

• Do you have any program that markets an introductory rate for membership? What are the guiding principles and assumptions of the program?

• How are dues collected? How often are members billed for dues? How many reminders do they receive? What happens if the member is in arrears?

• What happens when a member does not renew? Is an exit interview done? What happens with the information that is collected?

## Welcoming New Members

What happens when a new member joins the synagogue? Who does the initial intake—the executive director, the office receptionist, a layperson, the rabbi? There may be a New Member's Shabbat where recruits are welcomed formally to the congregation; some congregations even do creative things such as providing a Shabbat "welcome wagon" basket of candles, wine, and challah. In a synagogue of programs, the assumption is made that the people will find something that fits their needs. By and large, however, most new members are left on their own to connect to the sacred community in some meaningful way. In a synagogue of the twenty-first century, this is the key moment requiring a well-developed induction process that brings the individual into a synagogue of relationships.

### *Establishing Relationships*

At the root of the retention problem is the false assumption that once a person joins the congregation there is no need to continue building the relationship between the new member and the community. Unless a new member already has a social network that is part of the congregation, the person is left on her or his own to navigate the social fabric of the community. Some succeed at this task, others never do. Yet the stakes are high. Rick Warren, the pastor of Saddleback, discovered that when members of his congregation connect with just five to seven people, they are more likely to maintain their involvement in the congregation. This is why small groups are so important in the synagogue of the future.

Think of your own experience in joining the congregation. How did you meet new people? How did you create friendships? What contact did you have with the clergy, the staff, the lay leadership? Did you go to services and/or classes? Did you meet peers in your children's preschool or religious school classes? Did you volunteer for a committee, attend a program, work on a project?

Creating a relationship with the congregation mainly depends on creating a relationship with other members of the sacred community. It is true that synagogue members talk about "my rabbi" or "my cantor" often with a true sense of ownership borne of relationship. But with hundreds of people in a medium-size congregation, it is virtually impossible for the rabbi and cantor to establish and maintain a meaningful relationship with the majority of members. But if the community fosters a relationship between the members *themselves,* the chances of a person remaining part of the community increase dramatically.

I cannot emphasize enough the importance of relationships. The very sacredness of the community depends on the *quality* of the relationships that are established within it, to the degree to which members have taken upon *themselves*—not deferred to the professionals—the values of *b'tzelem Elohim* and *hachnasat orchim.* When a congregation lives and breathes these values, the sacred community comes alive; it becomes a place other people want to make a part of their lives. A sacred community is built on sacred relationships.

## Inducting New Members

When a new member joins a synagogue, they have moved from the Crowd to the Congregation. They have signed up, paid their dues, and received the written material about the synagogue to which they now belong. But what do they really know about this sacred community? Who do they know? And what does the synagogue know about them and their Jewish journeys? Instead of leaving this crucial beginning stage of relationship building to chance, we experimented with the creation of new member induction programs in Synagogue 2000 pilot congregations.

It was our research into the megachurches that gave us the idea of establishing a deliberate process of inducting new members into the congregation and setting them on a path of spiritual growth. Sacred communities are organisms alive with their own very specific cultures, with sets of norms, values, behaviors, and expectations. How are these communicated to new members—or even current members, for that matter? How might synagogues enculturate their members into the life of a spiritual community?

Imagine you are a brand-new member of a congregation and you are offered an opportunity to share the story of your spiritual journey, to consider what you are passionate about, to explore your God-given gifts and talents. Of course, you would also hear information about the congregation—its committees, structure, values, and mission. You would meet the clergy and key lay leaders. You would also meet a group of other new members. And you would be encouraged to take steps to connect to the congregation in a meaningful way.

When we asked whether any congregation had created such a process, we discovered that, once again, it was the innovative leadership of B'nai Jeshurun who was experimenting with this kind of new member orientation.

The BJ new members orientation is held over three separate meetings within a ten-day period, usually offered in November, December, and January. New members are invited to sign up for the orientation, although it is not required. About half of the two to three hundred new members signing up each year take advantage of the experience.

Session 1 is held in the home of a BJ member over a catered light supper on a weekday evening, and eight to ten new members are invited to share their stories of "what brought me to BJ" in moderated small groups. Then, a lay leader gives a brief history of the congregation, followed by an explanation of how members can get involved with the congregation by working on various committees, social justice projects, and the like.

Session 2 is held on the Friday night of that same week, when the new members gather at the synagogue for Kabbalat Shabbat services and Shabbat dinner. They are welcomed at the service and one of the clergy leads the group in Torah study after the meal.

Session 3 is held on a weeknight during the following week, when the group is invited to another BJ member's home for a potluck dinner. The featured event of the evening is a session with one of the rabbis who gives a brief talk about the congregation and answers any questions the new members may have about the synagogue or Judaism.

The leadership of BJ considers this work so important that it has a full-time professional staff person—a membership director—whose main responsibility is to recruit and induct new members and deepen the connectedness of current members to the congregation. The membership director reports that these new members who participate in the orientation process tend to become more involved and more connected more quickly than those who do not.

### Creating a New Membership Covenant

Our research uncovered other attempts to share the values of the sacred community and its hopes for creating a relationship with members. One of the most interesting is the idea of sanctifying this relationship through the establishment of a *brit* (covenant). The notion of *brit* is central in Judaism. God's covenant with Abraham and Sarah and us is the basis of our relationship with God. We celebrate the coming of age of our children in the ceremony of the Bar and Bat Mitzvah, children of "commandments." Yet, when it comes to initiating members into the synagogue, the only contract they make is for dues. The only expectation we place on them is financial. We often get what we ask for—checks—yet we also get long lists of members who are disconnected, uninvolved, or absent.

What would happen if we began to ask our new members to make Jewish commitments—commitments to establishing a relationship with God, commitments to other members of the synagogue community, commitments to repairing the world, commitments to their own deepening of their connections to Judaism. What might a membership covenant actually look like? Following are two examples from Synagogue 3000 Leadership Network participants.

## Tips

## *Membership Covenant*

**Rabbi Ed Feinstein**
**Valley Beth Shalom (Conservative)**
**Encino, California**

> *Bra'sheet (In the beginning …)*: I share the responsibility of creating a community of holiness at Valley Beth Shalom, a community that embraces and embodies the ideals, ethics, faith, and culture of the Jewish people.
>
> *Sh'mot (These are the names …)*: I will deepen my own Jewish identity and nurture my Jewish soul

through *Torah*/Learning, *Avodah*/Worship, *Gemilut Hesed*/Action, and *Hevrah*/Fellowship.

*Va'yikra (And God called ...)*: I will answer the call to become God's partner in bringing wholeness and holiness to the world. I will answer the call to repair the world's brokenness and heal its suffering.

*Bamidbar (In the wilderness ...)*: I will seek *shalom*, the blessings of wholeness, peace, and solidarity in my family, my circle of relations, my community, in my city, and in the world.

*Devarim (These are the words ...)*: I share the responsibility of transmitting Judaism to a new generation.

### Rabbi Dan Zemel
### Temple Micah (Reform)
### Washington, D.C.

"Rabbi Simon taught that the world rests on three pillars—Torah, prayer, and good deeds."

This statement represents the values that define Temple Micah. We ask each member to participate actively in the life of our community by supporting these three pillars.

Torah: I recognize that our community prizes Torah learning as a way to nurture the soul and guide our lives. I will engage in Torah learning through one of Micah's many offerings both to deepen myself and make our community a more learned place.

Prayer: I recognize that through prayer my soul can grow in holiness. I also understand that our community gathers and meets each other at Shabbat worship. This is where we come together and we begin to know each other's faces. I will strive to make community prayer a regular part of my Shabbat.

Good Deeds: At Micah we try and do our part in repairing the world. I understand that it is part of my responsibility to participate as a partner in this work of *tikkun* with my community.

## Establishing Member Mentors

In the Roman Catholic Church, new initiates are paired with veteran members of the congregation as they learn the requirements of membership. These "sponsors" often become friends, ombudspeople, and advisors to the initiates. In the Mormon Church, every family is visited once a month by two members of the local congregation, usually in their homes. These home visitors come equipped with resources, act as links to the programs of the church, and assist in times of need. They become the personal representatives of the church to the family.

In our synagogues, we could establish personal mentoring programs for members to help them on their Jewish journeys. These personal mentors would be able to advise individuals and families on taking the next steps on their Jewish journeys: how to become involved in the synagogue, how to live Jewishly, how to celebrate holidays and lifecycle events, and how to connect to the resources of the congregation. They would be able to help plan a Bar or Bat Mitzvah or wedding, provide meals and a *minyan* for a *shivah* home, arrange visits to a member in the hospital, or help build a *sukkah*. Whatever the member's next step on the Jewish road, the personal mentor would be there to help plan it.

## Welcoming Non-Jewish Members of Jewish Households

With the intermarriage rate in North America hovering at nearly 50 percent, it is an inevitable fact of synagogue life that many Jewish households have within them a non-Jewish person. According to the 2000 National Jewish Population Survey, only about 33 percent of these households are committed to raising Jewish children. If this figure could be raised to 50 percent, the future Jewish population would

## BMH-BJ Congregation (Orthodox)
## Denver, Colorado

Consider this creative idea:

*Our S2K team is leading the effort to create a synagogue "face book," similar to those found on college campuses to help people identify each other. We are inviting every individual and family member to have a photo taken or submitted. Instead of our usual annual directory of names, addresses, and phone numbers, we believe the face book will add to our sense of community.*

## Hebrew Institute of White Plains (Orthodox)
## White Plains, New York

Or this one:

*The S2K team spawned the idea of establishing a committee to ensure that new members have meal invitations for their first month of Shabbatot when they join the congregation. Veteran synagogue members inform the committee of their interest and availability for hosting new families for meals, and the committee links veteran and new members.*

hold steady. If the figure exceeded 50 percent, it could result in increased numbers of Jews in the future.

This is a very sensitive issue among synagogue leaders. Many congregations barely acknowledge the fact that non-Jews are a part of their member families. Even liberal synagogues have struggled over the years to find ways to maintain what they consider to be appropriate boundaries, while at the same time welcoming non-Jewish family members.

As I posited earlier, it is my contention that synagogue leaders should be far more proactive about encouraging conversion and/or the raising of Jewish children among intermarried families. A place to start might be to follow the lead of Rabbi Janet Marder who, on Yom Kippur morning in 2004, made an extraordinary gesture in her congregation that has reverberated throughout the Jewish community. Rabbi Marder invited all the non-Jewish spouses of Jewish members of her congregation to ascend the pulpit, whereupon she thanked them and blessed them for committing to creating a Jewish home and raising Jewish children. According to first-person accounts, the response in the congregation was electric, moving most people to tears. Here is Rabbi Marder's blessing:

> What we want to thank you for today is your decision to cast your lot with the Jewish people by becoming part of this congregation, and the love and support you give to your Jewish partner. Most of all, we want to offer our deepest thanks to those of you who are parents, and who are raising your sons and daughters as Jews.

Welcoming non-Jews and encouraging conversion are complex issues, yet both the Reform and Conservative Movements have recently faced up to the reality that a much more aggressive approach is called for in the years ahead. Once again, my own view is that all of the people within the reach of the Jewish community—Jews and non-Jews alike—should hear a call of *aliyah* to Judaism, an invitation to commit to a life of Torah as a joyous and enriching path for one's spiritual journey.

### Tips

## *Ideas for Recognizing and Celebrating New Members*

There are a variety of ways new members can be welcomed into the congregation:

- • Take complimentary photos of the individual or family and feature them in the lobby of the congregation. Give a copy to the family as a gift.

- Hold a new members' Shabbat dinner, hosted by the congregation. Ask the new members to offer a few words of testimony about their Jewish journeys at the celebration.
- Offer an *aliyah* to new members during a Shabbat service.
- Have the rabbi host a Rabbi's Chat in her or his home once or twice during the year to which new members are invited.
- Send cards on birthdays and the anniversary of the first year of membership.
- Recognize new members in the bulletin.
- Reserve a prime parking spot for the new member(s) of the month.
- Distribute items with the congregational logo.
- Be sure that someone has responsibility for staying in touch with a new member for an entire year. Do not just greet them and then forget them.

## Deepening the Connectedness of All Members to the Sacred Community

Let's go deeper into this issue of membership. If the new member induction process is successful, there is reason to believe that the relationship between the individual and the congregation will be off to a good start. But even this is just a first step in what is required to create a lifelong sacred relationship with the congregation. We know that our congregations are filled with mostly members who stay at the Congregation level, with a much smaller percentage reaching the Committed level, and an even smaller number becoming part of the Core. How can we create a deeper connectedness?

There are two secret ingredients for deepening the membership experience and for encouraging those who are disengaged to move

toward the Committed and the Core circles. These two ingredients
are *people* and *purpose.*

## People and the Meaning of Membership

A congregation is, by definition, a group of people. If a peripheral
member meets like-minded others who then become friends and role
models, there is some likelihood that the person will become more
deeply connected to the congregation.

Friendship is a key factor in forming "reference communities"—
those places where we find people with whom we want to associate,
people we admire, people we want to emulate, people we want to
learn from and with, and people we enjoy being around. Because we
"refer" ourselves to these people, they influence us in a variety of
ways—impacting our values, our behaviors, and even our beliefs. In
many congregations, members of the Committed and Core circles will
say that most of their best friends are members of the congregation.
Those who pay their dues but are not part of these circles often do
not have friends or even acquaintances in the synagogue.

People join congregations for many reasons. The initial motivation
for joining is because the congregation provides something: religious
education for children, worship services, a community of friends, a
rabbi when needed. Interestingly, most of the reasons for remaining at
a synagogue are less tangible and pertain to the heart and to the soul—
a sense of belonging and a sense of meaning. So we have to find ways
for new and disengaged congregants to acquire that sense of belonging and meaning. The obligation of members of a sacred community
is to be aware and conscious of such individuals and families so that
they do not remain peripheral and unconnected.

## Purpose and the Meaning of Membership

To deepen the meaning of membership, we suggest that each congregant be encouraged to discover his or her own purpose for belonging
to the spiritual community that is the synagogue. We will call this
purpose by the Hebrew term *shlichoot.* The root of *shlichoot* is *shaliach* (male) or *shlichah* (female), literally "a messenger." In a spiritually centered synagogue where everyone is considered an image of

## Temple Beth Abraham (Reform)
## Tarrytown, NY

If every congregation in North America did this one act of welcoming, imagine the impact on how people think about synagogues:

*Following a suggestion we heard at an S2K conference, we called all of our congregants (approximately 470) on the Monday before the High Holy Days to wish them a Shanah Tovah. Most of our organized contact with our congregants either is purely informative (bulletin) or is in making requests for their time or money. This initiative had no strings attached. Our intent was solely to wish all of our congregants a healthy and sweet new year. We simply have never reached out to the entire congregation in this way before. With only six people, we finished in one and a half hours. It was a relatively easy task and a nice experience for both the callers and the congregants. Our congregants were very surprised to receive such a call. After our good wishes, there was usually a silent pause as though they were waiting for us to ask for something, and when we didn't, they relaxed and told us repeatedly how nice it was for us to call them. Everyone seemed very happy and appreciative.*

God, we are God's messengers on earth. We are God's partners in the ongoing work of creation. Our task, then, is to discover our purpose—our *shlichoot*—our way of doing God's work.

Perhaps that purpose is to do the work of *tikkun olam*, repairing the world. Perhaps that purpose is to improve one's understanding and knowledge of Judaism. Perhaps that purpose is to teach others. Perhaps that purpose is to ensure the ongoing vitality of the congregation. Perhaps that purpose is to lead others in prayer. Perhaps that purpose is to help create a caring community.

Why is discovering such a personal purpose in relation to the synagogue so important? Because having a purpose creates meaning.

When I understand, in a deep way, the purpose of my membership, the meaning of my membership becomes clearer. When I visit a *shivah* at the home of a fellow member who is in mourning and understand why I am doing it, my membership in the community becomes meaningful. When I join with my friends to feed the hungry at a homeless shelter because my purpose is to reach out to others and help heal the world, my membership in the community becomes meaningful. When I sing with others in prayer as an expression of my thanks to God, my membership in the community becomes meaningful.

On the other hand, individuals have difficulty finding their purpose. How do they come to know what their *shlichoot* might be?

Another word for *shlichoot* is "passion." What is their passion? What keeps them up late at night? People naturally excel at the things they are passionate about. Find their passion and how it can serve the synagogue, and you will have found their purpose. What are the natural abilities and talents they have? Recruiting, researching, writing, landscaping, building, promoting, interviewing, decorating, planning, entertaining, selling, drawing, teaching, repairing, cooking—these are all gifts that can be used in the service of the congregation.

The sort of personality someone has will also help determine their purpose. Some people are extroverted, making friends easily and greeting strangers with ease; some work best alone; others are terrific collaborators. Find a service that fits their personality. What kinds of experiences have shaped their lives?

Five areas of experience are important to consider:

1. Educational experiences: What were your best subjects in school?
2. Vocational experiences: What jobs have you enjoyed?
3. Spiritual experiences: What have been your most meaningful encounters with God?
4. Volunteer experiences: How have you served congregations before?

5. Emotional experiences: What joys, hurts, and challenges have you experienced, and what did you
   learn from them?

The search for meaning is what drives our spiritual journey. Many are
seeking, but not all are finding. Congregations whose members experience belonging in their relationships with other people, and congregations whose members experience meaning in their relationship
to the synagogue, will see that many people become part of the
Committed and Core circles.

## Meetings vs. Missions

A major reason many synagogue members are not active in actually
serving the congregation is that most of their time is spent in meetings. The single most valuable asset people can give to the synagogue
is their time. Time is often the most important commodity we own.
Today, people have less leisure time than ever. Serving on a committee does not necessarily mean serving the congregation.

At Saddleback Church, there are no committees, but there are
seventy-nine different lay ministries. What's the difference between a
committee and a lay ministry? Committees discuss, but ministries do.
Committees argue; ministries act. Committees maintain; ministries
minister. Committees talk and consider; ministries serve and care.
Committees evaluate needs; ministries meet needs. In most synagogues, the laypeople handle the administration of the synagogue
through committees, while the rabbi is supposed to do all of the ministry. In a sacred community, the laypeople are empowered to do ministry as the clergy and Core members lead. The most difficult
challenge clergy and lay leadership can face is the empowerment of
the congregation to be *shlichim*. Congregants will want the rabbi at
the *shivah minyan*, to make the hospital visit, to do all the speaking.
But in a large synagogue, it is impossible for the clergy to do all the
work. Not only is it impossible, it is undesirable. To do so is to create
a synagogue that is person-driven, not purpose-driven.

Moreover, the talent and energy of hundreds of members might
be lost if they are not called upon for a mission. Congregants often
assume "the rabbi and professional staff will do it," and perhaps they

will, but that leads to burnout of professionals and members. The ideal is to empower every member to serve as a *shaliach*. Imagine the power!

## The Value of Commitment

In order to minister to the congregation, members have to be willing to make a commitment. People make commitments all the time (to causes, to civic groups, to political parties). The question is not whether people will make a commitment to something, but rather, who or what is going to get their commitment. The synagogue will not get a commitment without asking for it. We are pretty good at asking for financial commitments. In fact, many synagogue members report the only time they are visited in their homes by representatives of the synagogue is when there is money to be raised. People want to be committed to something that gives their lives significance and meaning. They are attracted by a well-articulated and challenging vision. One year, Rabbi Harold Schulweis of Valley Beth Shalom replaced the synagogue's annual High Holy Day appeal for money with an appeal for commitment. He created a pledge card that had turn-down tabs for people to indicate which synagogue activities they wanted to commit to and what life-changing practices they wanted the synagogue to teach them.

## Faith-Based Community Organizing

Some congregations have adopted the strategies pioneered by Saul Alinsky in organizing their spiritual communities to further their work in the world. At Temple Israel of Boston, congregants were invited to have one-on-one conversations about their social justice concerns in order to raise awareness and to assess issues that the synagogue might tackle. In addition to mobilizing action, these conversations linked members with one another in a way rarely seen before in the congregation, building community in a palpable way. Valley Beth Shalom, under the lay leadership of Janice Kamenir-Reznik, has launched Jewish World Watch, a synagogue-based social justice movement to address human crises such as the genocide in Darfur.

### Personal Spiritual Maturity

The Jewish notion of spirituality is quite different from the image of cloistered mystics. It is most assuredly not only the province of rabbis, cantors, and professional Jews. And it is not true that only the *frum* (religiously observant) can attain higher levels of spirituality. Jewish spirituality is found in the doing, not only in the praying. Judaism is a proactive religion, emphasizing the here and now. For the rabbis, Jewish spirituality came from quite mundane and practical pursuits. They found spiritual meaning in breaking bread, in reciting a blessing when observing a rainbow, when putting a child to sleep. There is spirituality to be found in the still, small voices as much as in the shofar blasts of Rosh Hashana.

Spiritual maturity is demonstrated by behavior rather than by beliefs. Judaism has always emphasized the doing over the believing—*na'aseh v'nishma* (we will do and we will understand). The extent of one's Jewish knowledge is not the proof of spirituality. Clearly, there are people with the ability to quote biblical passages and recite Jewish law who are hardly spiritual role models. By adopting a regimen of spiritual habits, Jews can reach a higher spiritual plane. Just as it takes regular exercise to become physically fit, it takes regular practice of certain exercises and good habits to become spiritually fit. Spiritual growth takes time. There may be instant coffee, instant oatmeal, and even instant weight loss, but there is no such thing as instant spirituality. It is possible to get a glimpse of higher spiritual feelings during spiritually welcoming worship, unusually moving healing services, or other moments of deep meaning, but we arrive at spiritual maturity as a result of a journey. And the journey lasts a lifetime.

There are many paths to Jewish spiritual maturity. For some, immersion in Jewish study leads to spiritual growth. For others, immersion in works of *tzedakah* and social justice enhance one's spiritual life. For some, adopting a Jewish lifestyle informed by the mitzvot is the way. For others, meditation and deeper understanding of Jewish prayer can lead to spiritual renewal. Whatever the path, the notion of commitment to the journey is central in the spiritual quest. Affiliation, even attendance at the occasional worship service, is certainly not enough to lead to spiritual maturity.

Jewish spirituality, unlike some Eastern religious traditions, is not primarily a personal and private matter. Jews need relationships to grow. Judaism requires a *minyan* of ten for communal prayer. We develop our spiritual selves in relationship not only to God but to others. In fact, it is impossible to love God without loving others. This is the essence of what Martin Buber called the I-Thou relationship. Jewish spiritual maturity is found in the context of community.

It takes a variety of spiritual experiences with God to produce spiritual maturity. It requires having a heart that worships and praises God, building and enjoying loving relationships, using your talents in service, and sharing your journey with others. Worship, study, community, deeds of loving-kindness, and healing—all these are required to reach spiritual maturity. Moreover, affective experiences are as important as cognitive ones. Study without practice is insufficient.

## Tips

## *Ways of Cultivating Jewish Spiritual Maturity*

- Set up one or more classes for congregants whose goal is to strive for spiritual maturity.
- Create pledge cards for people to indicate which new Jewish practice they are committed to adopting in the coming year. The response to these calls for commitment is often unusually positive. Some may be afraid to ask for big commitments, afraid that it will drive people away. The opposite is true: People are inspired to make a great commitment if there is a great purpose behind it. People respond to a passionate vision of Judaism, not a need the synagogue might have. Focus on the vision of the

synagogue, not the needs of the synagogue. Generalities won't inspire commitments. "Be a good Jew" means nothing. Spell out a variety of specific commitments that can lead people to higher spirituality—study, good deeds, *tzedakah*, celebrations, mitzvot—and provide ways for people to act on them.

• Emphasize the benefits of commitment to Jewish practice on every occasion. God was the first great practitioner of benefit advertising. God asks Abraham for a huge commitment: "Go, leave your house, and go to a place I will show you." And what's the benefit? "You shall be a blessing and your descendants as numerous as the stars in the sky." There are tremendous personal, family, and communal benefits to living a Jewishly committed lifestyle. Shabbat offers rest to the weary and overstressed. Helping others help themselves helps the community.

• Build a positive attitude toward commitment in small steps. Start with people wherever they may be on their spiritual path. Help them take the next small step. Celebrate these small steps, as well as the big ones.

The largest crowd of the year at many synagogues (besides the High Holy Days) is the Shabbat celebrating those members who become adult *B'nai Mitzvah*. These people have committed two years of their lives to learning Hebrew, the prayer service, and how to chant from the Torah and Haftorah. Their participation in the service is one of the most inspiring moments in the synagogue all year. Engage in the core spiritual exercises of Judaism:

- Learning. The Talmud asks, "Which is greater: study or good deeds?" The answer: "Study, for it leads to good deeds." Learning about Judaism goes hand in hand with experiencing Jewish living.
- Mitzvot. Living a Jewish life, celebrating Shabbat and Jewish festivals, observing Jewish practices—this is the fuel for the Jewish journey.
- Prayer. As difficult as accessing Jewish worship may be for some, finding ways to praise and petition God are indispensable for spiritual maturity.
- Community. Establishing relationships with others is the essence of belonging to a synagogue.
- *Tzedakah* and acts of loving-kindness. Judaism views as a spiritual act the giving of one's resources and talents to better the world.

### Jewish Journey Groups

The lifeblood of a synagogue of the twenty-first century is small spiritual support groups that members join to explore an interest or to pursue a purpose. In Synagogue 2000, we developed Jewish journey groups to act as the small group mechanism for connecting individuals more closely to the congregation.

**Tips**

## Ways of Fostering Small Groups

- Find out how many people belong to existing small groups.
- Find ways to revitalize these small groups if necessary.
- Organize additional small groups for congregants to become a part of. These might be

multi-session Jewish journey groups, focused on a particular topic or issue. These might also be multi-session workshops or classes, also focused on a particular topic. For classes to function in the same way as small groups, they must be organized and taught so that people can get to know one another and make contacts that might result in lasting connections.

Most synagogues already have a number of small groups, called boards or committees, that bring people together. But the agendas for these groups is nearly always "corporate"; they do the business of the congregation. Consider transforming these existing small groups by introducing S2K-style components of "meeting." How could each of the following groups in your own synagogue manifest a spirituality of welcoming?

- The board
- Committees of the board
- Study groups
- Social action groups
- *Bikkur Cholim* (visiting the sick) group
- *Nichum Aveilim* (comforting the mourner) group
- *Chevra Kadisha* (attending to the deceased) group
- School committees
- Bar and Bat Mitzvah families
- Parents of children who attend school together
- *Havurot*
- Choir
- Sisterhood
- Brotherhood or men's club
- Youth groups
- Torah readers
- Daily *minyan*
- Adult education classes
- Senior groups

There are several advantages to creating small groups within the larger synagogue community.

Small groups help foster friendships. Many synagogue members report that having a group of friends in the congregation is one of the most important benefits of belonging. Friendships are the bedrock of community.

Small groups personalize the congregation. If the congregation is larger than five hundred households, it is easy for individual members to feel disconnected. This is especially true in "megagogues" of a thousand or more membership units. Small groups are the vehicles for enabling members to connect to the congregation in a meaningful way.

Small groups also encourage personal growth. Spiritual growth often happens in small group settings that are intimate and supportive. Jewish journey groups enable people to check in with each other, to share the stories of personal journeys, and to study and pray together.

## Shaarei Tikvah (Conservative)
## Scarsdale, New York

*Our most recognized contribution from S2K is the Jewish journey group (JJG) entitled Talking About God. After a four-part lecture series about revelation in Conservative Judaism, the JJG gave us a forum to discuss some ideas from the lectures. Led by team member Alison Kellner, fifteen men and women of varying ages journeyed together. Each one brought his or her personal history and belief system about God. No two of them believed exactly the same thing. The exciting result was that the JJG worked exactly (if not better than!) we were told it would. People talked, discussed, listened, and struggled with ideas of God and bonded to each other in a way they weren't used to doing in other synagogue venues. No one wanted it to end, saying it was something they looked forward to attending.*

## Bet Torah (Conservative)
## Mt. Kisco, New York

*The S2K team of Bet Torah decided to give other groups in the congregation a feel for the S2K culture by meeting three times, on three consecutive weeks, with the chairpeople of five major Bet Torah committees (men's club, sisterhood, nursery school, Hebrew school, and youth commission). The meetings were run according to S2K format and each lasted about one and a half hours. During the meetings we discussed questions found in the S2K curriculum about how Bet Torah is important in our lives, the most important aspects of Bet Torah to each of us, and so on. At the conclusion, each participant came away with a sense of what S2K hopes to accomplish.*

## Young Israel of Scarsdale (Orthodox)
## Scarsdale, New York

*The Young Israel of Scarsdale created its own Jewish journey group with a curriculum centering on community responses to death and mourning. The theme emerged when we analyzed the demographics of our congregation and realized that, while most members of the congregation are baby boomers, our parents are in their seventies and eighties. We make many shivah visits in the course of a year and we recognized that the issues of death and mourning are ones all of us have faced or will face. The themes are sober and important. The curriculum will examine Jewish views towards death and the proper behavior and response of the community to those in our congregation who are mourning the loss of loved ones.*

## *Workshops for Disengaged Members*

In addition to a new members orientation seminar, consider offering a seminar for disengaged members—well-planned and intense workshop organized to encourage current members to deepen their relationship to the synagogue. A strong engagement workshop need not necessarily mean a long engagement workshop. It might be only four hours in one day or evening, yet if it is both personal and purposeful and addresses heart, mind, and soul it could produce a high level of commitment. Or, a workshop might be organized as an elective series so that individuals could come to the workshop segment that most speaks to them.

Following are some session ideas for engagement workshops:

### The Story of the Synagogue
At Disney University, the Walt Disney Company's employee training arm, a period of time is devoted to a program called, of all things, "Traditions." Through video clips and other forms of presentation, the history and achievements of the Disney Company are shared. Everyone comes to feel a sense of pride in being part of the Disney "family."

- What is the story of this synagogue?
- What are the critical moments in its life?
- What are the important memories people have of synagogue experiences?
- What are the things in which people take pride?

### Beliefs, Values, and Practices
We rarely take the time to reflect and report on our own beliefs, ambivalences, doubts, anxieties, and personal religious practices. This segment should be experiential as well as informational.

- What do we believe as Jews?
- How do we practice Judaism in this congregation?
- How do we practice Judaism in our lives?
- What kind of congregation are we, and why?
- What are the reasons for living a Jewish life?
- What do we, individually, believe in?

- What does Judaism say about learning, mitzvot, prayer, community, and *tzedakah/gemilut chasadim* (charity/acts of loving-kindness)?
- What are the how-tos of Jewish living?

**The Purposes of the Synagogue**
- What is the history of the synagogue in the Jewish tradition?
- Why does the synagogue exist?
- What is our synagogue's mission?
- What is our vision of what a synagogue can be?
- What do we do to actualize our vision?
- In our experience, where does the synagogue miss the mark?

**The Benefits of Membership**
- What benefits will you get from being a member of this congregation?
- What can the synagogue do for you?
- What do you want from the synagogue?

**The Responsibilities of Membership**
- What does the synagogue expect from you?
- What are your commitments to the congregation?
- What are your commitments to yourself as a member of a sacred community?

**The Organization of This Synagogue**
- How is the synagogue structured?
- How does the lay board work?
- Who are the professional and support staff?
- How does the synagogue pay its bills?
- Who do you go to with a problem?
- How do you make your voice heard?

**Involvement Opportunities**
- What small groups can I belong to?
- What committees can I join?
- How can I find my *shlichoot,* my purpose, my way to be involved in synagogue?

## *Teaching the Purposes*

The synagogue of the twenty-first century will do all that it can to induct and enculturate people into a sacred community that is committed to deepening the spiritual lives of its members. There is no substitute for teaching the purposes of a congregation. The main purpose of a synagogue is to encourage Jews to explore their Judaism, to find a level of spirituality in their lives, to connect them to community and to mobilize them to do God's work in the world. The synagogue is a community where worship is important, *hevrah* is cherished, and service to others is valued. We want to form and transform, not merely inform. Transformation does not happen by chance.

This is about taking a lifelong journey. Each step in the journey should lead to a deeper commitment. We don't want to lose people along the way; we don't want them to trip over stumbling blocks or to get lost. That is why it is important to lead a person step by step into a life of commitment. At key steps along the way, covenants and responsibilities are agreed to before moving ahead. Most people will begin the journey; some will get to deeper levels. If we only doubled the small percentage of synagogue members who move from the Congregation level of commitment to the Committed and from the Committed to the Core from 10 percent to 20 percent, it would transform our sacred communities.

## Structure, Staffing, and Funding for Growth

A synagogue of the twenty-first century will have a radically different structure, staffing, and funding than the typical synagogue of the last century. First, we have to change the way we talk about the reach of synagogues. Instead of referring to synagogue membership units, typically family units, it is much more accurate to speak of the raw actual numbers of individuals within the sacred community. For example, a synagogue with five hundred membership units may very well have two thousand or more individuals. A congregation with fifteen hundred units could have five thousand individuals. Count the number of seats or tickets you need for the High Holy Days, including the children, and you will have a number that is fairly accurate.

This counting is important in order to make the point that synagogues have tremendous reach into the community and deserve community funding. As mentioned earlier, I believe federations should fund synagogues, directly and substantially. Synagogues are the "retail outlets" for Judaism with the greatest potential reach of any Jewish institution. Some synagogues get indirect federation support through subsidies from the local Bureau of Jewish Education for teacher's salaries and professional development. But it is not nearly enough. In exchange for this vital community support, the synagogue should commit to 100 percent participation in the annual UJA/federation campaign. Synagogues must also be assertive about securing funds from philanthropists and foundations who engage in donor-directed giving.

Synagogues of the twenty-first century will have far more leaders organized to do the work of the synagogue. The anticipated growth in numbers and contributions will allow more professional staff to be engaged in the work of reaching in and reaching out. Plus, the empowerment of more laypeople to act as paraprofessionals with specific tasks to accomplish will swell the ranks of workers for the congregation.

Synagogues need more clergy—period. I have been involved in any number of congregations that were stymied by the questions Should we hire an assistant rabbi? Should we have a *hazzan sheini* (second cantor)? You should hire *three* assistant rabbis and at least two cantors! I can hear you now: How are we going to pay for them? The answer is in growth; growth of numbers and dollars. If you have faith and a plan to grow your congregation and to deepen the commitment of your current membership, you will find that the energy and excitement generated will attract the support you need to add to your staff.

In many twentieth-century synagogues, the new staff position of program director was created. I hope by now you are getting my message: More programs are not the answer to revitalizing synagogue life. Here are some ideas for new positions that might be created instead:

**Membership Director**
Consider hiring a full-time professional dedicated to implementing your plan for reaching out to the Community, building a Crowd, and inducting each and every individual into the life of the Congregation.

**Synagogue Nurse**
Don't laugh; the leadership of one of our S2K pilot congregations, Congregation Agudath Israel in Caldwell, New Jersey, did just that. They approached a member of the community who happened to be a registered nurse and asked her to organize Jewish journey groups centering on lifecycle issues such as bereavement and healing. The experiment was so successful that the congregation invited her to join the professional staff.

**Jewish Family Educator**
Families constitute the majority of the membership in most congregations. The challenge of family education is to engage the adults in the family and encourage them to take the next steps on their Jewish journey. If the family educator can develop strong relationships between families in Jewish journey groups and family education programs, they will have a strong connection to the congregation, which should decrease the fall-off in membership when their youngest child becomes Bar or Bat Mitzvah.

**Artists-in-Residence**
Musicians, singers, and song leaders can join the clergy in teaching the congregation to pray, to sing, to move, and to learn.

**Security Staff that Double as Greeters**
With the threat of terrorism, virtually every synagogue in North America has had to institute some level of security screening at their front doors, often at considerable expense. This can be an obstacle or an opportunity. Train the security staff in the art of greeting and you will get more return for your investment.

Adding staff to the chronically understaffed congregation is necessary but by no means sufficient. The empowerment of the Core of lay leadership to act as paraprofessionals working alongside the paid staff is essential for the synagogue of the twenty-first century to create the congregation imagined here.

The organization of the congregation will look different, too. Committees, as we have discussed, are very often a waste of time. Instead of recruiting new members to committees, recruit them to lay leadership positions. Begin the planning of your new organizational chart by thinking through the purpose of each group of lay leaders. Then, substitute "team" for "committee" and gather both professionals and lay leaders who have a particular *shlichoot,* the gifts and talents that will assist in achieving the identified purpose.

One of the first teams to establish is the welcoming team. The purpose of this team is to work on creating a spiritually welcoming ambience in the congregation. The target audience of the team is the Community, and its job is to train a group of greeters to offer warm welcome to guests and members at services, to evaluate the building and identify ways it can be more accessible and welcoming, and to review initial contact points with potential members, such as how the phones are answered in the office. Their task is to encourage those in the unaffiliated community to return, *teshuvah,* to come home. Similarly, organize a worship team, a membership team, an outreach team and a *shlichoot* team.

## Broadcasting the Message

The synagogue of the twenty-first century will use every available communication strategy to send the message that the congregation is "doing synagogue differently." Advertising experts agree that a message must constantly be repeated before it is heard and takes hold in the imagination of people. Here are some of the ways your message can be sent:

### Sermons and *Divrei Torah*

The clergy can influence the creation of a new culture through teaching from the pulpit, in classes, and via columns in the bulletin.

### Publications in the Pews

Most synagogues publish a weekly handout distributed to those attending services. This is an opportunity to send your message, to tell your story, and to invite people to connect.

### Website, Podcasting, and E-mail

Many synagogues have mounted websites, some with downloadable podcasts of sermons and music, and communicate with congregants via e-mail. These are powerful tools to help send your message and organize your teams.

### Newsletters

If you still publish and distribute a weekly or monthly mailing, be sure that your message is consistent and highlighted in each and every publication.

### Advertising

In some communities, competition for new members can be intense, particularly in the months leading up to the High Holy Days. What message are you sending to prospective members?

### School Communications

Do not overlook the power of sending home messages about the congregation to the parents of religious and/or day school children.

In sum, keep your eye on the twin goals of welcoming membership to reach out and welcome new members into the congregation, and to reach in and connect every single person who belongs to the congregation to some purpose that will provide meaning and value to membership in the sacred community. If you can find a way to create a welcoming ambience that is palpable the instant someone interacts with the congregation, if you can offer welcoming worship that engages someone immediately, and if you can establish a well-conceived strategy of welcoming membership that both inducts new members into the life of the congregation and encourages a deep and meaningful connection, then the transformation of your congregation into a sacred community of the twenty-first century will be within reach.

# IN GRATITUDE

I still love synagogues. After more than thirty years of working with congregations and ten years of intensive action research with the S2K sites, my faith in the synagogue remains unshaken. Yes, there is much we must do to improve, to deepen, and to transform congregations. But at their core, synagogues are the bedrock institution of the Jewish community and their importance in the twenty-first century will only increase.

I also love the people of synagogues. They are good people, hard-working and well-meaning volunteers, devoting extraordinary energy and time to the business of congregational life. They know that most of our congregations are good and they are open to ideas for making them better, for going deeper. I have met hundreds of lay leaders who resonate with the call for transforming congregations into sacred communities; specifically, these members of the nearly one hundred S2K teams have been an inspiration to me.

Synagogues are led by extraordinarily dedicated clergy and staff—rabbis, cantors, executive directors, educators, program directors, membership directors, teachers, youth advisors, office staff, and custodians—all who give their lives for the sacred task of creating sacred communities. They are on the front lines every single day, giving their hearts and souls to this work. *Yi'asher kochechem*—may God continue to strengthen them.

In spite of the tremendous importance of synagogues in Jewish life, there has been no action research center devoted to the study and improvement of synagogue life, until now. After a strategic planning process based on a careful review of the results of Synagogue 2000, the decision was reached to create Synagogue 3000, an independent, nonprofit entity. Initially, there will be two initiatives sponsored by S3K: (1) the S3K Leadership Network, a transdenominational gathering of courageous spiritual leaders who share the vision of synagogue articulated here and who represent the cutting edge of excellence in synagogue life, and (2) the S3K Synagogue Studies Institute, an academic research center for the study of synagogues, the Jewish address in the broader field of congregational studies. I invite you to connect with the developing work of S3K through our website, www.synagogue3000.org.

As we transition to this new effort, it is appropriate to offer thanks to those who have been so instrumental in the success of Synagogue 2000.

From the moment I shared that cup of stale coffee with Larry Hoffman, I have been blessed with his colleagueship and friendship. Surmounting enormous personal challenges, Larry has been our intellectual visionary and teacher, unfailingly provocative, supportive, and present. The North American synagogue has been forever transformed by his teachings and his many disciples.

Synagogue 2000, and now Synagogue 3000, would never exist without the support of a dedicated and passionate group of lay leaders, foundations, and philanthropists. When the history of American Judaism in the late twentieth century is written, virtually all of the creative innovations will be traced to one person: Rabbi Rachel Cowan. In her work with the Nathan Cummings Foundation, Rachel blazed the trail for everyone—practitioners, academics, and other foundations. Joining her early on in support of Synagogue 2000 were Bruce Whizin and Shelley Whizin from the Shirley and Arthur Whizin Foundation. Bruce and Shelley have been wonderful partners and friends. Marge Tabankin and Rachel Levin from Steven Spielberg's Righteous Persons Foundation discovered our dream early in their search for projects that could make a difference, and their support through the years has been crucial to our success. Along the way, our three major funders were joined by a number of other foundations and federations, including the William Ludwig and Susan R. Ludwig Family Trust, the Richard and Lois England Family Foundation, the Gaia Fund, the Rose Community Foundation, the Joseph and Rebecca Meyerhoff Awards Committee, the Bulova Gale Foundation, the Allied Jewish Federation of Colorado, the Jewish Federation of Metropolitan Detroit, William Davidson, Rita J. and Stanley H. Kaplan Family Foundation, Janet and Jeff Beck, Beatrice Fox Auerbach Foundation Fund, Crown Family Foundation, M. L. Sturm Foundation, Terry Rosenberg and Donald Rosenberg, William Rosenberg Family Foundation, Laurence J. and Shuling H. Smith, Jewish United Fund/Jewish Federation of Metropolitan Chicago, Dr. Ruth Durschlag, Marion Blumenthal Philanthropic Fund, Susan K. Freedman and Rabbi Rick Jacobs, Don and Janie Friend, Lee M. Hendler Philanthropic Fund, UJA-Federation of New York, and the Union of Reform Judaism. Most recently, Bernie Marcus and the Marcus Foundation of Atlanta have been very generous in supporting the new work of Synagogue 3000. Special thanks to my friend and colleague Jay Kaiman for spearheading this partnership.

The Synagogue 2000/3000 board, led by our capable chairperson, Terry Rosenberg, has lent steadfast support. Many thanks to all those who have served as members: Larry Akman, Marion Blumenthal, Lili Bosse, Rabbi Rachel Cowan, Rabbi Ed Feinstein, Don Friend, Lee Meyerhoff Hendler, Rabbi Rick Jacobs, Mark Schlesinger, Steve Silberman, Larry Smith, Rabbi Aaron Spiegel, Melanie Sturm, Bonnie Tisch, Beryl Weiner, Bruce Whizin, and Shelley Whizin. Shifra Bronznick and Didi Goldenhar have been especially helpful in guiding the transition from Synagogue 2000 to Synagogue 3000.

We have been so fortunate to attract a group of phenomenal rabbis, cantors, musicians, composers, choreographers, educators, and artists who became Synagogue 2000 fellows, teaching at our conferences and lending their support: Cantor Rosalie Boxt, Rabbi/Cantor Angela Buchdahl, Rabbi Rachel Cowan, Penny Dannenberg, Rabbi Elliot Dorff, Rabbi Paula Mack Drill, Rabbi Amy Eilberg, Rabbi Helaine Ettinger, Rabbi Ed Feinstein, Rabbi Nancy Flam, Karen Frank, Debbie Friedman, Rabbi Dan Freelander, Rabbi Elyse Frishman, Joel Grishaver, Dr. Carol Hausman, Rabbi Rick Jacobs, Rabbi Sam Joseph, Risa Jaroslow, Dr. Elli Kranzler, Rabbi Lawrence Kushner, Amichai Lau-Lavie, Liz Lerman, Rachel Levin, Danny Maseng, Rabbi Roly Matalon, Cantor Jack Mendelson, Rabbi Kerry Olitzky, Hazzan Ari Priven, Rabbi Jonathan Rosenblatt, Cantor Benjie Ellen Schiller, Rabbi Ron Shulman, Rabbi Alan Silverstein, Rabbi Jonathan Slater, Rabbi Joel Soffin, Craig Taubman, Richard Vosko, Ph.D., Rabbi Elaine Zecher, and Rabbi Dan Zemel.

Special thanks to those who facilitated the creation of our cohort groups: Harlene Appelman, Bob Aronson, John Ruskay, Alisa Kurshan, Rabbi Deborah Joselow, Lisa Farber Miller, Rabbi Eric Yoffie, Rabbi Dan Freelander, Susan Spero, Rabbi Sue Ann Wasserman, Rabbi Kim Geringer, Steve Posen, Julie Falbaum, Dale Rubin, Shere Kahn, Ros Begun, Vickie Marx, Karen Lustig, and Elliot Forchheimer.

I am indebted to our devoted staff of professionals who have poured their talents into our work: Merri Lovinger Arian, Joshua Avedon, Dr. Adrianne Bank, Cantor Ellen Dreskin, Ellen Franklin, Fran Heller, Dr. Joel Hoffman, Rabbi Yoel Kahn, Rabbi Leora Kaye, Linda Klonsky, J. Shawn Landres, Harriet Lewis, Judy Mann, Dr. Amy Sales, Rabbi Randy Sheinberg, Rhonda Slater, Rabbi Robyn Tsesarski and Rabbi Ruth Zlotnick. Hebrew Union College–Jewish Institute of Religion in New York and the Whizin Center for the Jewish Future of American Jewish University in Los Angeles have been hospitable hosts of our project.

I have learned much from the megachurches and their model of outreach. At every church and conference, I was warmly welcomed and assisted with whatever information I required. A special word of thanks to Rick Warren, the extraordinary pastor of Saddleback Church, who has responded to every request we have made in our quest to tap into his genius. Rick has hosted our conferees and kindly accepted our invitation to meet with the S3K Leadership Network at an historic encounter on June 15, 2005. When we last met, I told him that I was working on "translating" many of the concepts in his groundbreaking book on congregations, *The Purpose-Driven Church,* for application (not replication!) in synagogues. Characteristically, Rick was overwhelmingly enthusiastic and encouraging. I have also been warmly received by the leadership of Willow Creek Church, the Crystal Cathedral, the Leadership Network, the Indianapolis Center for Congregations, the Hartford Seminary, the Fuller Theological Seminary, the Alban Institute and, most recently, by Emergent-U.S., the pioneers of the emergent movement.

I am grateful, as always, to the terrific people of Jewish Lights Publishing, beginning with their visionary leader, Stuart M. Matlins, along with Emily Wichland, Mark Ogilbee, Ilana Kurshan, and the entire staff.

Many thanks to those who read early drafts of this book and offered valuable comments and critique: Terry Rosenberg, Lee Meyerhoff Hendler, Ellen Dreskin, Merri Lovinger Arian, Shawn Landres, Jay Kaiman, Craig Taubman, and Larry Hoffman. Special thanks to my rabbi and neighbor, Ed Feinstein, with whom I share morning musings about the future of synagogue life as we meet at the end of our driveways, picking up the morning newspapers in our pajamas.

Of course, I want to thank you, the reader, for spending this time with me. I pray that you have been challenged and inspired. As you embark on the journey of synagogue transformation, I welcome your comments and suggestions. Please feel free to write to me at ron@synagogue3000.org. Remember: *You can do this!* I look forward to hearing about your success!

Finally, I am blessed with an amazing family that inspires me daily. My parents, Bernice and Alan Wolfson, made certain that synagogue was an important part of my life and they encourage me daily to work for their improvement. Most of this book was written in a hospital room at the Mayo Clinic where my father-in-law, Abe Kukawka, underwent open-heart surgery at the age of 95. Just months before he fell ill, he bought a brand-new car—and insisted on a ten-year warranty! He asked the Mayo surgeon for the same deal on his new heart valve. May he live to 120! I have dedicated this book to him and to the memory of my beloved mother-in-law, Hildegard Kukawka, and to the sweetest man in the world, our Uncle George (Gedale) Kukawka, and their family, who perished in the Holocaust. Many thanks to Bob and Sibby Wolfson and Doug and Sara Wolfson who supported us during our long stay in Omaha and Rochester. As always, there are no adequate words to express the depth of my love for Susan Kukawka Wolfson who unfailingly warmly welcomes my colleagues and supports my work in every way. My prayer is that our children Havi Michele and Michael Louis and ultimately their families will find and help create synagogues that are true sacred communities for the twenty-first century.

May God bless your sacred work!
Ron Wolfson
Encino, California

# ACTION GUIDE FOR CONGREGATIONAL LEADERS

*The Spirituality of Welcoming: How to Transform Your Congregation into a Sacred Community* can be used as a basic text for synagogue leadership wishing to engage in a serious consideration of how to establish a truly welcoming culture in the congregation.

Each member of the board and the professional staff should have a copy of the book for reading. Construct a plan to read the book over the course of several board meetings according to the following syllabus:

## Session One: Envisioning Ourselves as a Twenty-First-Century Synagogue

Read Chapter 1, "Introduction," and Chapter 2, "The Synagogue 2000 Theory of Synagogue Transformation."

Discussion: Establish ground rules for the conversation using the S2K Statement of Values as a guide. Choose from the following three sets of questions:

1. Have each person share when they joined the congregation and why. What initially attracted them? Why have they stayed? When and why did they become a leader?

2. Consider this question: If someone met you in the grocery store and asked what you love about your synagogue, what would you say? If they asked what your synagogue is known for, what would you say? (Answer in this way: "I belong to Congregation So-and-So because ... " "We're known for ... " "We're proud of our ... ") If someone wanted to experience what your synagogue is known for, what would you invite them to do: attend services, take a class, participate in a social justice project, or hear a sermon?

3. Are there times when we are not pleased with what happens in our congregation? When do we "blow it"?

## Session Two: Welcoming Ambience

Read Chapter 3, "Welcoming Ambience."

Take the entire group out to the parking lot and experience the synagogue walk-through. Do the exercises in this chapter. Develop a list of issues to address that will increase the warmth of the welcome for guests and members. Appoint a subgroup of the board to monitor these improvements. Appoint a team to work with the executive director to train the frontline staff in quality service.

## Session Three: Welcoming Worship

Read Chapter 4, "Welcoming Worship."

Recall a time when you were spiritually moved by a worship service. What was it about the experience that worked? Identify categories for discussion: music, space, learning, liturgy, clergy. Invite the rabbi and cantor to answer this question: When you are on vacation, what kind of worship service do you seek for yourself? Compile lists of what works for both the laity and the clergy; you will have a list of what everyone considers effective in worship (a better strategy than criticizing what you have now). Then ask, What is stopping us from having a service that reflects what we like? How can we overcome the obstacles?

## Session Four: Welcoming Membership

Read Chapter 5, "Welcoming Membership."

Appoint a "mystery shopper" to call the synagogue pretending to be a typical shul-shopper of a certain demographic; for example, a couple in their mid-thirties with one child, a 38-year-old single, a 78-year-old single. Have the mystery shopper inquire about membership in the congregation and track carefully what happens. Review the process of joining your congregation. Develop a list of ways to improve the experience.

Remember, you can find additional resources for your synagogue transformation journey at the Synagogue 3000 website, www.synagogue3000.org

# SUGGESTIONS FOR FURTHER READING

Addison, Howard A., and Barbara Eve Breitman, eds. *Jewish Spiritual Direction: An Innovative Guide from Traditional and Contemporary Sources.* Woodstock, VT: Jewish Lights, 2006.

Amann, Paula. *Journeys to a Jewish Life: Inspiring Stories from the Spiritual Journeys of American Jews.* Woodstock, VT: Jewish Lights, 2007.

Anderson, Kristin, and Ron Zemke. *Delivering Knock Your Socks Off Service.* New York: American Management Association, 2006.

Aron, Isa. *Becoming a Congregation of Learners: Learning as a Key to Revitalizing Congregational Life.* Woodstock, VT: Jewish Lights, 2000.

————. *The Self-Renewing Congregation: Organizational Strategies for Revitalizing Congregational Life.* Woodstock, VT: Jewish Lights, 2002.

Bass, Diana Butler. *The Practicing Congregation: Imagining a New Old Church.* Herndon, VA: Alban Institute, 2004.

Carroll, Jack W., and Wade Clark Roof. *Bridging Divided Worlds: Generational Cultures in Congregations.* San Francisco: Pfeiffer, 2002.

Cohen, Norman J. *Moses and the Journey to Leadership: Timeless Lessons of Effective Management from the Bible and Today's Leaders.* Woodstock, VT: Jewish Lights, 2008.

Cohen, Steven M. "Engaging the Next Generation of American Jews: Distinguishing the In-Married, Inter-Married, and Non-Married." *Journal of Jewish Communal Service,* Fall/Winter 2005, pp. 43–52.

Cohen, Steven M., and Arnold Eisen. *The Jew Within: Self, Family and Community in the United States.* Bloomington, IN: Indiana University Press, 2000.

Collins, Jim. *Good to Great.* New York: HarperBusiness, 2001.

Disney Institute. *Be Our Guest: Perfecting the Art of Customer Service.* New York: Disney Editions, 2003.

Fishburn, Janet Forsythe, ed. *People of a Compassionate God: Creating Welcoming Congregations.* Nashville: Abingdon Press, 2003.

Frazee, Randy. *The Connecting Church.* Grand Rapids, MI: Zondervan, 2001.

Freiberg, Kevin and Jackie. *Nuts! Southwest Airlines' Crazy Recipe for Business and Personal Success.* New York: Crown Business, 1998.

Friedman, Dayle A., ed. *Jewish Pastoral Care,* 2nd Ed.: *A Practical Handbook from Traditional & Contemporary Sources.* Woodstock, VT: Jewish Lights, 2010.

Gallup, George Jr., and D. Michael Lindsay. *The Gallup Guide: Reality Check for 21st Century Churches.* Princeton, NJ: Gallup Organization, 2002.

Gibbs, Eddie, and Ryan K. Bolger. *Emerging Churches: Creating Christian Community in Postmodern Cultures.* Grand Rapids, MI: Baker Academic, 2005.

Gitomer, Jeffrey. *Customer Satisfaction Is Worthless, Customer Loyalty Is Priceless.* Atlanta: Bard Press, 1998.

Gladwell, Malcolm. *Blink: The Power of Thinking Without Thinking*. New York: Little, Brown, 2007.

Hoffman, Lawrence A. *The Art of Public Prayer*, 2nd Ed.: *Not for Clergy Only*. Woodstock, VT: SkyLight Paths, 1999.

———. *Rethinking Synagogues: A New Vocabulary for Congregational Life*. Woodstock, VT: Jewish Lights, 2006.

Hybels, Bill and Lynne. *Rediscovering Church: The Story and Vision of Willow Creek Community Church*. Grand Rapids, MI: Zondervan, 1997.

Laufer, Nathan. *The Genesis of Leadership: What the Bible Teaches Us about Vision, Values and Leading Change*. Woodstock, VT: Jewish Lights, 2008.

Marcus, Bernie, and Arthur Blank. *Built From Scratch: How a Couple of Regular Guys Grew The Home Depot from Nothing to $30 Billion*. New York: Crown Business, 2001.

Mitchell, Jack. *Hug Your Customers*. New York: Hyperion, 2003.

Pine, B. Joseph, and James H. Gilmore. *The Experience Economy*. Boston: Harvard Business School Press, 1999.

Rendle, Gilbert R. *Leading Change in the Congregation: Spiritual and Organizational Tools for Leaders*. Bethesda, MD: Alban Institute, 1997.

Sanders, Betsy. *Fabled Service: Ordinary Acts, Extraordinary Outcomes*. San Francisco: Jossey-Bass, 1997.

Sarna, Jonathan. *American Judaism*. New Haven: Yale University Press, 2005.

Schmitt, Bernd H. *Experiential Marketing*. New York: Free Press, 1999.

Schwarz, Sidney. *Finding a Spiritual Home: How a New Generation of Jews Can Transform the American Synagogue*. Woodstock, VT: Jewish Lights, 2003.

Summit, Jeffrey. *The Lord's Song in a Strange Land: Music and Identity in Contemporary Jewish Worship*. New York: Oxford University Press, 2003.

Teutsch, David A. *Spiritual Community: The Power to Restore Hope, Commitment and Joy*. Woodstock, VT: Jewish Lights, 2005.

Twist, Lynne. *The Soul of Money*. New York: W. W. Norton, 2006.

Waltz, Mark L. *First Impressions: Creating Wow Experiences in Your Church*. Loveland, CO: Group, 2005.

Warren, Rick. *The Purpose-Driven Church*. Grand Rapids, MI: Zondervan, 1995.

———. *The Purpose-Driven Life*. Grand Rapids, MI: Zondervan, 2007.

Weinzweig, Ari. *Zingerman's Guide to Giving Great Service*. Ann Arbor, MI: Zingerman's, 2004.

Wolfson, Ron. *God's To-Do List: 103 Ways to Be an Angel and Do God's Work on Earth*. Woodstock, VT: Jewish Lights, 2006.

———. *The Seven Questions You're Asked in Heaven: Reviewing and Renewing Your Life on Earth*. Woodstock, VT: Jewish Lights, 2009.

Zevit, Rabbi Shawn Israel. *Offerings of the Heart: Money and Values in Faith Communities*. Herndon, VA: Alban Institute, 2005.

# GUIDE TO TIPS AND EXERCISES

## Tips

## Exercises

# AVAILABLE FROM BETTER BOOKSTORES.
# TRY YOUR BOOKSTORE FIRST.

## Bar/Bat Mitzvah

**The JGirl's Guide:** The Young Jewish Woman's Handbook for Coming of Age
*By Penina Adelman, Ali Feldman and Shulamit Reinharz* This inspirational, interactive guidebook helps pre-teen Jewish girls address the many issues surrounding coming of age. 6 x 9, 240 pp, Quality PB, 978-1-58023-215-9 **$14.99** *For ages 11 & up*
Also Available: **The JGirl's Teacher's and Parent's Guide**
8½ x 11, 56 pp, PB, 978-1-58023-225-8 **$8.99**

**Bar/Bat Mitzvah Basics, 2nd Edition:** A Practical Family Guide to Coming of Age Together *Edited by Helen Leneman; Foreword by Rabbi Jeffrey K. Salkin*
6 x 9, 240 pp, Quality PB, 978-1-58023-151-0 **$18.95**

**The Bar/Bat Mitzvah Memory Book, 2nd Edition:** An Album for Treasuring the Spiritual Celebration *By Rabbi Jeffrey K. Salkin and Nina Salkin*
8 x 10, 48 pp, 2-color text, Deluxe HC, ribbon marker, 978-1-58023-263-0 **$19.99**

**For Kids—Putting God on Your Guest List, 2nd Edition:** How to Claim the Spiritual Meaning of Your Bar or Bat Mitzvah *By Rabbi Jeffrey K. Salkin*
6 x 9, 144 pp, Quality PB, 978-1-58023-308-8 **$15.99** *For ages 11–13*

**Putting God on the Guest List, 3rd Edition:** How to Reclaim the Spiritual Meaning of Your Child's Bar or Bat Mitzvah *By Rabbi Jeffrey K. Salkin*
6 x 9, 224 pp, Quality PB, 978-1-58023-222-7 **$16.99**; HC, 978-1-58023-260-9 **$24.99**
Also Available: **Putting God on the Guest List Teacher's Guide**
8½ x 11, 48 pp, PB, 978-1-58023-226-5 **$8.99**

**Tough Questions Jews Ask:** A Young Adult's Guide to Building a Jewish Life
*By Rabbi Edward Feinstein* 6 x 9, 160 pp, Quality PB, 978-1-58023-139-8 **$14.99** *For ages 11 & up*
Also Available: **Tough Questions Jews Ask Teacher's Guide**
8½ x 11, 72 pp, PB, 978-1-58023-187-9 **$8.95**

## Bible Study/Midrash

**The Modern Men's Torah Commentary:** New Insights from Jewish Men on the 54 Weekly Torah Portions *Edited by Rabbi Jeffrey K. Salkin*
A major contribution to modern biblical commentary. Addresses the most important concerns of modern men by opening them up to the messages of Torah.
6 x 9, 368 pp, HC, 978-1-58023-395-8 **$24.99**

**The Genesis of Leadership:** What the Bible Teaches Us about Vision, Values and Leading Change *By Rabbi Nathan Laufer; Foreword by Senator Joseph I. Lieberman*
6 x 9, 288 pp, Quality PB, 978-1-58023-352-1 **$18.99**

**Hineini in Our Lives:** Learning How to Respond to Others through 14 Biblical Texts and Personal Stories *By Rabbi Norman J. Cohen, PhD* 6 x 9, 240 pp, Quality PB, 978-1-58023-274-6 **$16.99**

**A Man's Responsibility:** A Jewish Guide to Being a Son, a Partner in Marriage, a Father and a Community Leader *By Rabbi Joseph B. Meszler*
6 x 9, 192 pp, Quality PB, 978-1-58023-435-1 **$16.99**; HC, 978-1-58023-362-0 **$21.99**

**Moses and the Journey to Leadership:** Timeless Lessons of Effective Management from the Bible and Today's Leaders *By Rabbi Norman J. Cohen, PhD*
6 x 9, 240 pp, Quality PB, 978-1-58023-351-4 **$18.99**; HC, 978-1-58023-227-2 **$21.99**

**Righteous Gentiles in the Hebrew Bible:** Ancient Role Models for Sacred Relationships *By Rabbi Jeffrey K. Salkin; Foreword by Rabbi Harold M. Schulweis; Preface by Phyllis Tickle* 6 x 9, 192 pp, Quality PB, 978-1-58023-364-4 **$18.99**

**The Triumph of Eve & Other Subversive Bible Tales** *By Matt Biers-Ariel* 5½ x 8½, 192 pp, Quality PB, 978-1-59473-176-1 **$14.99** *(A book from SkyLight Paths, Jewish Lights' sister imprint)*

**The Wisdom of Judaism:** An Introduction to the Values of the Talmud
*By Rabbi Dov Peretz Elkins* 6 x 9, 192 pp, Quality PB, 978-1-58023-327-9 **$16.99**
Also Available: **The Wisdom of Judaism Teacher's Guide**
8½ x 11, 18 pp, PB, 978-1-58023-350-7 **$8.99**

*Or phone, fax, mail or e-mail to:* **JEWISH LIGHTS** Publishing
Sunset Farm Offices, Route 4 • P.O. Box 237 • Woodstock, Vermont 05091
Tel: (802) 457-4000 • Fax: (802) 457-4004 • www.jewishlights.com
*Credit card orders:* (800) 962-4544 (8:30AM–5:30PM ET Monday–Friday)
Generous discounts on quantity orders. SATISFACTION GUARANTEED. Prices subject to change.

# Inspiration

**The Seven Questions You're Asked in Heaven:** Reviewing and Renewing Your Life on Earth *By Dr. Ron Wolfson*
An intriguing and entertaining resource for living a life that matters.
6 x 9, 176 pp, Quality PB, 978-1-58023-407-8 **$16.99**

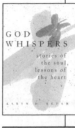

**Happiness and the Human Spirit:** The Spirituality of Becoming the Best You Can Be *By Rabbi Abraham J. Twerski, MD*
Shows you that true happiness is attainable once you stop looking outside yourself for the source. 6 x 9, 176 pp, Quality PB, 978-1-58023-404-7 **$16.99**; HC, 978-1-58023-343-9 **$19.99**

**A Formula for Proper Living:** Practical Lessons from Life and Torah
*By Rabbi Abraham J. Twerski, MD*
Gives you practical lessons for life that you can put to day-to-day use in dealing with yourself and others. 6 x 9, 144 pp, HC, 978-1-58023-402-3 **$19.99**

**The Bridge to Forgiveness:** Stories and Prayers for Finding God and Restoring Wholeness *By Rabbi Karyn D. Kedar* 6 x 9, 176 pp, HC, 978-1-58023-324-8 **$19.99**

**The Empty Chair:** Finding Hope and Joy—Timeless Wisdom from a Hasidic Master, Rebbe Nachman of Breslov *Adapted by Moshe Mykoff and the Breslov Research Institute*
4 x 6, 128 pp, Deluxe PB w/ flaps, 978-1-879045-67-5 **$9.99**

**The Gentle Weapon:** Prayers for Everyday and Not-So-Everyday Moments—Timeless Wisdom from the Teachings of the Hasidic Master, Rebbe Nachman of Breslov *Adapted by Moshe Mykoff and S. C. Mizrahi, together with the Breslov Research Institute*
4 x 6, 144 pp, Deluxe PB w/ flaps, 978-1-58023-022-3 **$9.99**

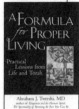

**God Whispers:** Stories of the Soul, Lessons of the Heart *By Rabbi Karyn D. Kedar*
6 x 9, 176 pp, Quality PB, 978-1-58023-088-9 **$15.95**

**God's To-Do List:** 103 Ways to Be an Angel and Do God's Work on Earth
*By Dr. Ron Wolfson* 6 x 9, 144 pp, Quality PB, 978-1-58023-301-9 **$16.99**

**Jewish Stories from Heaven and Earth:** Inspiring Tales to Nourish the Heart and Soul *Edited by Rabbi Dov Peretz Elkins* 6 x 9, 304 pp, Quality PB, 978-1-58023-363-7 **$16.99**

**Life's Daily Blessings:** Inspiring Reflections on Gratitude and Joy for Every Day, Based on Jewish Wisdom *By Rabbi Kerry M. Olitzky* 4½ x 6½, 368 pp, Quality PB, 978-1-58023-396-5 **$16.99**

**Restful Reflections:** Nighttime Inspiration to Calm the Soul, Based on Jewish Wisdom
*By Rabbi Kerry M. Olitzky and Rabbi Lori Forman* 4½ x 6½, 448 pp, Quality PB, 978-1-58023-091-9 **$15.95**

**Sacred Intentions:** Daily Inspiration to Strengthen the Spirit, Based on Jewish Wisdom
*By Rabbi Kerry M. Olitzky and Rabbi Lori Forman* 4½ x 6½, 448 pp, Quality PB, 978-1-58023-061-2 **$15.95**

# Kabbalah/Mysticism

**Ehyeh:** A Kabbalah for Tomorrow
*By Rabbi Arthur Green, PhD* 6 x 9, 224 pp, Quality PB, 978-1-58023-213-5 **$18.99**

**The Flame of the Heart:** Prayers of a Chasidic Mystic
*By Reb Noson of Breslov; Translated and adapted by David Sears, with the Breslov Research Institute*
5 x 7¼, 160 pp, Quality PB, 978-1-58023-246-3 **$15.99**

**The Gift of Kabbalah:** Discovering the Secrets of Heaven, Renewing Your Life on Earth
*By Tamar Frankiel, PhD* 6 x 9, 256 pp, Quality PB, 978-1-58023-141-1 **$16.95**

**Kabbalah:** A Brief Introduction for Christians
*By Tamar Frankiel, PhD* 5½ x 8½, 208 pp, Quality PB, 978-1-58023-303-3 **$16.99**

**The Lost Princess & Other Kabbalistic Tales of Rebbe Nachman of Breslov**
**The Seven Beggars & Other Kabbalistic Tales of Rebbe Nachman of Breslov**
*Translated by Rabbi Aryeh Kaplan; Preface by Rabbi Chaim Kramer*
Lost Princess: 6 x 9, 400 pp, Quality PB, 978-1-58023-217-3 **$18.99**
Seven Beggars: 6 x 9, 192 pp, Quality PB, 978-1-58023-250-0 **$16.99**

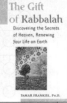

**Seek My Face:** A Jewish Mystical Theology *By Rabbi Arthur Green, PhD*
6 x 9, 304 pp, Quality PB, 978-1-58023-130-5 **$19.95**

**Zohar:** Annotated & Explained *Translation & Annotation by Dr. Daniel C. Matt; Foreword by Andrew Harvey* 5½ x 8½, 176 pp, Quality PB, 978-1-893361-51-5 **$15.99**
*(A book from SkyLight Paths, Jewish Lights' sister imprint)*

See also *The Way Into Jewish Mystical Tradition* in The Way Into... Series.

# Life Cycle

## Marriage/Parenting/Family/Aging

**The New Jewish Baby Album:** Creating and Celebrating the Beginning of a Spiritual Life—A Jewish Lights Companion
*By the Editors at Jewish Lights; Foreword by Anita Diamant; Preface by Rabbi Sandy Eisenberg Sasso*
A spiritual keepsake that will be treasured for generations. More than just a memory book, *shows you how—and why it's important*—to create a Jewish home and a Jewish life. 8 x 10, 64 pp, Deluxe Padded HC, Full-color illus., 978-1-58023-138-1 **$19.95**

**The Jewish Pregnancy Book:** A Resource for the Soul, Body & Mind during Pregnancy, Birth & the First Three Months *By Sandy Falk, MD, and Rabbi Daniel Judson, with Steven A. Rapp* Medical information, prayers and rituals for each stage of pregnancy. 7 x 10, 208 pp, b/w photos, Quality PB, 978-1-58023-178-7 **$16.95**

**Celebrating Your New Jewish Daughter:** Creating Jewish Ways to Welcome Baby Girls into the Covenant—New and Traditional Ceremonies *By Debra Nussbaum Cohen; Foreword by Rabbi Sandy Eisenberg Sasso* 6 x 9, 272 pp, Quality PB, 978-1-58023-090-2 **$18.95**

**The New Jewish Baby Book, 2nd Edition:** Names, Ceremonies & Customs—A Guide for Today's Families *By Anita Diamant* 6 x 9, 320 pp, Quality PB, 978-1-58023-251-7 **$19.99**

**Parenting as a Spiritual Journey:** Deepening Ordinary and Extraordinary Events into Sacred Occasions *By Rabbi Nancy Fuchs-Kreimer, PhD*
6 x 9, 224 pp, Quality PB, 978-1-58023-016-2 **$17.99**

**Parenting Jewish Teens:** A Guide for the Perplexed
*By Joanne Doades* Explores the questions and issues that shape the world in which today's Jewish teenagers live and offers constructive advice to parents.
6 x 9, 176 pp, Quality PB, 978-1-58023-305-7 **$16.99**

---

**Judaism for Two:** A Spiritual Guide for Strengthening and Celebrating Your Loving Relationship *By Rabbi Nancy Fuchs-Kreimer, PhD, and Rabbi Nancy H. Wiener, DMin; Foreword by Rabbi Elliot N. Dorff, PhD*
Addresses the ways Jewish teachings can enhance and strengthen committed relationships. 6 x 9, 224 pp, Quality PB, 978-1-58023-254-8 **$16.99**

**The Creative Jewish Wedding Book, 2nd Edition:** A Hands-On Guide to New & Old Traditions, Ceremonies & Celebrations *By Gabrielle Kaplan-Mayer*
9 x 9, 288 pp, b/w photos, Quality PB, 978-1-58023-398-9 **$19.99**

**Divorce Is a Mitzvah:** A Practical Guide to Finding Wholeness and Holiness When Your Marriage Dies *By Rabbi Perry Netter; Afterword by Rabbi Laura Geller*
6 x 9, 224 pp, Quality PB, 978-1-58023-172-5 **$16.95**

**Embracing the Covenant:** Converts to Judaism Talk About Why & How
*By Rabbi Allan Berkowitz and Patti Moskovitz* 6 x 9, 192 pp, Quality PB, 978-1-879045-50-7 **$16.95**

**The Guide to Jewish Interfaith Family Life:** An InterfaithFamily.com Handbook
*Edited by Ronnie Friedland and Edmund Case*
6 x 9, 384 pp, Quality PB, 978-1-58023-153-4 **$18.95**

**A Heart of Wisdom:** Making the Jewish Journey from Midlife through the Elder Years
*Edited by Susan Berrin; Foreword by Rabbi Harold Kushner*
6 x 9, 384 pp, Quality PB, 978-1-58023-051-3 **$18.95**

**Introducing My Faith and My Community:** The Jewish Outreach Institute Guide for the Christian in a Jewish Interfaith Relationship
*By Rabbi Kerry M. Olitzky* 6 x 9, 176 pp, Quality PB, 978-1-58023-192-3 **$16.99**

**Making a Successful Jewish Interfaith Marriage:** The Jewish Outreach Institute Guide to Opportunities, Challenges and Resources *By Rabbi Kerry M. Olitzky with Joan Peterson Littman*
6 x 9, 176 pp, Quality PB, 978-1-58023-170-1 **$16.95**

**A Man's Responsibility:** A Jewish Guide to Being a Son, a Partner in Marriage, a Father and a Community Leader *By Rabbi Joseph B. Meszler*
6 x 9, 192 pp, Quality PB, 978-1-58023-435-1 **$16.95**; HC, 978-1-58023-362-0 **$21.99**

**So That Your Values Live On:** Ethical Wills and How to Prepare Them
*Edited by Rabbi Jack Riemer and Rabbi Nathaniel Stampfer*
6 x 9, 272 pp, Quality PB, 978-1-879045-34-7 **$18.99**

# Holidays/Holy Days

## Who by Fire, Who by Water—Un'taneh Tokef
*Edited by Rabbi Lawrence A. Hoffman, PhD*
Examines the prayer's theology, authorship and poetry through a set of lively essays, all written in accessible language.
6 x 9, 272 pp, HC, 978-1-58023-424-5 **$24.99**

## Rosh Hashanah Readings: Inspiration, Information and Contemplation
## Yom Kippur Readings: Inspiration, Information and Contemplation
*Edited by Rabbi Dov Peretz Elkins; Section Introductions from Arthur Green's These Are the Words*
An extraordinary collection of readings, prayers and insights that will enable you to enter into the spirit of the High Holy Days in a personal and powerful way, permitting the meaning of the Jewish New Year to enter the heart.
Rosh Hashanah: 6 x 9, 400 pp, Quality PB, 978-1-58023-437-5 **$19.99**; HC, 978-1-58023-239-5 **$24.99**
Yom Kippur: 6 x 9, 368 pp, Quality PB, 978-1-58023-438-2 **$19.99**; HC, 978-1-58023-271-5 **$24.99**

## Jewish Holidays: A Brief Introduction for Christians
*By Rabbi Kerry M. Olitzky and Rabbi Daniel Judson*
5½ x 8½, 176 pp, Quality PB, 978-1-58023-302-6 **$16.99**

## Reclaiming Judaism as a Spiritual Practice: Holy Days and Shabbat
*By Rabbi Goldie Milgram* 7 x 9, 272 pp, Quality PB, 978-1-58023-205-0 **$19.99**

## 7th Heaven: Celebrating Shabbat with Rebbe Nachman of Breslov
*By Moshe Mykoff with the Breslov Research Institute*
5⅛ x 8¼, 224 pp, Deluxe PB w/ flaps, 978-1-58023-175-6 **$18.95**

## Shabbat, 2nd Edition: The Family Guide to Preparing for and Celebrating the Sabbath *By Dr. Ron Wolfson*
7 x 9, 320 pp, Illus., Quality PB, 978-1-58023-164-0 **$19.99**

## Hanukkah, 2nd Edition: The Family Guide to Spiritual Celebration
*By Dr. Ron Wolfson* 7 x 9, 240 pp, Illus., Quality PB, 978-1-58023-122-0 **$18.95**

## The Jewish Family Fun Book, 2nd Edition: Holiday Projects, Everyday Activities, and Travel Ideas with Jewish Themes *By Danielle Dardashti and Roni Sarig; Illus. by Avi Katz*
6 x 9, 304 pp, 70+ b/w illus. & diagrams, Quality PB, 978-1-58023-333-0 **$18.99**

## The Jewish Lights Book of Fun Classroom Activities: Simple and Seasonal Projects for Teachers and Students *By Danielle Dardashti and Roni Sarig*
6 x 9, 240 pp, Quality PB, 978-1-58023-206-7 **$19.99**

# Passover

## My People's Passover Haggadah
### Traditional Texts, Modern Commentaries
*Edited by Rabbi Lawrence A. Hoffman, PhD, and David Arnow, PhD*
A diverse and exciting collection of commentaries on the traditional Passover Haggadah—in two volumes!
Vol. 1: 7 x 10, 304 pp, HC, 978-1-58023-354-5 **$24.99**
Vol. 2: 7 x 10, 320 pp, HC, 978-1-58023-346-0 **$24.99**

## Leading the Passover Journey: The Seder's Meaning Revealed, the Haggadah's Story Retold *By Rabbi Nathan Laufer*
Uncovers the hidden meaning of the Seder's rituals and customs.
6 x 9, 224 pp, Quality PB, 978-1-58023-399-6 **$18.99**; HC, 978-1-58023-211-1 **$24.99**

## The Women's Passover Companion: Women's Reflections on the Festival of Freedom
*Edited by Rabbi Sharon Cohen Anisfeld, Tara Mohr and Catherine Spector; Foreword by Paula E. Hyman*
6 x 9, 352 pp, Quality PB, 978-1-58023-231-9 **$19.99**; HC, 978-1-58023-128-2 **$24.95**

## The Women's Seder Sourcebook: Rituals & Readings for Use at the Passover Seder
*Edited by Rabbi Sharon Cohen Anisfeld, Tara Mohr and Catherine Spector*
6 x 9, 384 pp, Quality PB, 978-1-58023-232-6 **$19.99**

## Creating Lively Passover Seders: A Sourcebook of Engaging Tales, Texts & Activities
*By David Arnow, PhD* 7 x 9, 416 pp, Quality PB, 978-1-58023-184-8 **$24.99**

## Passover, 2nd Edition: The Family Guide to Spiritual Celebration
*By Dr. Ron Wolfson with Joel Lurie Grishaver* 7 x 9, 416 pp, Quality PB, 978-1-58023-174-9 **$19.95**

# Theology/Philosophy/The Way Into... Series

The Way Into... series offers an accessible and highly usable "guided tour" of the Jewish faith, people, history and beliefs—in total, an introduction to Judaism that will enable you to understand and interact with the sacred texts of the Jewish tradition. Each volume is written by a leading contemporary scholar and teacher, and explores one key aspect of Judaism. The Way Into... series enables all readers to achieve a real sense of Jewish cultural literacy through guided study.

### The Way Into Encountering God in Judaism
*By Rabbi Neil Gillman, PhD*
For everyone who wants to understand how Jews have encountered God throughout history and today.
6 x 9, 240 pp, Quality PB, 978-1-58023-199-2 **$18.99**; HC, 978-1-58023-025-4 **$21.95**
Also Available: **The Jewish Approach to God:** A Brief Introduction for Christians
*By Rabbi Neil Gillman, PhD*
5½ x 8¼, 192 pp, Quality PB, 978-1-58023-190-9 **$16.95**

### The Way Into Jewish Mystical Tradition
*By Rabbi Lawrence Kushner*
Allows readers to interact directly with the sacred mystical texts of the Jewish tradition. An accessible introduction to the concepts of Jewish mysticism, their religious and spiritual significance, and how they relate to life today.
6 x 9, 224 pp, Quality PB, 978-1-58023-200-5 **$18.99**; HC, 978-1-58023-029-2 **$21.95**

### The Way Into Jewish Prayer
*By Rabbi Lawrence A. Hoffman, PhD*
Opens the door to 3,000 years of Jewish prayer, making anyone feel at home in the Jewish way of communicating with God.
6 x 9, 208 pp, Quality PB, 978-1-58023-201-2 **$18.99**

Also Available: **The Way Into Jewish Prayer Teacher's Guide**
*By Rabbi Jennifer Ossakow Goldsmith*
8½ x 11, 42 pp, PB, 978-1-58023-345-3 **$8.99**
Download a free copy at www.jewishlights.com.

### The Way Into Judaism and the Environment
*By Jeremy Benstein, PhD*
Explores the ways in which Judaism contributes to contemporary social-environmental issues, the extent to which Judaism is part of the problem and how it can be part of the solution.
6 x 9, 288 pp, Quality PB, 978-1-58023-368-2 **$18.99**; HC, 978-1-58023-268-5 **$24.99**

### The Way Into *Tikkun Olam* (Repairing the World)
*By Rabbi Elliot N. Dorff, PhD*
An accessible introduction to the Jewish concept of the individual's responsibility to care for others and repair the world.
6 x 9, 304 pp, Quality PB, 978-1-58023-328-6 **$18.99**; 320 pp, HC, 978-1-58023-269-2 **$24.99**

### The Way Into Torah
*By Rabbi Norman J. Cohen, PhD*
Helps guide you in the exploration of the origins and development of Torah, explains why it should be studied and how to do it.
6 x 9, 176 pp, Quality PB, 978-1-58023-198-5 **$16.99**

### The Way Into the Varieties of Jewishness
*By Sylvia Barack Fishman, PhD*
Explores the religious and historical understanding of what it has meant to be Jewish from ancient times to the present controversy over "Who is a Jew?"
6 x 9, 288 pp, Quality PB, 978-1-58023-367-5 **$18.99**; HC, 978-1-58023-030-8 **$24.99**

# Theology/Philosophy

**Jewish Theology in Our Time:** A New Generation Explores the Foundations and Future of Jewish Belief *Edited by Rabbi Elliot J. Cosgrove, PhD; Foreword by Rabbi David J. Wolpe; Preface by Rabbi Carole B. Balin, PhD*
A powerful and challenging examination of what Jews can believe—by a new generation's most dynamic and innovative thinkers.
6 x 9, 240 pp, HC, 978-1-58023-413-9 **$24.99**

**Maimonides, Spinoza and Us:** Toward an Intellectually Vibrant Judaism
*By Rabbi Marc D. Angel, PhD* A challenging look at two great Jewish philosophers and what their thinking means to our understanding of God, truth, revelation and reason. 6 x 9, 224 pp, HC, 978-1-58023-411-5 **$24.99**

**The Death of Death:** Resurrection and Immortality in Jewish Thought
*By Rabbi Neil Gillman, PhD* 6 x 9, 336 pp, Quality PB, 978-1-58023-081-0 **$18.95**

**Doing Jewish Theology:** God, Torah & Israel in Modern Judaism *By Rabbi Neil Gillman, PhD*
6 x 9, 304 pp, Quality PB, 978-1-58023-439-9 **$18.99**; HC, 978-1-58023-322-4 **$24.99**

**Ethics of the Sages:** Pirke Avot—Annotated & Explained
*Translation & Annotation by Rabbi Rami Shapiro* 5½ x 8½, 192 pp, Quality PB, 978-1-59473-207-2 **$16.99***

**Hasidic Tales:** Annotated & Explained *Translation & Annotation by Rabbi Rami Shapiro*
5½ x 8½, 240 pp, Quality PB, 978-1-893361-86-7 **$16.95***

**A Heart of Many Rooms:** Celebrating the Many Voices within Judaism
*By Dr. David Hartman* 6 x 9, 352 pp, Quality PB, 978-1-58023-156-5 **$19.95**

**The Hebrew Prophets:** Selections Annotated & Explained
*Translation & Annotation by Rabbi Rami Shapiro; Foreword by Rabbi Zalman M. Schachter-Shalomi*
5½ x 8½, 224 pp, Quality PB, 978-1-59473-037-5 **$16.99***

**A Jewish Understanding of the New Testament** *By Rabbi Samuel Sandmel; Preface by Rabbi David Sandmel* 5½ x 8½, 368 pp, Quality PB, 978-1-59473-048-1 **$19.99***

**Jews and Judaism in the 21st Century:** Human Responsibility, the Presence of God and the Future of the Covenant *Edited by Rabbi Edward Feinstein; Foreword by Paula E. Hyman*
6 x 9, 192 pp, Quality PB, 978-1-58023-374-3 **$19.99**; HC, 978-1-58023-315-6 **$24.99**

**A Living Covenant:** The Innovative Spirit in Traditional Judaism
*By Dr. David Hartman* 6 x 9, 368 pp, Quality PB, 978-1-58023-011-7 **$25.00**

**Love and Terror in the God Encounter:** The Theological Legacy of Rabbi Joseph B. Soloveitchik *By Dr. David Hartman* 6 x 9, 240 pp, Quality PB, 978-1-58023-176-3 **$19.95**

**The Personhood of God:** Biblical Theology, Human Faith and the Divine Image
*By Dr. Yochanan Muffs; Foreword by Dr. David Hartman*
6 x 9, 240 pp, Quality PB, 978-1-58023-338-5 **$18.99**; HC, 978-1-58023-265-4 **$24.99**

**A Touch of the Sacred:** A Theologian's Informal Guide to Jewish Belief
*By Dr. Eugene B. Borowitz and Frances W. Schwartz*
6 x 9, 256 pp, Quality PB, 978-1-58023-416-0 **$16.99**; HC, 978-1-58023-337-8 **$21.99**

**Traces of God:** Seeing God in Torah, History and Everyday Life *By Rabbi Neil Gillman, PhD*
6 x 9, 240 pp, Quality PB, 978-1-58023-369-9 **$16.99**

**We Jews and Jesus:** Exploring Theological Differences for Mutual Understanding *By Rabbi Samuel Sandmel; Preface by Rabbi David Sandmel* 6 x 9, 192 pp, Quality PB, 978-1-59473-208-9 **$16.99***

**Your Word Is Fire:** The Hasidic Masters on Contemplative Prayer
*Edited and translated by Rabbi Arthur Green, PhD, and Barry W. Holtz*
6 x 9, 160 pp, Quality PB, 978-1-879045-25-5 **$15.95**

## I Am Jewish
### Personal Reflections Inspired by the Last Words of Daniel Pearl
Almost 150 Jews—both famous and not—from all walks of life, from all around the world, write about many aspects of their Judaism.
*Edited by Judea and Ruth Pearl* 6 x 9, 304 pp, Deluxe PB w/ flaps, 978-1-58023-259-3 **$18.99**
**Download a free copy of the *I Am Jewish Teacher's Guide* at www.jewishlights.com.**

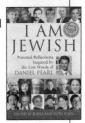

**Hannah Senesh:** Her Life and Diary, The First Complete Edition
*By Hannah Senesh; Foreword by Marge Piercy; Preface by Eitan Senesh; Afterword by Roberta Grossman*
6 x 9, 368 pp, b/w photos, Quality PB, 978-1-58023-342-2 **$19.99**

---

**A book from SkyLight Paths, Jewish Lights' sister imprint*

# Social Justice

## There Shall Be No Needy
Pursuing Social Justice through Jewish Law and Tradition
*By Rabbi Jill Jacobs; Foreword by Rabbi Elliot N. Dorff, PhD; Preface by Simon Greer*
Confronts the most pressing issues of twenty-first-century America from a deeply Jewish perspective.
6 x 9, 288 pp, Quality PB, 978-1-58023-425-2 **$16.99**; HC, 978-1-58023-394-1 **$21.99**
Also Available: **There Shall Be No Needy Teacher's Guide**
8½ x 11, 56 pp, PB, 978-1-58023-429-0 **$8.99**

## Conscience: The Duty to Obey and the Duty to Disobey
*By Rabbi Harold M. Schulweis*
This clarion call to rethink our moral and political behavior examines the idea of conscience and the role conscience plays in our relationships to government, law, ethics, religion, human nature, God—and to each other.
6 x 9, 160 pp, Quality PB, 978-1-58023-419-1 **$16.99**; HC, 978-1-58023-375-0 **$19.99**

## Judaism and Justice: The Jewish Passion to Repair the World
*By Rabbi Sidney Schwarz; Foreword by Ruth Messinger*
Explores the relationship between Judaism, social justice and the Jewish identity of American Jews.
6 x 9, 352 pp, Quality PB, 978-1-58023-353-8 **$19.99**; HC, 978-1-58023-312-5 **$24.99**

## Spiritual Activism: A Jewish Guide to Leadership and Repairing the World
*By Rabbi Avraham Weiss; Foreword by Alan M. Dershowitz*
6 x 9, 224 pp, Quality PB, 978-1-58023-418-4 **$16.99**; HC, 978-1-58023-355-2 **$24.99**

## Righteous Indignation: A Jewish Call for Justice *Edited by Rabbi Or N. Rose, Jo Ellen Green Kaiser and Margie Klein; Foreword by Rabbi David Ellenson, PhD*
Leading progressive Jewish activists explore meaningful intellectual and spiritual foundations for their social justice work.
6 x 9, 384 pp, Quality PB, 978-1-58023-414-6 **$19.99**; HC, 978-1-58023-336-1 **$24.99**

# Spirituality/Women's Interest

## New Jewish Feminism: Probing the Past, Forging the Future
*Edited by Rabbi Elyse Goldstein; Foreword by Anita Diamant*
Looks at the growth and accomplishments of Jewish feminism and what they mean for Jewish women today and tomorrow.
6 x 9, 480 pp, HC, 978-1-58023-359-0 **$24.99**

## The Divine Feminine in Biblical Wisdom Literature
Selections Annotated & Explained
*Translation & Annotation by Rabbi Rami Shapiro*
5½ x 8½, 240 pp, Quality PB, 978-1-59473-109-9 **$16.99**
*(A book from SkyLight Paths, Jewish Lights' sister imprint)*

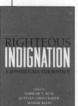

**The Quotable Jewish Woman:** Wisdom, Inspiration & Humor from the Mind & Heart
*Edited by Elaine Bernstein Partnow* 6 x 9, 496 pp, Quality PB, 978-1-58023-236-4 **$19.99**

## The Women's Haftarah Commentary: New Insights from Women
Rabbis on the 54 Weekly Haftarah Portions, the 5 Megillot & Special Shabbatot
*Edited by Rabbi Elyse Goldstein* Illuminates the historical significance of female portrayals in the Haftarah and the Five Megillot.
6 x 9, 560 pp, Quality PB, 978-1-58023-371-2 **$19.99**

## The Women's Torah Commentary: New Insights from Women
Rabbis on the 54 Weekly Torah Portions
*Edited by Rabbi Elyse Goldstein*
Over fifty women rabbis offer inspiring insights on the Torah, in a week-by-week format.
6 x 9, 496 pp, Quality PB, 978-1-58023-370-5 **$19.99**; HC, 978-1-58023-076-6 **$34.95**

See Passover for *The Women's Passover Companion: Women's Reflections on the Festival of Freedom* and *The Women's Seder Sourcebook: Rituals & Readings for Use at the Passover Seder.*